Jews and Booze

THE GOLDSTEIN-GOREN SERIES
IN AMERICAN JEWISH HISTORY
General Editor: Hasia R. Diner

*We Remember with Reverence and Love: American Jews and
the Myth of Silence after the Holocaust, 1945–1962*
Hasia R. Diner

Is Diss a System? A Milt Gross Comic Reader
Edited by Ari Y. Kelman

*All Together Different: Yiddish Socialists, Garment Workers, and
the Labor Roots of Multiculturalism*
Daniel Katz

Jews and Booze: Becoming American in the Age of Prohibition
Marni Davis

Jews and Booze

Becoming American in
the Age of Prohibition

Marni Davis

NEW YORK UNIVERSITY PRESS
New York and London

NEW YORK UNIVERSITY PRESS
New York and London
www.nyupress.org

References to Internet Websites (URLs) were accurate at the time of writing.
Neither the author nor New York University Press is responsible for URLs
that may have expired or changed since the manuscript was prepared.

Library of Congress Cataloging-in-Publication Data

Davis, Marni.
Jews and booze : becoming American in the age of prohibition / Marni Davis.
p. cm. — (The Goldstein-Goren Series in American Jewish History)
Includes bibliographical references and index.
ISBN 978-0-8147-2028-8 (cl : alk. paper)
ISBN 978-0-8147-8384-9 (ebook)
ISBN 978-0-8147-4409-3 (ebook)
1. Jews—Alcohol use—United States—Attitudes. 2. Alcoholic beverage industry—
United States—History—19th century. 3. Alcoholic beverage industry—
United States—History—20th century. 4. Alcohol—Law and legislation—
United States. 5. United States—Ethnic relations. I. Title.
HV5185.D38   2011
363.4'1089924073—dc23   2011028199

New York University Press books are printed on acid-free paper,
and their binding materials are chosen for strength and durability.
We strive to use environmentally responsible suppliers and materials
to the greatest extent possible in publishing our books.

Manufactured in the United States of America
10 9 8 7 6 5 4 3 2 1

Contents

Illustrations

Acknowledgments

It is with great pleasure that I thank the many individuals who helped me through the research and writing of this book. I have relied on mentors, colleagues, archivists, librarians, and loved ones throughout, and I am forever in their debt.

Jonathan Prude and Eric L. Goldstein are foremost on this list. They have both influenced me profoundly, not only by guiding me through the process of getting an early version of this book on paper, but also by teaching me how to be a historian, by instruction and by example. I am fortunate to have been a beneficiary of their knowledge and intellectual generosity; their contributions are manifest in every aspect of this book.

Scholars at many other institutions, as well as independent historians, have also taken time to comment on my work and offer critiques and suggestions. Jonathan Sarna, Hasia Diner, Rebecca Kobrin, Jack S. Blocker, Jr., Daniel Okrent, Lee Shai Weissbach, Thomas R. Pegram, and Hollace Ava Weiner all read parts of this manuscript and gave me their scholarly insights, as did David Sehat, Michael Galchinsky, Clifford Kuhn, and Vincent Lloyd, my colleagues at Georgia State University. Sander Gilman, Glenn Dynner, Rebecca Edwards, Leonard Rogoff, Deborah Weiner, Marcia Hertzman, Stuart Rockoff, and Libby Garland shared their research with me, and made me aware of resources and historical connections I would never have unearthed on my own. I had the great luck of finding research collaborators while a graduate student: H. Paul Thompson and I mapped out the ethno-racial makeup of Atlanta's saloon culture; and Mollie Lewis and I undertook Yiddish translation projects together, including Leonard Landes's idiosyncratic contribution to American temperance literature. My research assistants at Georgia State—Mindy Clegg, Mike Castellini, and Haley Aaron—also helped me immeasurably.

I have collaborated with many conscientious and meticulous editors over the years, and their attentions have made this a better book. Jennifer Hammer at NYU Press has been a pleasure to work with; thanks as well to Gabrielle Begue, and to Despina Papazoglou Gimbel and Nicholas Taylor for their careful copyediting and their patience. I want to express my appreciation, too, to the anonymous readers at NYU Press whose many valuable comments on early versions of this book helped me to sharpen my thinking and my prose.

Many thanks to the institutions that have supported my work. The History Department at Georgia State University, as well as the History Department, the Tam Institute for Jewish Studies, and the Graduate School at Emory University granted me funds and fellowships while I undertook this project. The grants I received from the National Foundation of Jewish Culture, the Southern Jewish Historical Society, and the American Jewish Archives provided research support that made this book possible.

I am grateful to the many librarians who were so gracious and generous with their time and energies at both Emory University's Woodruff Library and at the Georgia State University Library. Kevin Proffitt and his staff at the American Jewish Archives were heaven-sent, and I look forward to working with them again. Many thanks to the archivists at the American Jewish Historical Society in New York; the Jewish Museum of Maryland in Baltimore; the Western Jewish Americana archives of the Magnes Collection of Jewish Art and Life; the Filson Archives and the special collections at the University of Louisville; Newark Public Library; the Jewish Historical Society of MetroWest; the Sonoma County Library; and the William Breman Jewish Heritage Museum in Atlanta. Thanks to the Harvard Business School, and to Dun & Bradstreet, for enabling my access to and granting permissions for use of the R. G. Dun & Co. Collection.

My deepest thanks go to three people. My parents, Barry and Rachelle Davis, both had long teaching careers. They taught me to love books and to cherish education, and they loved their jobs, which made me want to teach, too—a most sublime inheritance. Finally, my everlasting gratitude, and my heart, goes to Eric Entrican Wilson. His patience, love, and encouragement made it possible for me to write this book, and for that reason it is dedicated to him.

Introduction

Prohibition agent Izzy Einstein was stationed in the Jewish quarter of the Lower East Side, waiting to arrest a truck driver due to make a delivery of contraband alcohol, when he spotted an elderly gentleman wheeling a rickety baby carriage down the sidewalk. The man was a "strange looking mama," Einstein wrote later; he had surmised from the fellow's long beard that he was a Jewish immigrant, and Jewish patriarchs were not often seen pushing prams around the neighborhood. Einstein knew this intimately, since he, too, was a Jewish immigrant, and the Lower East Side had been his home since childhood. Working on a hunch that the carriage was transporting booze instead of babies, Einstein sidled up to the man and peered in, but "the baby was so covered that you couldn't see his face." So he pulled back the coverlet to get a better look. Lo and behold, "it was a gallon—the cutest 'tot of whiskey' I ever saw." Within the hour, Einstein had deposited the liquor and the carriage at the local precinct, "accompanied by the old fellow, who was weeping profusely."[1]

This image of two Jews standing side by side at a police station with a bottle of whiskey between them represents a peculiar moment in American Jews' long and complicated relationship to one of the most divisive issues in the nation's history: the "liquor question." Einstein and his partner, another Jewish Lower East Sider named Moe Smith, fashioned themselves as enforcers of a law brought into being by decades of activism on the part of Protestant lobbyists and anti-immigrant interests. It was an atypical and culturally anomalous choice on their part, since American Jews had been fierce critics of temperance and prohibition activists' efforts since the 1870s. Jews had opposed the anti-alcohol movement because they sensed its underlying moral coercion and cultural intolerance, but also for economic reasons: beer, wine, and liquor commerce had served as a source of both individual and communal upward mobility for American Jews since before the Civil War. But the Eighteenth Amendment to the Constitution had declared the "manufacture, sale, or transportation of intoxicating liquors" to be a criminal act, and, like everyone else, Jews were obligated to conform to the law or suffer the consequences. Few Jews, though, showed as much enthusiasm for Prohibition as Einstein and Smith, who arrested more than four thousand bootleggers during their tenure with the Bureau of Prohibition.[2]

The success of the American anti-alcohol movement upended Jews' long-standing commercial relationship with alcohol.[3] It also posed new and stressful challenges to Jewish status and identity in the United States that reverberated well beyond their economic pursuits. For decades, American Jewish attitudes toward alcohol had provided them with opportunities to engage in national debates in ways that demonstrated their deep and simultaneous attachment to both Jewish and American culture. They boasted of their reputation as a historically "sober people" with little interest in alcohol-induced stupefaction—or, as one nineteenth-century American rabbi wrote, "the Jew drinks, but he . . . knows when to stop"—which allowed them to highlight their ethno-religious distinctiveness at the same time as they pointed to themselves as upstanding members of their communities.[4] When they inveighed against the politics of the anti-alcohol movement, they positioned themselves as an ethnic interest group, but also as staunch defenders of the Constitution and champions of religious pluralism and political liberalism, tenets that they endorsed as quintessentially American. And their productivity in the American alcohol trade, they suggested, proved that Jews, widely regarded as an essentially and categorically commercial people, contributed to the nation's economic growth.

Jews' relationship to alcohol, in other words, confirmed the value of their Jewishness, even while it helped them establish their bona fides as American citizens. As late as 1918, only a year before the ratification of the Eighteenth Amendment, some American Jews still offered their communal relation to alcohol as testament to their positive qualities. "The liquor business always proved attractive to our people," claimed Pittsburgh's *Jewish Criterion*, "despite the fact that they themselves [*sic*] are universally known as a temperate people." How to explain this paradox? "Liquor is a stable and marketable product," the *Criterion* proposed, "which from a purely business point of view would appeal to persons with a keen business sense."[5]

Alas, as the old bootlegger's unlucky run-in with Einstein demonstrated, liquor proved to be an unstable product indeed, eventually marketable only by illegal means. By the time Prohibition became national law, American Jewish attitudes toward alcohol had rendered their political and social standing unstable as well. When the industrial titan, prohibition advocate, and anti-Semitic propagandist Henry Ford declared that "the Jews are on the side of liquor and always have been," he intimated that the history of Jewry's economic ties to alcohol and their political opposition to prohibition classified them as eternally un-American, incapable of abiding by the morality of the dominant culture.[6] Jews' past involvement in the alcohol trade—a resource for social integration, cultural adjustment, and economic mobility for generations—had become a liability.

"There is no question," the sociologist Nathan Glazer has written, "that a people's relation to alcohol represents something very deep about it."[7] This is true, but there is more to it than that: a people's relation to alcohol also represents something deep about their relation to other people, and to the culture in which they live. Jews' engagement in this vexed and increasingly despised sector of the American economy, and their advocacy of alcohol's legal availability, shaped the image of the Jew in United States, a nation with its own troubled and ambivalent relation to alcohol. As American anti-Semitic sentiment intensified at the turn of the century, Jews' history in the alcohol trade acted as confirmation of suspicions about Jewish economic behavior, in ways that mirrored broader concerns about their presence in American society. A new cast of villains emerged in prohibitionist rhetoric: the wealthy arriviste Jewish distiller and wholesaler; the Jewish saloon-keeper and liquor store owner who sold alcohol in impoverished communities; and, after the Eighteenth Amendment gained force of law in 1920, the Jewish bootlegger. Though their connection to alcohol had previously been a subject of communal pride, Jews now faced a distressing choice: refashion their attitudes toward alcohol commerce and consumption so that they aligned with the dominant culture, or maintain their historical connection to alcohol and risk marginalization. Their struggle to negotiate between these options shows how difficult it was for American Jews to unite their ethnic and American identities—especially during the late nineteenth and early twentieth centuries, when the terms of American identity were themselves profoundly unsteady.

It might seem strange to suggest that alcohol could have so profound an impact on American Jewish life. Today, Americans tend to scoff at the intensity of the debates over alcohol that so roiled the nation a hundred years ago. The government has been fighting a "war on drugs" since the Nixon administration, and a national crack cocaine epidemic has given way to a national methamphetamine epidemic. A war on "demon rum," by comparison, seems downright quaint. Yet these debates were impassioned, often bitter, and freighted with deep cultural meaning. As one prohibition advocate wrote, alcohol epitomized "the acme of evil, the climax of iniquity, the mother of abominations, and the sum of villainies."[8] Alcohol both represented and created personal and societal disorder, its enemies insisted. It undermined morality and debased the political system. It impoverished workers and their families, endangered public health, and, by impeding immigrant acculturation, endangered national security as well. Its legal availability enabled venal businessmen to exploit vulnerable communities for their own financial gain, and the taxes levied on alcohol production rendered government complicit in this exploitation. The magnitude of the anti-alcohol movement's total (albeit brief) victory—a constitutional amendment, a federal law, and the creation of a bureaucracy devoted to the prosecution of that law—shows that prohibitionists succeeded in convincing a critical mass of Americans that the nation's alcohol problem could only be solved by banishing the substance.

Historians of the American anti-alcohol movement have come to a range of conclusions about its underlying motivations.[9] Some take seriously reformers' concerns about the alcohol industry's offenses and the injuries done to Americans by excessive drink. These scholars point out that nineteenth-century workers and others with limited power, such as women and middle-class African Americans, saw temperance as a force of economic and social uplift. In addition, they insist, white middle-class progressives of the early twentieth century championed prohibition as a reform that would, as William Jennings Bryan contended, "bring the highest good to the greatest number without any injustice to any."[10] Others offer a far less sympathetic view, framing temperance and prohibition activists as provincial moralists and antimodern reactionaries. These scholars have been influenced, primarily, by Richard Hofstadter's claim that prohibition was a "pseudo-reform"; they regard prohibitionists as seeking not the improvement of democratic politics or the amelioration of urban poverty, but rather the reestablishment of rural and small-town WASP dominance in American society.[11]

Whether the anti-alcohol movement's intentions were beneficent or malevolent—whether it sought to improve American society for the benefit of all, or intended to set limits on American identity in order to exclude those who failed to conform—is not a question this book seeks to answer in any definitive way. Anti-alcohol activists, as a group, were too varied in their broader value commitments to be characterized so simply. Further, as nuanced historical evaluations of the movement point out, prohibition wove together liberal and conservative ideological strands so that paternalism, even outright bigotry, could motivate even the most progressive-minded activists.[12]

Focusing on the relationship between the anti-alcohol movement and American Jews (a portion of the population that, with few exceptions, ardently objected to that movement) serves as a reminder that prohibition provoked substantial opposition, whose partisans staked as assertive a claim to American principles as did the prohibitionists—a subject that has received minimal attention from historians of the era.[13] An investigation of the broader significance of Jews' relation to alcohol during the years of the American temperance and prohibition movements helps to clarify the terms of the debate itself, and shows how the discourse shifted over time. By examining how anti-alcohol activists and American Jews considered one another—sometimes with guarded wariness, and sometimes with unmitigated hostility—we can better understand what was at stake for both sides, and for American culture, during these decades.

The primary intent of this book is to shed new light on Jewish immigrants' experiences with the processes of "becoming" American, and to consider the function of Jews' relation to alcohol in their acculturation. Of course, Jews have not been the only immigrant population to struggle with the process of Americanization, and to confront the tensions between their commitments to the cultures they brought with them and their desire to fit in to the larger society.[14] But the issue has been a consistently thorny one for Jews; while the maintenance of group distinctiveness and minority consciousness has always been a fundamental component of Jewish identity, most American Jews—both immigrant and native born—have wanted to be (and to be seen as) unambiguously American. Jews have sometimes been hard-pressed to merge these two aspects of their communal character, and have struggled to balance or synthesize their allegiances to their in-group and to American culture.[15]

So did Jews' participation in the alcohol trade and their opposition to anti-alcohol movements help or hinder their efforts to be accepted within American society? And how did it affect their sense of themselves, both individually and collectively, as an ethnically, religiously, and historically distinct group? These questions can be answered only by looking at Jews' relation to alcohol within the broader context of the changing political and cultural discourse. For most of the nineteenth century, Jewish ideas about alcohol consumption and commerce fit within the wide spectrum of the national discussion on the subject. But between the 1870s (when the modern temperance movement began) and the 1930s (when the nation's "noble experiment" with national prohibition came to an end), that discussion narrowed significantly, as white native-born Protestants increasingly approved of the anti-alcohol movement's most absolute objectives. Jews stayed in place on the issue while

American culture changed around them, and they eventually found themselves not only on the losing side of the national debate, but also distrusted, even vilified, for ever having been "on the side of liquor."

As a result, American Jews' relation to alcohol during these critical decades exacerbated the inherent and inevitable tensions between their efforts to blend in and their efforts to stand apart. Their changing relationship to the anti-alcohol movement (which was itself undergoing constant transformation) made abundantly clear that adaptation and integration could be a bumpy and nonlinear process. For a time, producing, selling, and consuming alcohol, and defending Americans' right to do so, helped Jews to fulfill their ambition to become fully American while remaining meaningfully Jewish. But as negative attitudes toward alcohol became more prevalent, they overlapped, and sometimes intertwined, with other anxieties; prohibitionists regarded alcohol commerce not just as a sinister force in American society, but also as an un-American product foisted on the nation by venal commercial forces and immoral immigrants. By 1920, when the Eighteenth Amendment went into effect, the political stance and entrepreneurial choice Jews had embraced for decades became a mark of marginality and a source of shame. Jews' economic practices and cultural attitudes now came into direct conflict with the nation's prevailing moral and political ideals, and with American law as well.

The anti-alcohol movement's rise and demise roughly coincided with two successive waves of Jewish immigration to the United States, first from central Europe, then from the Pale of Settlement, Galicia, and elsewhere in eastern Europe. Jews had been engaged in the alcohol trade in these regions for centuries, and these immigrants arrived in the United States familiar with some of the skills needed to make and sell alcohol. But Jews' relation to alcohol predated their experience in Europe by millennia, and harks back to the foundations of rabbinic law. Jews are linked to alcohol production and consumption by the dietary regulations of kashrut, which require Jews to use wine in their religious rituals and forbid consumption of wine produced or even handled by non-Jews.[16] This doctrine protects Jews from inadvertently drinking *yayin nesekh*, or wine sanctified for use in gentile religious ritual. But *stam yeinam*, or wine produced by gentiles for non-sacramental purposes, is also deemed *treyf* (unkosher). These restrictions were meant to prevent certain kinds of conviviality between Jews and non-Jews. Drinking, it has been said, can lead to dancing, and the rabbis who codified the laws of kashrut feared that if Jews consumed wine with their non-Jewish neighbors, social integration and diminished communal identity would result.[17]

Jews' relation to alcohol, in this regard, both symbolized and imposed Jewish difference by creating a barrier between them and others. At the same time, this aspect of rabbinic law also created a commercial niche. If Jews were to have the wine they needed, they had to oversee and control every step of its production and purveyance, from the harvesting of the grapes to the raising of the kiddush cup. Perhaps because of their familiarity with wine production—and because the mainstream of rabbinic Judaism never placed any taboo on alcohol—Jews have also brewed, distilled, and sold all varieties of intoxicating beverages to both Jews and gentiles since the beginning of the Diaspora. Centuries before the Common Era, prominent members of Persian Babylon's Jewish community made a living by brewing beer.[18] In the Islamic empire during the Middle Ages, where prevailing interpretations of the Koran proscribed practicing Muslims from having any contact with alcohol, those Muslims who drank wine anyway relied on Jewish merchants and vintners as their suppliers.[19] In medieval and early modern Europe, where Jews were frequently forbidden from owning land, they produced beer, wine, and distilled liquor by buying surpluses of grapes and grains from Christian farmers.[20] They also acted as middlemen and brokers, purchasing agricultural products in bulk and making them available to alcohol producers elsewhere, or moving the finished product between manufacturers and faraway retailers and wholesalers. Intoxicating beverages were among the many commodities Jews trafficked as intermediaries, and this socioeconomic activity situated Jews centrally in the creation of commercial markets in both urban centers and the rural countryside.[21]

This history can help us appreciate the frustration and pathos of Izzy's carriage-pushing bootlegger. When Jewish immigrants took up alcohol entrepreneurship in the United States, they forged a powerful link between their past and their present. But their new national context exerted a force of its own. The American alcohol industry grew spectacularly during these years, aided by both technological improvements that facilitated the mass manufacture and marketing of all kinds of consumer goods, and population increase, which expanded the number of consumers. Alcohol was the nation's fifth-largest industry at the turn of the century, contributing one-third of the tax revenue in federal coffers—staggering statistics that point to the importance of the alcohol business in all aspects of American life.[22]

Jews were among the tens of thousands who availed themselves of the opportunities offered by the expansion of the American alcohol trade. They took up these practices in ways that evinced continuity with their longtime historical engagement in alcohol commerce and attentiveness to entrepreneurial opportunities in the American context. Examining this entrepreneurial choice—which until now has never been investigated in depth by historians of the American Jewish experience[23]—offers a new perspective on the role that Jews have played in American commercial life. Much of the historical scholarship on Jews and American commerce has focused on their experiences as wageworkers in the garment trade or as participants in national and international labor movements in major industrial cities, where the majority of American Jewish immigrants settled and adjusted to life in their new country.[24] The consumer practices of Jewish immigrants (and especially Jewish women) have also received robust attention, though those studies that regard consumption as an expression of Jewish ethnicity generally ignore Jewish manufacturers and purveyors of consumer goods.[25] Jews' experiences as American entrepreneurs, and the ways in which they shaped both American and American Jewish culture, have been given relatively short shrift—perhaps out of wariness that any focus on Jews as petty capitalists and members of the merchant middle class could perpetuate anti-Semitic stereotypes or essentialist presumptions about Jews' economic proclivities.[26]

The historian Lucy Dawidowicz, best known for her scholarship on the Holocaust and the lost world of eastern European Yiddish culture, as well as for her pugnacious anti-Communism, lamented this lacuna in the historiography. When she died in 1990, she was reportedly at work on a history of American Jewry that, she hoped, would not only identify American Jewish entrepreneurs, but also, she wrote, "show how they served the American economy," and "restore to the [Jewish] merchant and businessman the recognition of their social usefulness."[27] Dawidowicz readily admitted that she came to this research with a political and ideological bias: resuscitating and celebrating the history of the American Jewish merchant, she declared, would controvert "those ideas which for generations have denigrated trade and commerce, and which have romanticized the peasant and idealized the proletariat. It is strange," she continued, that "we are still captive to Marxist notions about the unproductivity of the middleman."[28]

I share neither Dawidowicz's broader political commitments, nor her hope to "restore" any category of historical figure in the affections of American Jewish memory. But I do think that she was correct to call on scholars of the Jewish experience to think of economic history as "a variant or subcategory of social history," and I, too, regard Jews' engagement in American commercial life as central to the history of "other kinds of social processes, such as acculturation and assimilation."[29] Entrepreneurship created socioeconomic spaces where Jews interacted with their neighbors, as colleagues and collaborators, as competitors, and as buyers and sellers who assessed one another from across the retail counter. Where Jews and gentiles felt themselves to be engaged in mutually beneficial economic endeavors, these interactions could provide entrée into ecumenical communal life. But the nature of the commodity Jewish entrepreneurs were selling mattered, too, sometimes powerfully, such as when Jews trafficked in a controversial substance like alcohol.[30] As John Higham noted, Americans have historically viewed Jewish entrepreneurial activity with a mix of admiration and revulsion, and economic anti-Semitism in the United States was often "blurred by a lingering respect." But at the end of the century this ambivalence frequently shaded toward hostility, and "the unattractive elements in the economic stereotype grew more pronounced."[31] Because Jewish engagement in the alcohol trade played a role (and in some instances a dominant one) in the development in this stereotype, an examination of the Jewish alcohol entrepreneur—his lived experience, as well as his representation in the prohibitionist imagination—is in order.

Unfortunately for the historian of Jewish economic life, it is difficult to ascertain trends in American Jewish entrepreneurship in *any* sector on a national scale. The best possible historical resource for occupational data, the U.S. census records, does offer information on the number of saloonkeepers, liquor dealers, brewers, and other jobs in the alcohol trade. The Census Bureau also aggregated data on the nativity of individuals in these occupations. But the bureau did not take note of individual religious affiliation, except in cases where immigration authorities classified adherents to a particular religion as members of a racial group—as they did with "Hindus," for instance, in the early twentieth century. American Jewish communal leaders, fearing that the categorization of Jews as a race (and, potentially, as nonwhite) would undermine their status as citizens, prevailed on the bureau to eliminate any classification that would differentiate Jews from other whites in census data.[32] As a result, for historians of American Jewish workers and entrepreneurs, the U.S. census's massive troves of occupational data can serve as only the bluntest of instruments. The fact that of the 71,385 individuals engaged in saloonkeeping as an occupation in 1890, 38,888 (54 percent) were foreign-born—19,309 emigrants from Germany; 7,575 from Ireland; 1,955 from Scandinavia; 1,134 from Italy; 421 from Russia; and so forth—does not tell us enough.[33] American Jewish organizations also undertook demographic studies of Jewish occupational trends during the late nineteenth and early twentieth centuries, but their researches were often severely limited in regional scope, and their statistics frequently combined occupations into broad categories like "manufacturing," "trade," "retail," or "agriculture."

In short, no authoritative record of American Jewish occupational history currently exists. Scholars and genealogists who seek to fill this gap use other historical resources—like immigrant ship manifests, religious and social organization membership rosters, Jewish publications, and marriage and burial records, as well as the information that the census does provide, such as individual names, nativity, parents' places of birth, and native languages. By using these resources, I have found that in cities and towns all over the country, Jews were frequently active in local alcohol industries. What's more, in some places their presence in the local liquor trade was proportionally far greater than their presence in the general population.

By distilling liquor and brewing beer, as vintners, saloonkeepers, liquor store owners, and as liquor and wine wholesalers, Jews joined other Americans, both immigrant and native born, in this busy sector of the American economy. Whether they did so primarily because of their past or their present would be difficult to determine in any definitive way. These were choices made by individuals, based on their personal and familial histories, as well as opportunities made available in their sites of settlement; whether they succeeded or failed was the result of both acumen and luck. But as we shall see, American Jews engaged the trade visibly and vigorously, and they championed the trade because it helped them to be simultaneously insiders and outsiders, both a part of the American people and a people apart—at least, it did for a while.

Jews and Booze is divided into three parts, each of which comprises a pair of chapters. In part I, "Alcohol and Acculturation," the first chapter examines American Jews' growing presence in the alcohol industry during the nineteenth century, and the second looks at American Jews' critique of the temperance movement. Part I focuses on the "second wave" of Jewish immigration to the United States: approximately 250,000 newcomers who were primarily of central European birth and descent. An acculturated and upwardly mobile lot (thanks in part to the liquor business), these Jews regularly spoke out against organizations like the Woman's Christian Temperance Union, which sought to impose Protestant values on American politics and culture. When this generation of Jewish immigrants excoriated prohibitionists as theocrats and fanatics, they were asserting and reinforcing their belief that American civic life should be devoid of sectarian religious content. By taking the side of the "wets" (against the "drys"), and pointing to their reputation for moderation and self-restraint in their own alcohol-consumption habits, American Jews intended to undercut prohibitionist reformers' claims that American national identity centered on Christian morality. For these American Jews, alcohol acted as a force for inclusion.

The two chapters in part II, "Alcohol and Anti-Semitism," examine the "third wave" of Jewish immigration to the United States during the late nineteenth and early twentieth centuries, when hundreds of thousands of eastern European Jews arrived in American ports and cities. Chapter 3 shows that these Jewish immigrants also took up the alcohol trade in their sites of settlement, at a time when both Jewish immigrants and alcohol traffickers were subjected to increasingly hostile scrutiny. Chapter 4 explains the emergence of a toxic image of the Jewish alcohol purveyor—a new iteration of the image of the Jewish economic villain in the United States, though one that had already surfaced in other countries. Prohibitionist agitation exacerbated American anti-Semitic sentiment, especially as it related to Jewish economic behavior. Accusations that Jews had monopolized this controversial commodity reflected broader concerns about their presence in the American economy. Anti-Semitism and prohibitionism provided parallel ideological settings for Americans to express alarm about economic stratification and the increasingly urban and commercial nature of the American economy. For some—and here I am mostly in alignment with Hofstadter's assessment of the anti-alcohol movement—the growth of both the alcohol industry and the American Jewish population were manifestations of the erosion of white Protestants' political, economic, and cultural dominance.

Part III, "Jews and the Prohibition Era," looks at the events leading to the passage of the Eighteenth Amendment and the years that the National Prohibition Act was in effect. This was Izzy Einstein's heyday, but it was also the heyday of Meyer Lansky, Longy Zwillman, and their cohort of Jewish bootleggers. Prohibition introduced a great deal of uncertainty for those American Jews who feared that the illegal acts of a few would endanger the reputation and status of the larger group. Making matters even more complicated, the Volstead Act (which codified federal Prohibition law) granted special dispensation for sacramental wine used in religious ceremonies. But was it wrong for Jews to partake of a commodity that was denied to their fellow Americans? Should Jews insist on "special rights" for the sake of their own historical continuity, or break with the past for the sake of assimilation? They also disagreed about how to react to Jews who used the sacramental wine exemption to break the law, flooding the illegal alcohol market with kosher wine and liquor and seemingly proving the accusation made by Ford and others that Jews constituted a prodigious proportion of American bootleggers.

Chapter 5 maps Jews' bootlegging activities, with particular attention to the "rabbinic wine scandals" engendered by the Volstead Act's sacramental wine dispensation. Chapter 6 shows that American Jewish leaders struggled both publicly and privately to agree on a communal response to these developments. Should they defend their history in the trade and fight the new law on political grounds? Or should they abandon alcohol in the interest of national cohesion? American Jewish leaders tried their best to prove that their communities embraced the law, and feared the repercussions of their ultimate failure to create a unified communal front. Prohibition and the phenomenon of Jewish bootlegging demonstrated that no subset of Jews, no matter how acculturated, could easily enforce a set of cultural mores and socioeconomic practices that would unite the religiously, economically, and regionally diverse American Jewish community. As it turned out, they could not even convince all assimilated, middle-class American Jews to obey the law.

American Jews' reactions to anti-alcohol politics changed over time, as did depictions of "the Jew" in the American prohibitionist imagination. The temperance and prohibition movements played a key role in debates about what it meant to be American during the late nineteenth and early twentieth centuries. Jewish responses to Americans' inconstant relation to alcohol encapsulated their efforts to clarify and defend their communal and civic identities, both to their fellow Americans and to themselves.

PART I

Alcohol and Acculturation

1

Setting up Shop

Jews Becoming Americans in the
Nineteenth-Century Alcohol Trade

"The history of those who produce and sell liquor," the historian Jack S. Blocker, Jr., has written, must be "part of any examination of the social use of and response to beverage alcohol."[1] One of the foremost students of both the American alcohol industry and the movement against it, Blocker was pointing out the lopsided nature of scholarly production on the topic. While the shelves are crammed full to bursting with historical studies of alcohol's consumers and alcohol's critics,[2] with a few important exceptions historians have paid little mind to those who made and sold the alcohol Americans were drinking.[3]

But the producers, distributors, and purveyors of beer, wine, and liquor need to be incorporated into the story as well. Participants in the American alcohol industry made and moved a product that carried profound and contentious meaning in their national culture. They chose to traffic in a controversial commodity, and they themselves constituted a faction in national debates. Their incentives, as well as their experiences in the trade, can help us to understand what alcohol represented to its supporters during these decades.

For nineteenth-century American Jews, alcohol commerce represented both a connection with their past and a means to improve their present. Their pre-migrational familiarity with the processes of production and distribution dovetailed with the structure of the American alcohol trade, creating opportunities for aspiring entrepreneurs—and sometimes for entire extended families—to establish themselves in their new country. The alcohol industry facilitated economic mobility and served as a force of acculturation, even while it created and sustained Jewish communities through ethnic entrepreneurial networks.

Isaac Wolfe Bernheim's trajectory into the alcohol industry illustrates a few of these forces. The son of a Jewish wine wholesaler, Bernheim had emigrated from Baden to New York at the end of the Civil War, joining a wave of mid-nineteenth-century Jewish emigrants from German-speaking central Europe, where exclusion, economic marginalization, and, in some cases, violent religious persecution pushed Jews to seek better lives elsewhere.[4] After struggling as a peddler in rural Pennsylvania, he made his way to Paducah, Kentucky, a town of fewer than ten thousand residents with "neither club nor theater" but "a good many saloons," he later wrote. Paducah was situated about two hundred miles from Louisville, a national hub for both the production and distribution of whiskey, and Paducah's economy relied heavily on Louisville's muscular presence in that industry. Several of Paducah's more prominent Jews were already engaged in the trade—including Meyer Weil, who twice served as the town's mayor. In 1868, fellow Jewish immigrants Moses Bloom and Reuben Loeb offered Bernheim the position of bookkeeper in their liquor-wholesaling firm, and he took it without a moment's hesitation.[5]

Isaac soon sent for his brother Bernhard, who came from Germany to join him at Bloom, Loeb, and Co. The ambitious brothers "outgrew their connection" with Loeb and Bloom not long after, and in 1872 they started their own firm with the help of local investors of both Jewish and Christian background. "In the back room of a small country store," Bernheim recalled, "the two potential distillers and a negro helper founded a 'business.'" They expanded their operations in 1888, purchasing a distillery in Louisville and moving their administrative operations to that city. By the turn of the century, Bernheim Bros. was one of the nation's leading whiskey distillers. They produced thousands of gallons of whiskey yearly in a state-of-the-art facility and achieved international renown for their I. W. Harper elite brand of bourbon whiskey.[6] Their company "stands to-day in the very front rank," declared a liquor industry trade magazine in 1901, "not only of the commercial institutions of Louisville but of the whiskey houses of the world."[7]

Jews gravitated toward different sectors of American alcohol production and distribution with varying degrees of enthusiasm and continuity. The distilled liquor business, and the whiskey industry in particular, proved most attractive to Jewish immigrants during the nineteenth century. Perhaps whiskey's nationalistic significance played some role in their choice. While Americans often associated wine and beer with European tastes and European immigrants, producers and consumers of domestically produced whiskey championed it as a deeply American product. Initially produced by Scots-Irish distillers who developed the craft in the British Isles and practiced their skills in the Appalachian frontier where they settled, whiskey replaced rum as the national liquor of choice after the Revolution.[8] Never mind that the Scots-Irish, too, were European immigrants. These pioneers of Anglo-American frontier settlement represented a quintessential version of national identity in the American imagination: white, Protestant, and skeptical of authority.[9] The bourbon whiskey they produced stood as a symbol for American authenticity and political autonomy, even as it served as a practical means to turn excess and perishable agricultural stock into a valuable commodity.

Jewish immigrants may have reveled in attaching themselves to whiskey's symbolic power. But the structure of whiskey production and distribution likely played a greater role in propelling Jews into the trade. Because vertical integration—the organization of commodity manufacture and distribution so that a single entity controls all its stages—affected the whiskey industry less than it did other alcohol production networks, it was possible to participate in whiskey traffic at many levels of the process. One could supply raw materials such as grains or flavoring, distill raw alcohol, rectify alcohol into "blended" whiskey, purchase whiskey in bulk from distillers and rectifiers and distribute it to retailers, or sell it directly to consumers. European Jews engaged in similar intermediary market roles, moving goods among agricultural producers, mass manufacturers, and distributors.[10] The American whiskey industry enabled them to take up all of these roles in their new country: it was a familiar line of trade, organized in a familiar manner.

It was also a relatively easy trade to enter, even though starting and running a licensed distillery could be prohibitively expensive—especially as mass production of liquor became increasingly mechanized in the late nineteenth century. But a wholesaling business required little more than access to a stock of liquor and clients to whom to sell it. Because American whiskey production was almost entirely unregulated until the passage of the "Bottled-in-Bond" Act of 1897, one could also become a rectifier easily, by purchasing straight whiskey from distillers and adding raw alcohol and flavoring agents to make blended whiskey or liqueur. This unbridled business environment lent itself to unscrupulous practices; some rectifiers labeled blended whiskey as straight, or misled consumers about the age of the whiskey they sold, or even added toxic adulterants to their "bourbon." By the turn of the century, rectifiers were regarded as disreputable swindlers who willingly degraded their product and sullied the whiskey industry itself for a profit—an accusation that, as we shall see, attached itself to Jewish whiskey dealers in the early twentieth century.[11]

Isaac Wolfe Bernheim's story shows how European Jewish culture and the opportunities made available in the American context drew Jews into this line of work: his family's experience familiarized him with alcohol commerce, a trade in which local Jews were already active. Other Jews engaged in the whiskey business in Louisville had done similar work in Europe, or came from alcohol-purveying families. Hilmar Ehrmann, for example, came to Louisville in 1887 from Tirnau, in western Hungary, where he had been trained as a maker of cordials and liqueurs. Soon after his arrival, he discovered that he needed to rethink his livelihood. According to his son, Ehrmann "found to his great disappointment that Kentuckians didn't give a damn about effeminate drinks like cordials." So he adjusted to local ideas about gender and alcohol consumption, and began to deal in a more "manly" product for a male drinking culture. Although he continued to manufacture European-style liqueurs, his wholesaling business dealt primarily in whiskey.[12] By 1900, Jews made up 25 percent of the whiskey distillers, rectifiers, and wholesalers in Louisville, a city where the Jewish population was about 3 percent of the municipal whole.[13]

The structure and culture of the American brewing industry, by contrast, impeded Jews' long-term participation in that trade. By the 1880s, the brewing industry had instituted the "tied-house" system, which structured beer supply networks so that brewers provided their product directly to saloon-keepers. (This was before the advent of home refrigeration, so saloons acted as the only beer retail outlets. Those who wished to drink their beer at home would send someone to the local saloon with a can or a bucket to fill, a practice commonly referred to as "rushing the growler.") This practice effectively cut out the middleman, and as a result, middlers and "jobbers," a position occupied by Jews in a gamut of European and American industries, played little role in the beer trade.[14]

The ethnic culture of American brewing also discouraged Jewish involvement in the beer industry. Between half and three-quarters of brewers and maltsters working in the United States were of German birth; the brewing industry also attracted native-born descendants of German immigrants, although those numbers were not formally tallied.[15] In American cities where large German populations had settled—such as Milwaukee, St. Louis, and Cincinnati in the Midwest, San Antonio in the Southwest, and New York, Brooklyn, Philadelphia, and Newark in the Northeast—local brewing industries contributed substantially to German ethnic economies, as employers and as local symbols and organizers of community life.[16] The industry's ethnic identity was so overly determined that the United States Brewers' Association, which was founded in 1862 as the industry's lobbying organization, did all their internal business in the German language until 1875.[17]

Jewish and non-Jewish German immigrants coexisted (and sometimes cooperated) in some occupations, such as general merchandizing and skilled labor in the garment trade. Wherever German immigrants constituted the majority of brewers and brewery employees, however, Jews were rarely to be found in that industry. This was partly the result of occupational experience—or, rather, the lack thereof. Jews infrequently participated in the central European brewing industry because brewers' guilds, like other German craft guilds, maintained policies that excluded Jews.[18] While Jews might have interacted with the brewing industry as suppliers of raw materials like hops, malt, and wheat—as commercial intermediaries between grain farmers and beer producers[19]—they rarely found work within the breweries or established a brewery of their own. Jewish immigrants seeking similar employment in the United States thus had little practical knowledge in industrial beer production.

In a disconcerting twist, the six-pointed hexagram—most familiar today as the Magen David, or Jewish star—was the insignia of the medieval European brewers' guild. Beginning in the fourteenth century, central European brewers branded their barreled product with the *brauerstern*, which symbolically alluded to purity and elemental balance. This practice continued in the United States, where German American brewers regularly used the star in their logo designs. Producers of other alcoholic beverages, from absinthe to whiskey, included the star in their insignias as well. Although Jews have used the hexagram for as long, if not longer—and although some American Jewish whiskey distillers and wholesalers incorporated the star into their branding motifs—its modern association with Jews as a people bears no direct relation to its use by alcohol manufacturers.

Despite structural impediments, a few Jewish brewers proved to be exceptions to the general rule. The Prussian immigrant Joseph Phillipson opened the first brewery in St. Louis in 1815. Another Prussian Jew, Frederick Zadek Solomon, cofounded the first brewery in Denver in 1859. A few years later, Solomon Goldstein, who emigrated from Poland to Anaheim, established that city's first brewery.[20] These Jewish brewers shared decisive characteristics: all three men figured among the earliest Jewish settlers in their cities,

1. Bar sign advertising George Ehret's New York City brewery, date unknown.

2. Advertisement for Star Whiskey, ca. 1859.

3. Letterhead from Rosskam, Gerstley & Co., Philadelphia, 1880. (Courtesy of Karen S. Franklin)

Medieval alchemists and brewers commonly used the hexagram to represent their crafts, and producers of other alcoholic beverages made use of the symbol as well. Of these nineteenth-century American alcohol manufacturers, only Isaac Rosskam and the Gerstley family were Jewish. It is unknown if they incorporated the star into their letterhead design because of its religious significance, or because it was a conventional practice for their trade.

and they all pioneered beer production in places where local economies were too new and in flux for alcohol purveyance to be oriented around ethnic community. Such sites provided a relatively open arena for ambitious entrepreneurs, regardless of religious background or immigrant status. When consumer interest was met with a dearth of local producers for that item, Jews took the opportunity and stepped into the gap.

In some environments, religious and other cultural pressures that kept local producers and purveyors of alcohol in relatively short supply created entrepreneurial possibilities for Jews. In the American South, negative attitudes toward alcohol came to permeate the dominant religious culture. Even though many white southerners were enthusiastic alcohol consumers, and still more opposed legislative restriction on alcohol's availability (since they associated temperance and prohibition activism with abolitionist movements and government interference in "home rule"), most were hesitant to go against the prevailing opinions of their neighbors and fellow church members by taking up the liquor trade themselves. This opened opportunities to southerners whose cultures and religions did not regard alcohol as taboo, such as Jews, Catholics, and Lutherans. A historian of the alcohol trade in Mississippi has observed that the business "appealed to ethnic minority groups"—Germans and Italians as well as Jews—who sold beer and liquor to native-born Protestants who "did not object to purchasing liquor" from a cultural outsider. A similar dynamic shaped beer production in Atlanta, a city that hosted a German community of approximately six hundred persons in 1880, many of whom were Jewish. Several German-owned breweries came and went in Atlanta's early years, and by 1885 only one remained: the Atlanta City Brewery, owned by the central European Jewish immigrant Albert Steiner.[21]

In Brooklyn, an environment where a German brewing culture was already well entrenched, there lived one family of Jewish immigrants whose pre- *and* post-migrational entrepreneurial choices defied conventional cultural practices. Samuel Liebmann was a Jewish freethinker and advocate of political reform and republicanism in his native Württemberg, where he owned an inn and brewery. According to family history, Liebmann styled his establishment as a gathering place for liberal-minded politicians and military officers, but after the failed republican revolution of 1848, the king of Württemberg declared Liebmann's tavern off limits to soldiers. By 1855, Samuel and his sons had immigrated to the United States, settling in Bushwick, a Brooklyn neighborhood famous in the mid-nineteenth century for its abundance of German immigrant–owned lager breweries. The Liebmanns built their operation on "Brewers' Row," and in the 1880s S. Liebmann and Sons Brewery began to produce Rheingold Beer, for which they would eventually become nationally known.[22]

Demography and entrepreneurial opportunity drew the Liebmanns and their small cohort of Jewish brewers into an industry that American Jews generally avoided. Whatever their individual circumstances, they were all motivated by the fact that beer was, to put it mildly, a growth industry during the late nineteenth century. Wine, on the other hand, was not. American wine producers, in comparison to their beer- and liquor-manufacturing counterparts, yielded a mere trickle. In 1870, the national wine industry reported production of only $2.25 million worth of wine, while $55 million worth of beer flowed out of American breweries and distilleries made $36 million worth of hard liquor. Ten years later, American wineries were still producing less than $3 million worth of wine, whereas beer and liquor production had nearly doubled in value. In 1890, the same story: twice as much beer and liquor as ten years before, and less than $3 million worth of wine.[23]

American indifference toward wine inhibited industry growth. Few Jews took up wine production in the United States, and the paucity of American Jewish vintners during the nineteenth century shows how an aspiring entrepreneur's context could overpower his ethnic history and culture. But would not American Jews' demand for kosher wine have inspired Jewish involvement in wine production, regardless of the general state of the industry? In fact, it did not, because that demand remained too low to stimulate production. While it is impossible to know how rigorously American Jews kept kosher during the nineteenth century, we do know that many were inconsistent in their observance. This shift away from tradition was not sui generis when it came to wine consumption; proscriptions against nonkosher wine had begun to wither centuries earlier.[24] The relative liberalism and openness of American society, and Jews' eagerness to participate in their surrounding culture, facilitated a degree of Jewish integration that was novel in modern Jewish life. For many immigrants, especially those who settled or traveled in regions with few fellow Jews, the appeal of casual sociality with neighbors, customers, and business contacts lessened the religious taboo against "gentile wine." The growth of Reform Judaism, which endorsed an Americanized mode of Jewish religious practice and encouraged its adherents to dispense with kashrut's anachronistic demands, amplified this trend.

Even Jews who drank nonkosher wine for most of the year, however, would likely have sought out kosher wine during major Jewish holidays and for religious functions. But another factor inhibited the establishment of a manufacturing niche to serve this demand: Jews could make kosher wine themselves. The historian Jonathan Sarna has noted that in the American context, home-made raisin wine was generally deemed an acceptable substitute when regular kosher wine was unavailable.[25] Unlike producers of kosher meat, who needed ritual knowledge as well as access to livestock and slaughtering facilities, making kosher wine did not necessitate religious training or occupational specialization. For wine to be kosher, the primary requirement is that only Jews who observe the Sabbath and adhere to the laws of kashrut be involved in its production, from crushing the grapes to bottling the finished product, and that any additives, utensils, and vessels used also be deemed kosher. This allowed religious Jews to make wine at home, and cheaply; all you needed was raisins, water, sugar, spices, and a clean, *kashered* container.[26] Nineteenth-century American Jews who desired kosher wine could produce it at their own hearth or acquire it from their more observant neighbors, and the informal market of home and neighborhood production met the needs of those American Jewish consumers who maintained this traditional religious practice.

The scarcity of advertisements for kosher wine in Jewish publications until the last quarter of the nineteenth century—even during the Passover holiday season, when the laws of kashrut are especially rigorous—points to its near-total absence from the commercial marketplace. The earliest record of kosher wine commerce in the United States dates back to 1848, when forty-two casks were sent from Jerusalem to New York City. This shipment of wine, which was guaranteed "pure and holy, and fit for religious purposes" by a Jerusalem rabbi, is the first known instance of any trade between American and Palestinian Jews. It would be the last such importation for decades, since the importers failed to sell all the wine at auction.[27] Grocers in New York, San Francisco, and Charleston advertised kosher wine for sale during the Passover seasons of 1859, 1861, and 1866, respectively; while neither the New York nor the Charleston shopkeepers specified the provenance of the wine, the San Francisco wine dealers claimed to have produced kosher muscat at their own Los Angeles vineyard.[28] The *American Israelite*, the national publication founded by Isaac Mayer Wise—the rabbi who developed and promoted the institutions of American Reform Judaism—had offered advertisements for *shochetim* (kosher butchers) and matzo bakers offering their Passover wares since the 1850s. But the first advertisements for "kosher l'Pesach" wine did not appear in the paper until 1867. [29]

Commercially produced kosher wine was more accessible in the 1870s and 1880s, after improvements in commercial shipping methods led to a general increase in wine importation from Europe. While most kosher wine consumed

4. Benjamin Dreyfus's winery, Anaheim, 1884. Known as the "king of the Anaheim winemakers," Ben Dreyfus (*fourth from left*) was the first vintner to produce kosher for Passover wine in California—and likely the first to do so in the United States. (Courtesy of the Anaheim Public Library)

in the United States originated in central Europe,[30] an emergent wine industry in Southern California, centered on the "German colony" of Anaheim, also captured a share of this small market.[31] A handful of Jewish immigrants took up viticulture in the region—some working for other winemakers, a few investing in their own acreage.[32] But most of the kosher wine produced in Anaheim came from the vineyards of Benjamin Dreyfus, who had immigrated to the United States from Bavaria. After attaining citizenship in 1851, he set out for the new state of California, traveling first to Los Angeles, where he worked for a brewery. He moved to Anaheim in 1858, where he and a fellow German immigrant opened a dry goods store and then a hotel and tavern.[33]

Dreyfus began to participate in the colony's wine trade in the 1860s. He managed the Anaheim Wine Growers' Association, retailing and wholesaling Anaheim wines through the association's offices in New York and San Francisco. He soon invested in a vineyard of his own. Kosher wine production was one of his earliest projects: in 1864, a San Francisco Jewish newspaper carried Dreyfus's advertisements for "Kosher wines, brandies, and white wine vinegar for *Pesach*," some of which he manufactured himself.[34] By 1876, Dreyfus ran the largest and most technologically modern winery in California, owned thousands of productive acres, and produced hundreds of thousands of gallons of wine a year.

How much kosher wine Dreyfus produced is unknown—though it was enough to attract Isaac Mayer Wise's attention. Wise took great pride in Dreyfus's status as the "king of the Anaheim winemakers," extolling Dreyfus's contributions to the industry in general and to the nation's Jewish population in particular. The successful promotion of domestically produced wines, kosher or otherwise, "is mostly due to the firm of B. Dreyfus and Co., of our country," Wise proclaimed in 1882. This industry was "one of our greatest interests," he wrote, although he was not likely to be enthusiastic about a California kosher wine industry facilitating increased observation of Jewish law. Rather, it would enhance the American Jewish ethnic economy and act as a contradiction to the commonly held stereotype that Jews did not work the land.[35]

Dreyfus and a handful of German Jewish winemakers in Southern California responded to specific market opportunities in their regional economic environment. Beyond such locations, few nineteenth-century Jewish immigrants entered the field, despite any number of cultural factors that would, under other circumstances, have led them to it.[36] But their presence in American viticulture proved short-lived. Domestic wine production in the United States dried up almost entirely during the late 1880s, when an agricultural ailment that destroyed vineyards all over the world decimated Southern California's wine industry. Dreyfus died in 1886, just as the extent of the crisis was becoming apparent. Anaheimers reorganized their local economy around other crops, such as citrus and walnuts.[37] Thus a brief phase of American Jewish participation in the wine industry, kosher or otherwise, ended. The next phase would begin not long after, when domestic wine grape production bounced back at the same time as eastern European Jewish immigration at the turn of the century radically transformed the American Jewish population and heightened the demand for traditional Jewish consumer goods.

Jews who remained active in wine commerce imported their stock from Europe, and often sold other products, most frequently domestic whiskey and other distilled liquors. Purveyors of services linked with alcohol retail, such as innkeepers, taverners, and proprietors of "kosher boarding houses" who advertised their establishments in Jewish publications, regularly announced that they served "imported Rhine wines," from Germany, in addition to "the most choice liquors," at their dinner and supper tables. (Whether this German wine was kosher, the innkeepers did not specify.) Liquor wholesalers frequently sold imported wines in addition to spirits and cordials. But wine did not figure as centrally in American Jewish commercial life as it had in Europe; here, whiskies unquestionably took the lead.

Both cultural and contextual circumstances drew Jews into the liquor trade. At the same time, another aspect of American Jewish life proved decisive: Jewish alcohol entrepreneurs' hiring practices expanded their ethnic entrepreneurial network. A 1901 advertisement in Louisville's Young Men's Hebrew Association (YMHA) newsletter reached out to potential employees in a most explicit manner: "WANTED: 'Three Jewish young men to represent a leading whiskey house. Need have no experience but must be first class, tiptop salesmen and come well recommended.'" A similar ad, for a "Jewish young man to solicit trade in the wholesale liquor business," was placed in Pittsburgh's local Jewish newspaper the following year.[38]

These advertisements gave overt expression to a most common and conventional practice within a wide range of immigrant communities: in-group hiring and economic assistance. Nineteenth-century Chinese and Italian immigrants to the United States each developed networks that enabled new arrivals to find employment, often through a labor broker who was also a nonnative member of the same group. Immigrant communities established informal pools of capital, to be made available as loans to aspiring entrepreneurs from their ethnic group. These systems were not always benevolent; some labor brokers proved willing to exploit their own countrymen, and community loan associations might impose exorbitant interest rates. But for immigrants without the personal connections or language skills to seek employment on their own, or who could not qualify for a loan or credit because of ethnic discrimination or lack of assets, these might be their sole options. And for those who were both lucky and energetic, ethnic economic networks provided a means for financial security, and even for upward mobility.[39]

As did other ethnic minorities, Jewish immigrants in the United States availed themselves of in-group employment networks whenever possible, in all regions and industries.[40] The presence of a few Jewish whiskeymen in a city could have a profound effect on the occupational choices of other local Jews. Isaac Wolfe Bernheim entered the whiskey trade in this fashion, by finding opportunity with Bloom and Loeb. He then added another link to the chain by bringing his brother into the business—and once they had started their own firm, they hired their cousin, Barney Dreyfuss, to work as the Bernheim Distilleries accountant.[41]

The surest line to a job, in any field, was through family ties. Once established, an entrepreneur often hired a relative to work alongside him in the business. These employees might later open their own concerns, not only with their former boss's blessing but with his assistance as well. By supplying stock to former employees turned independent entrepreneurs, one wholesaler could generate a sizeable collective of similar, smaller businesses. These networks were of mutual benefit to both parties, since the more established entrepreneur gained new outlets for his stock. The more successful his protégés, the more he himself prospered. (Setting up one's sons-in-law in business, as many entrepreneurs did, could also contribute to a daughter's economic well-being.)

This dynamic helped to expand the cluster of Jewish whiskey entrepreneurs in Cincinnati. Like Louisville, Cincinnati served as a hub for the distilled alcohol trade, and here, too, Jewish immigrants found an occupational niche for themselves. In 1875, according to *Bonfort's Wine and Liquor Circular*, a national trade publication, Jewish entrepreneurs owned five of the fifteen biggest whiskey-rectifying businesses in the city.[42] In 1900, when Jews constituted around 5 percent of the metropolitan population, nearly a quarter (23.7 percent) of the city's whiskey entrepreneurs were Jews.[43]

Freiberg & Workum and S. Levi & Bros., two of the firms listed by *Bonfort's* in 1875, contributed significantly to the Cincinnati cluster. After the Prussian-born Solomon Levi brought his brothers Herman and Leopold into the business, their company hired several members of their family's younger generation as traveling salesmen and clerks. He then spun the younger men off into their own businesses and served as their main suppliers. All told, S. Levi & Bros. was responsible for the establishment of at least three more Jewish-owned wholesaling concerns.[44] Julius Freiberg was born in 1823 in the Rhine Province, and apprenticed at fifteen to a vintner and barrel maker. He immigrated to the United States in 1847, and in 1855 he founded a whiskey distillery and rectifying house in Cincinnati, in partnership with Levi Workum, a native-born Jew who was already involved in whiskey production. By 1900, at least four more whiskey-wholesaling concerns had been established by Freiberg family members.[45]

Some Jewish distillers and wholesalers extended their business pursuits beyond a single location, setting up offices in multiple cities and creating regional networks of relatives working together in their trade. The whiskey distiller and wholesaler Ferdinand Westheimer of St. Joseph, Missouri, sent five of his sons to Louisville, Cincinnati, and Baltimore in the late nineteenth century so that they could open affiliated branches in each city. The Bluthenthal brothers branched out similarly. After emigrating from southwestern Germany, the Bluthenthals established separate but related liquor wholesaling companies in Atlanta, Memphis, and Cincinnati (where one of the brothers married into the Freiberg distilling family). This practice increased the number of cities where Jews took up the trade, expanded employment opportunities for their fellow Jews, and demonstrated the possibility of engagement in the trade to other Jewish immigrants who aspired to self-employment.[46]

Just as family might serve as a source of business, business connections sometimes became family connections. Marriages between Jews whose families were in the same industry were a common outgrowth of Jewish socioeconomic life during the nineteenth century. Jews of a certain status within an industry socialized and worshipped together, did business with one another, and often lived in the same neighborhood. Since they were discouraged from associating too intimately with non-Jews of the opposite sex—both by injunctions imposed within Jewish culture and by prejudice against them from without—they had little choice but to seek one another out as potential spouses.[47]

Marriages within the whiskey industry facilitated the creation and enhancement of business partnerships. Isaac Bernheim married Amanda Uri, the daughter of one of the early investors and partners in the Bernheims' company. A year after Julius Freiberg and Levi Workum commenced their distilling venture in Cincinnati, Freiberg married Workum's sister Duffie. This dynamic held true for alcohol entrepreneurs outside the whiskey trade as well. In one instance of business creating a family connection that then enhanced business, in Brooklyn in 1895 Sadie Liebmann was wed to Samuel Simon Steiner. Sadie was the granddaughter of Samuel Liebmann, founder of S. Liebmann and Sons; Samuel was a scion of a prominent Jewish hops-trading family in Manhattan that maintained offices in both New York and their hometown of Laupheim. "Under these fortuitous family circumstances," a historian of the firm has written of this union, "beer production grew constantly."[48]

Jewish whiskeymen also looked beyond their immediate families for employees, apprentices, and partners, as Isaac Wolfe Bernheim's early career in Paducah and the job notice in the Louisville YMHA newsletter both indicate. Commercial apprenticeships and partnerships made possible by ethnic community connections helped Jews find positions in the alcohol industry and kept business within the in-group. Although intra-group cooperation was not unique to the alcohol trade or to Jewish communities, it does explain, at least in part, how certain ethnic communities came to hold so many jobs in a particular trade or industry.[49] Among Louisville's Jews, this dynamic was common enough to inspire a local in-joke. An 1895 issue of the city's YMHA newsletter included a short item about the organization's janitor, who, the piece claimed, was going into the distilling business; his capital stock was estimated at $100,000, and Isaac Wolfe Bernheim would be the company's vice president.[50] None of this was true, but readers in the know would surely have been amused. The idea that a janitor would join the ranks of Louisville's distillers, with Isaac Bernheim as his partner, was patently absurd and yet entirely possible. Since so many successful Jews in the alcohol trade had started their careers from modest origins and ascended into the entrepreneurial elite—Bernheim not least among them—why not a janitor, too?

Engagement in the alcohol trade throughout the nineteenth century enhanced American Jews' business, family, and ethno-religious networks, and served to strengthen Jewish community cohesion. Jewish alcohol entrepreneurs also actively sought to reinforce group unity by participating in and supporting local and national Jewish organizations. They were nearly ubiquitous among leading members of Jewish communal organizations, even at the nascent moments of American Jewish communities. Henry Hyman, the first Jew to settle in Louisville, made his living as the proprietor of a tavern called Hyman's Altar, and helped organize Louisville's first Jewish mutual aid society.[51] In Atlanta, the Bavarian immigrant David Mayer sold alcohol, clothes, and slaves for a living; in 1860, he spearheaded the purchase of a section of Atlanta's Oakland Cemetery for Jewish use, and later participated in the founding of the city's first synagogue.[52]

Whiskey distillers and wholesalers were well represented on executive committees and boards of directors in nineteenth-century Jewish institutions. In Cincinnati in 1873, at the foundational meeting of Isaac Mayer Wise's Union of American Hebrew Congregations (UAHC), Julius Freiberg, then president of that city's Congregation Bene Israel, addressed the delegates with words of welcome. He later became president of that organization, as did his son and business partner, J. Walter Freiberg.[53] Louisville's Jewish distillers Samuel Grabfelder and Louis Barkhouse both presided over Congregation Adas Israel, and Nathan Block served as director of the local YMHA. (Construction of the YMHA's building, it is worth mentioning, was funded by the Bernheims, and Isaac had earlier been president of the organization.)[54] The Jewish distillers of Peoria, Illinois—a city that produced more whiskey than the entire state of Kentucky at the end of the nineteenth century—could also be found in leadership roles in local denominational institutions. Samuel Woolner, a Hungarian immigrant whose family founded one of the city's largest distilleries, for years held the presidency of Congregation Anshai Emeth; the liquor wholesaler David Ullman served as his vice president.[55]

One might reasonably expect this phenomenon in cities where the alcohol industry was central to the local economy and alcohol entrepreneurs were both relatively numerous and accorded especially high status. When Louisville's Adas Israel sent a dozen delegates as representatives to the 1892 convention of the UAHC, at least six of these men made and sold alcohol for a living.[56] Yet that same year in Atlanta—not a city known for its alcohol industry—six of the fourteen officers of the Hebrew Benevolent Congregation were currently or had until recently been involved in the local alcohol trade.[57] Jewish alcohol entrepreneurs loomed larger in their communities than their numbers might indicate. They demonstrated eagerness to play an active role in Jewish life, and the most successful among them gained significant social standing. This simultaneously tightened the ties that bound them to their social and economic networks and raised their status further among their coreligionists.

All the above-named Jewish organizations, while varying in purpose and geographic reach, shared a common mission that corresponded to the worldview of these whiskeymen. American Jewish alcohol entrepreneurs of this era consistently gravitated toward communal institutions that encouraged and facilitated acculturation. Adas Israel in Louisville, Atlanta's Hebrew Benevolent Congregation (also known as "the Temple"), and Anshai Emeth in Peoria all favored a progressive, reformist vision of American Judaism. The Cincinnati campus of Hebrew Union College, the rabbinical seminary Wise founded in 1875 in order to train a liberal, modern American rabbinate, bears brick-and-mortar proof of whiskey entrepreneurs' abiding interest in an acculturated version of Jewish organizational life: the Freiberg family of Cincinnati provided the financial resources for building the campus gymnasium, and Isaac Wolfe Bernheim funded the construction of the library. Bernheim's ambition to modernize American Judaism grew over the course of his life, and his 1907 telegram to the UAHC announcing his donation made his intentions clear. "The construction of a modern college complete in its appointments," he wrote, "will mark an epoch in the history of progressive American Israel. It will prove that reform has taken deep root, and will enable it to blossom and bear fruit."[58]

This tendency to move away from traditional Judaism—away from what is today referred to as Orthodoxy—indicated a shift in nineteenth-century American Jewish religious and cultural practices. Among those American Jews who remained committed to religious identity and observance were tens of thousands who felt that the American context, which both provided opportunities for inclusion and imposed pressures to conform, required revision of Jewish liturgy and custom, and even, in some cases, rejection of those elements of Jewish law that clashed with American cultural practices. The reforms they implemented reveal a messy combination of motivations, sometimes purely practical and sometimes philosophically driven. Schisms within the movement showed that there was no single idea about how much change was too much.[59] But generally speaking, reformers (and Reformers) created a version of Judaism, and of Jewish identity, that its practitioners proudly considered modern, rational, and dignified enough to stand along-side mainstream American Protestantism. Most important, promoters of this progressive and acculturated version of American Judaism encouraged Jews to think of themselves as Americans, first and foremost—as free to participate in all aspects of American life, even while they continued to identify as Jews.[60]

The Young Men's Hebrew Association also responded to nineteenth-century American Jews' desire to participate more fully in American life. Modeled after the Young Men's Christian Association and similarly inspired by Victorian ideas about manliness, morality, and leisure, the YMHA offered literary and educational events and promoted vigorous physical exercise. They provided a Jewish-centered environment for socializing, and created opportunities for young Jewish men to edify themselves about Jewish history and literature.[61] At the same time, YMHAs (and similar secular Jewish clubs) encouraged personal growth through cosmopolitan pursuits, offering lectures on science and political issues as well as classes in European languages.

Sometimes they took a step beyond acculturation and actively facilitated integration. At the dedication of Louisville's YMHA building in 1896, the organization's secretary, a lawyer by vocation (and a close associate of Bernheim's), discussed with a reporter from the local newspaper the executive committee's decision to open YMHA membership to non-Jews. The secretary acknowledged that this was an unusual and controversial move, and explained that their goal was to "cultivate a closer and more intimate personal and social relationship" with non-Jewish Louisvillians. "In our business life we meet all our fellow citizens with the very happiest results, but this has been carried only to a limited degree into our social life. . . . There ought to be no distinction between Jew and Gentile in our social relations." The Jews of the YMHA, the secretary informed a local reporter, "invite all who are qualified by character and standing, Jew or Gentile, to join us."[62] Membership in a progressively minded Jewish social collective or congregation demonstrated Jews' eagerness to redefine Jewish identity and group unity so that it did not preclude integration.

Jewish alcohol entrepreneurs were exceptionally invested in this project because they worked in an industry that was predominantly non-Jewish. Acculturative forms of Jewish religious practice and social organization did not require Jews to remain segregated from their gentile neighbors, and nineteenth-century Jewish alcohol entrepreneurs found this philosophy to be especially useful. Their experience was unlike that of Jews in the dry goods and garment trades, both fields in which Jewish employees and entrepreneurs were heavily concentrated and where strong ethnic networks allowed Jews at all levels of the business to work together with less reliance on non-Jewish participation. By contrast, work in the alcohol business consistently put Jews in contact with industry agents and businessmen outside Jewish circles. They interacted regularly with gentile customers and competitors, and some even formed business partnerships with Christians.

Such experiences and relationships proved economically and psychologically beneficial for both Jewish alcohol entrepreneurs and their ethnic communities. Many sought to extend these relationships beyond their businesses and participated in a wide range of civic engagement. Those who proved capable leaders in local politics or national trade associations served as Jewish communities' representatives to American Christians. For Jews who hoped to be accepted as citizens of their cities and towns and to be incorporated into national life more largely, Jewish whiskeymen were among the vanguard, helping to forge a path toward admission into American society.

Alcohol entrepreneurs were not the only Jewish businessmen who acted as both formal and informal community liaisons during the nineteenth century. Jewish professionals, merchants, and workers of all kinds joined Masonic temples and chambers of commerce, whenever and wherever Jews were welcome within such organizations. They also entered the political arena, running for elected office and publicly commenting on elections and current events (sometimes to the dismay of other Jews, who feared accusations that they were pursuing a group agenda).[63] The frequency with which Jewish alcohol purveyors did these things, however, points to their relative comfort among non-Jews, as well as their interest in creating and nurturing social networks that connected them to their non-Jewish colleagues.

The specific nature of Jewish alcohol entrepreneurs' efforts toward civic engagement and cultural integration sometimes reflected the demographics of their locality. In late nineteenth-century Cincinnati, for instance, German immigrants made up as much as a fifth of the local population. In this context, Jews in the alcohol trade, themselves German immigrants, often participated in local German American culture. The Jewish distiller Samuel

N. Pike funded the construction of the city's Pike Opera House, a cultural center for performances of German theater and music, while Julius Freiberg held positions on the board of directors of a number of German American organizations.[64]

But most Jewish alcohol entrepreneurs set their sights beyond German cultural associations. Their interest in civic engagement occasionally led them into politics, and those who held elected offices acted as public representatives of both their ethnic and their business communities. In the 1870s and 1880s, Jews who made their livings as saloonkeepers and liquor dealers acted as city aldermen and justices of the peace in Little Rock and Helena, Arkansas. The Jewish liquor dealer and wholesale grocer Isaac Lowenberg was elected mayor of Natchez, Mississippi, and the Jewish saloonkeeper Cassius Tillman served as the town sheriff.[65]

During the same decade, Ben Dreyfus, the "wine king of Anaheim," served on the city council and then held that town's mayoral office.[66] The Cincinnatian Charles Fleischmann—a Hungarian Jewish immigrant whose manufacturing concerns included both distilled liquor and compressed baking yeast—was elected to the Ohio state senate several times before his death in 1898, and his son and business partner was the city's mayor from 1900 until 1906.[67]

Jewish distillers, wholesalers, and brewers also avidly took up membership and leadership of commercial interest collectives. By taking part in these groups, Jewish alcohol entrepreneurs intensified their cooperative relationships with non-Jewish colleagues and fellow businessmen, and together they rallied around a cause they could all agree on: local, regional, and national environments that encouraged business activity and economic growth. In 1900, when Atlanta's Chamber of Commerce announced the formation of a fund-raising committee of sixty-three local businessmen for the upcoming Southern Interstate Fair, three of the four participating Jews sold alcohol for a living: Albert Steiner, president of the Atlanta City Brewery; Aaron Bluthenthal, cofounder of the wholesaling enterprise Bluthenthal and Bickart; and Joseph Jacobs, whose chain of pharmacies also retailed liquor for both medicinal and beverage use.[68] In addition, Steiner and Bluthenthal were two of the three designates on the "Liquor Dealer" committee—a significant overrepresentation of Jews, who constituted less than 10 percent of the local trade.[69] These men enjoyed high esteem both among Jewish businessmen and within the general entrepreneurial community, and were eager (or, at least, willing) to lend their energies to municipal pro-business endeavors.

5. A. & M. Moses General Store, Natchez, Mississippi, date unknown. The store's sign announces the availability of "whisky, brandy, gin & wine." Jews played an active role in commercial and civic life in Natchez, as they did in cities and towns throughout the nineteenth-century South. Several of Natchez's Jewish liquor dealers and saloonkeepers served in positions of municipal authority. (Courtesy of the Goldring/Woldenberg Institute of Southern Jewish Life)

Jewish alcohol entrepreneurs participated in industry lobbying organizations as well. Advocacy on behalf of their industry enabled them to look after group interests, and their involvement acted as a retort to accusations that Jewish political and economic concerns differed from those of other Americans.[70] The Liebmanns of Brooklyn, for instance, helped found the United States Brewers' Association in 1862, and several family members served on the organization's executive board. Julius Barkhouse, a member of a prominent Louisville distilling family, helped to organize an association "devoted to the special interests of Kentucky distillation," and served as its secretary.[71] Cincinnati's Jewish whiskeymen were members of the city's Commercial Association, Business Men's Club, and Chamber of Commerce, and held leadership positions in the Ohio Wine & Spirit Association and the National Wholesale Liquor Dealers Association.[72] Samuel Woolner, Jr., of Peoria held the office of vice president of the latter organization, and Isaac Wolfe Bernheim served as its president.

These efforts toward cooperation and shared interest were generally successful. For the most part, non-Jewish alcohol entrepreneurs welcomed their Jewish colleagues into the trade and celebrated their successes as a boon to the larger industry. *Bonfort's Wine and Spirit Circular* regularly included friendly mentions and complementary longer pieces on thriving Jewish businessmen. Elias Block & Sons were described as "our enterprising Cincinnati friends" whose product would "elevate the taste for whiskies to a higher level." Isaac Bernheim's successes were extolled regularly, sometimes with humorous bite. *Bonfort's* noted in 1890 that Bernheim had recently attended Mardi Gras in New Orleans; "if he likes it he will buy it," the writer joked, "and travel it around the country as an advertisement" for his distillery's I. W. Harper whiskey brand. On a few occasions, *Bonfort's*, which was founded and published by German Lutheran immigrants, included a little Yiddish for their readers. What, for instance, did the Cincinnati wholesaler Samuel N. Weil want for Christmas in 1889? According to *Bonfort's*, he wanted a *Metziah*—the Yiddish word for "bargain."[73] Considering the friendliness of the editor's general attitude toward Jewish distillers and wholesalers, this comment should not be interpreted as an anti-Semitic slur, but rather a friendly ribbing—even though it played on stereotypes of Jewish economic behavior. *Bonfort's* occasional practice of sprinkling news stories with Yiddish acknowledged the prevalence of Jews in the American liquor trade.

The nineteenth-century alcohol industry's inclusiveness extended beyond the trade itself. Credit reports from these decades present another commercial context in which Jews in the beer, liquor, and wine industries were well regarded, or at least generally judged on their merits. In the mid-nineteenth century, several credit-reporting agencies began to offer their services to American wholesalers. R. G. Dun & Co., the predominant credit reference agency of the nineteenth century, hired correspondents all over the country to investigate the reputations and assess the financial standing of businessmen seeking to purchase stock on credit. In the past, businessmen had extended credit based on personal knowledge of their customers; but as commercial networks extended beyond the local, wholesalers came to rely on credit reporters for information about potential debtors hundreds, and sometimes even thousands, of miles away.[74]

The credit reports accumulated by R. G. Dun & Co. indicate that Jewish alcohol entrepreneurs were assessed as creditworthy—which is to say, trustworthy and capable of paying off their debts—on a regular basis. For instance, R. G. Dun's first mention of the Hoffheimer Brothers, a liquor wholesaling firm in Cincinnati, suggested that potential creditors should regard them with caution. "Here a short time," the reporter noted in 1855. "No one knows them—have a small stock and do but little business." But by 1858, according to the credit agency's local reporter, the company had found its feet: "Some of their Israelitish brethren think [the Hoffheimers] have been getting along too fast for the modest means with which they are known to have come from a few years ago. But those of their faith *in the same trade* say they have made considerable money. . . . Some of our largest liquor dealers here have full confidence and will sell them all they want."[75]

R. G. Dun's reporter had solicited the opinion of the Hoffheimers' fellow Jewish liquor wholesalers in town. He seems to have asked around about liquor dealers James and Albert Levy as well, and he noted them as "in good credit with their Hebrew brethren" in November 1866. In both cases, Cincinnati's Jewish economic networks were a source of valued information. When Jewish liquor businessmen gained the trust of "their Hebrew brethren," reporters pronounced them trustworthy, and creditworthy, to the general business community. In the liquor industry, Jewish and gentile economic networks did not generate mutually exclusive credit systems. Rather, they interacted with one another, and a Jewish businessman who did well and enjoyed the confidence of other Jews could be granted entrée into the larger world of alcohol entrepreneurs. The 1871 credit report on Jewish liquor wholesalers Simon and Joseph Silverman of Pomeroy, Ohio, described them as "very well liked here by Jew & Gentile," indicating that they operated comfortably in both Jewish and non-Jewish commercial networks.[76]

The fact that a businessman was Jewish also suggested that he had access not only to other sources of credit, but also to a ready-made customer base. R. G. Dun & Co. first reported on Julius Isaacs, who kept a liquor retail outlet in Newark, in 1876, after he had been in business for five years. His business was very small, worth no more than $1,000 all told. Regardless, the correspondent noted that Isaacs was an "attentive" businessman, and that he had "secured a good run of customers among his class of people (Israelites)." On that basis, Isaacs was assessed as "a fair risk for small wants."[77]

This picture contradicts much of the historiography on nineteenth-century American Jewish economic life. Historians often claim that R. G. Dun's reporters were universally dismissive of and insulting toward Jews. Some have argued that the reporters' negative assessments of Jewish businessmen made Jewish economic networks a necessity, without which Jews would have had no access to credit at all.[78] Yet an 1869 report on the Atlanta liquor wholesaler Levi Cohen—"We would not fear to credit them for any amount"—undermines that analysis. So does the report made that same year on Loeb and Bloom, Isaac Wolfe Bernheim's employers in Paducah: "They stand high for integrity and business capacity . . . are doing quite a business for this place: we think them entirely good."[79] Of 230 reports on Jewish liquor businesses found in R. G. Dun & Co.'s ledgers for four cities—Cincinnati, Louisville, Atlanta, and Newark—an overwhelming majority (180, or 78 percent of the total) were positive. Of those positive reviews, 32 could be deemed only moderately enthusiastic, usually because the businessmen dealt in very small amounts of stock, or because they refused to share their financial records with correspondents. In 50 cases (22 percent), the reporter recommended that the businessmen not be granted credit at all, and in only six of these reports did overt anti-Semitism stand out as a factor.

It is true that if one were looking for prejudice in the credit agency's ledgers, one could find it. Anti-Semitism and social discrimination against Jews escalated in the United States during the last third of the nineteenth century, as upwardly mobile Jewish businessmen and their families sought access to elite (and nearly homogenously white, native-born, and Protestant) cultural venues.[80] Suspicion of Jewish economic behavior influenced some R. G. Dun reporters, as when they referred to Jewish businessmen as "tricky" or "sharp," or as "strangers" whose general character was thus far unknown. Jews' occasional unwillingness to share their business records with reporters, alongside their status as newcomers, also rendered them less than entirely trustworthy in the eyes of the credit reporters.[81] Sometimes even positive assessments dripped with bigotry: "He is a Jew," an Iowa reporter wrote of a furniture and cloth salesman in 1868, "but he seems honest." In Grand Rapids, another backhanded compliment in an otherwise positive report on a clothier: "The worst thing we know of him is that he is a Jew." For some reporters, the best that could be said of a Jewish businessman was that he was "of the better sort."[82]

Jewish alcohol entrepreneurs were not immune from this development, although it is worth suggesting that some Jewish businessmen seem to have deserved the negative reviews they received. According to reports, the Cincinnati liquor storeowner Isaac Jacobs paid for his stock with a check from a bank in which he did not have an account, and when the bank tried to reclaim the merchandise, they found that Jacobs had removed the whiskey from the barrels and filled them with water. "Jacobs is considered a first class rogue," the reporter declared in 1856, "and his whole business life has been one swindling operation." In later years he was referred to as a "scamp" and "very slippery," and his affiliation with other liquor companies rendered them suspect in the eyes of R. G. Dun & Co.'s correspondents. But none of the entries mentions Jacobs's religious affiliation, so it is impossible to know whether anti-Semitism had any influence in this scathing report—that is, if Jacobs's malfeasances confirmed the correspondent's preconceptions of Jewish business practices, or if the reporter even knew that Jacobs was Jewish.[83]

Anti-Semitic intent is clearer in the reports on the Selig family, who sold dry goods, groceries, and liquor in Atlanta. In early 1877, the correspondent called them "energetic Germans" of "good habits," but also referred to them as being of "tricky stock"—a phrase that was sometimes used to refer to Germans as well as to Jews. The next report, later that year, is not as ambivalent or ambiguous. "This Class of Merchants," he wrote, "always takes care of 'Number One' in the event of an emergency."[84] This turn of phrase was regularly employed in credit assessments of Jewish businessmen, and the word choice made clear that the writer had preconceived notions about Jewish business ethics and entrepreneurial trustworthiness.

In general, however, the R. G. Dun & Co. ledgers present a full range of attitudes toward Jewish businessmen in the American alcohol trade, and in fact trend toward positive assessments. This might come as a surprise not only to historians of the American Jewish experience, but also to historians who have studied the credit rating agency's general ideological motivations. Its founder, Lewis Tappan, was an evangelical Christian and a temperance advocate, and made a point of hiring correspondents who shared his convictions. The historian Bertram Wyatt-Brown has noted that Tappan "piously refused to sell his service to a distillery."[85] A more thorough examination of the ledgers, however, evinces no principled discrimination against urban alcohol businessmen of any region, religion, or ethnicity. If their enterprise was at all profitable, and they did not enjoy their own product to excess, Tappan's agency was willing to appraise alcohol producers and purveyors positively, and to view them as entirely respectable. Reports from all over the country refer to brewers, wholesalers, and even saloonkeepers as "industrious" and "honest," and therefore worthy of credit. For the credit rating company's correspondents, entrepreneurial success usually overrode spiritual and political considerations, at least where alcohol was concerned. Business, as they say, was business.

The same attitude seems to have held for Jews within that industry. Even if hostility based on their ethnic and religious affiliation did affect the ability of some Jews to obtain positive credit reports, examination of R. G. Dun's records shows that anti-Semitism was not a consistent or even a frequent obstacle for Jewish alcohol entrepreneurs. Positive credit reports gave their recipients access to national credit networks, which enhanced their ability to participate in the American economy. Jews in the liquor trade were thus positioned both to help their fellow Jews (since they had access to more capital) and to strengthen the Jewish entrepreneurial presence in mainstream business circles.

For some, success in the alcohol business gave them the means to respond to social anti-Semitism. A few years after a hotelier denied the banker Joseph Seligman a room at the exclusive Union Hotel in Saratoga, New York, and an owner of another elite resort on Coney Island announced that he would exclude Jews from his hotel as well—anti-Semitic incidents that unnerved acculturated Jews all over the country—the distiller Charles Fleischmann purchased sixty acres of land in Griffin's Corners, several counties to the south of Saratoga. There in the Catskills, in 1883, the Fleischmann family established a summer colony of their own. They intended this upstate New York resort to cater to other wealthy central European Jewish immigrants and their descendants, so that they could vacation together and avoid the humiliation of rejection that Seligman had suffered.[86] If they were to be excluded from elite social environments, Fleischmann was determined to recreate the upper-class leisure milieu so that prosperous American Jews could comport themselves as did other wealthy Americans.

As worrying as social anti-Semitism was to nineteenth-century Jews, another development arguably concerned them more, for the repercussions threatened to be more dire: the growing campaign to "Christianize" American society and politics. The temperance and prohibition movements participated in this campaign, aspiring to significantly modify American life not only by removing beverage alcohol from the consumer market, but also by infusing American politics with Protestant religious ideology. As advocates of an interpretation of American politics and law that restricted the influence of religious sectarianism on the state—and, of course, as participants in the American alcohol traffic—Jews were compelled to take a position on the issue. In doing so, they utilized political and cultural debates about the place of alcohol, religion, and individual liberty that reinforced for themselves, and presented to their Christian fellow citizens, a notion of their own communal identity that was simultaneously, seamlessly, and proudly both Jewish and American.

2

"Do as We Israelites Do"

American Jews and the Gilded Age Temperance Movement

The ladies who gathered in Cleveland in November 1874 had set themselves an ambitious goal: they were going to establish a national women's organization that would work toward the total eradication of beverage alcohol from American life. Although both individually and institutionally affiliated with the Protestant church, they hoped that all American women would join their cause—an aspiration that generated a brief debate about the prudence of including the word "Christian" in the organization's name. One of the women present suggested that by referring so explicitly to their religious affiliation, they risked "shut[ting] out the Jews." But the majority dismissed this concern, and in the end they declared themselves the Woman's Christian Temperance Union (WCTU). "Since there was no creed test" for members, they assured themselves, the alienation of Jewish women "need not be feared."[1]

Twenty years later, an editorial in the monthly periodical *American Jewess* suggested that those initial concerns had been well-founded. The 1895 article, likely written by the editor and clubwoman Rosa Sonneschein, reported that at a recent WCTU conference, Frances Willard, the group's president, urged the organization to create alliances with Jewish and Catholic women. Though this indicated "tolerance and progress," Sonneschein proclaimed, she predicted that Jews would continue to avoid the organization, as they had done since its inception. That word, it seems, had indeed proved alienating; "the name *Christian*," she wrote, "indicates too narrow a sphere."[2]

Jews' main objection concerning the WCTU, however, was not its sectarian name but the cause it espoused. Jews consumed alcohol in their weekly home-based religious rituals and in their social gatherings, Sonneschein noted, yet "drunkenness is amongst them . . . only encountered in a few isolated cases." Alcohol abuse, in other words, was not a Jewish concern, and

Jews' moderate drinking habits indicated that the problem with alcohol was not located in the alcohol itself, but in the drinker who failed to exercise self-control. Because of their distinctive cultural relationship to alcohol, she concluded, Jews would forever remain "loath to subscribe to total abstinence" and would never join the ranks of temperance activists.[3]

American Jews supported moderation as a personal virtue and an admirable trait, and a few encouraged some regulation of alcohol commerce. But throughout the late nineteenth century, Jews generally rejected the anti-alcohol movement. Like Sonneschein, they dismissed the movement's claim that morally right-minded people never touched a drop, and pointed to themselves as proof that alcohol could be consumed in a spirit of self-restraint. Further, they protested that the movement's demand for the legal prohibition of the manufacture and sale of alcohol imposed unjust restrictions on personal behavior and commercial enterprise. And they expressed horror at the gendered nature of temperance politics, insisting that the woman's sphere did not include public demonstrations and acts of civil disobedience. In sum, American Jews regarded the anti-alcohol movement as politically wrong-headed—even repulsive—and certainly as inimical to the civil liberties guaranteed by the Constitution.

Jews' presence on the "wet" side of temperance and prohibition debates is not surprising, since the anti-alcohol movement threatened their own ancient religious rituals and contemporary social practices. Considering the prominence of alcohol producers and purveyors in many nineteenth-century Jewish communities, anti-alcohol movements also posed a danger to their entrepreneurial freedom and economic well-being. But Jewish criticism of the temperance movement was an act of communal self-protection with objectives beyond the right to drink and to traffic in commodities of their choosing; it was a defense of the idea of the nonsectarian state, which American Jews held dear. Jews' experience in the United States—where they could participate in economic and political life and join civic institutions to an extent impossible elsewhere—had facilitated the creation of a group identity that was acculturated and American but also unapologetically Jewish. The temperance movement's religious commitments signaled the expansion of nineteenth-century efforts to "Christianize" American life and reorganize its laws around Protestant values and morality. Jews feared that if these movements were successful, their equal status, even their citizenship, could be in peril.[4]

Jews could have responded to the temperance movement merely by disputing its claims to be consistent with American political practices, and by protesting that mandatory abstinence would infringe on all Americans' constitutional rights of conscience and property. That they did, and in doing so they refined their communal position on the relationship between religion and politics in the United States. They also joined other Americans who were skeptical of the temperance movement's call for sumptuary laws by insisting that "prohibition does not prohibit," and pointing out that simply making alcohol illegal would not keep people from finding a drink if they really wanted one. But they went a step further: American Jews presented themselves as a preferable counterpoint to both the drunkard and the teetotaler, and counseled their fellow Americans, as Rabbi Marcus Jastrow said in 1874, to "do as we Israelites do" by neither loving nor despising alcohol excessively. The prohibition debate provided Jews occasion to suggest that their distinctive historical and religious relationship to alcohol made them model citizens whose presence benefited the nation.

American debates surrounding the effect of alcohol consumption on politics, public health, and morality began well before the American Revolution. Colonists and citizens of the early republic acknowledged the presence of "strong drink" in all aspects of their culture. American and European observers alike expressed amazement and dismay at the ceaseless flow of liquor, in business dealings, at political gatherings, and in the home, where all family members, including women and children, consumed it. "Americans drank at home and abroad, alone and together, at work and at play, in fun and in earnest," the historian W. J. Rorabaugh has written. "They drank from the crack of dawn to the crack of dawn."[5] Benjamin Rush, the surgeon general of the Continental Army, took issue with the widely held belief that alcohol was an elixir of health, insisting that alcohol created rather than cured illness and inevitably led to physical and spiritual degeneracy. Others claimed that the steady flow of alcohol at civic events (especially elections) and in the military threatened the health of the body politic.

Early temperance advocates urged moderation rather than total abstention, encouraging their countrymen (and women) to avoid distilled liquors and choose wine, cider, and beer instead.[6] By the mid-nineteenth century, however, concerns shifted from *what* and *how much* Americans drank to *that* they drank at all. Thousands of temperance societies sprang up all over the nation (and in the Northeast and Midwest in particular) during the 1830s and 1840s, imploring citizens to pledge, formally and publicly, to renounce even moderate consumption of alcohol. Antebellum temperance activism was, in part, a response to the jarring changes wrought by the economic transformations of the day. The nation was growing increasingly urban, industrial, and commercially oriented. Internal migration and immigration from abroad, which filled cities and towns with newcomers who further upended the traditional social and political order, exacerbating the anxieties provoked by economic change. By swearing off indulgence in alcohol and drunken leisure, teetotalers hoped to master their bewilderment by becoming more productive and manifesting a heightened level of self-control.[7]

Although they aimed to embody industrial discipline and to control their own passions, in fact their ambitions extended beyond their own personal comportment. Temperance enthusiasts regarded alcohol consumption as a burden on the whole community. If a drinker spent his weekly wages on a payday drinking binge, they pointed out, his family starved. If he drank at work, his productivity (and thus the output of his workplace) suffered. If his alcohol consumption was heavy enough to render him a public nuisance—or worse, a pauper or a criminal—his community was obligated to spend its limited resources on him, and possibly on the family he had failed to support. The common good, some teetotalers insisted, required not only that alcohol be despised, but also that it be out of reach. Antebellum temperance activists most often employed moral suasion and sought to convince drinkers to abstain of their own free will. They regarded coercion, in the form of "no-license" laws and other legislation that limited or prohibited the availability of beverage alcohol, as another possible solution to the nation's liquor problem. Even as early as the 1850s, exhortations for personal temperance intertwined with demands for total prohibition; the latter philosophy soon dominated.[8]

The religious revivalism of the Second Great Awakening further influenced the growth and direction of the antebellum temperance movement. Protestant revivalists preached that once the nation had collectively abandoned sinful behavior and chosen Christian redemption, the Second Coming of the Messiah would soon be at hand. This marked a shift in American Protestant theology from Calvinist ideas of predestination to the belief that salvation was available to all who chose a righteous path. One achieved salvation via inner piety, and outwardly demonstrated it through church attendance, economic productivity, familial stability and contentment, and participation in the struggle against societal ills like poverty and crime. Not every churchgoing revivalist adhered to the principle of teetotalism; but for those whose zeal for temperance was influenced by millennialism, "ardent spirits" posed a singular danger to the nation's spiritual health—both individually and collectively, since drinking hardened men's hearts against both God and their fellow men. In addition to breeding paupers and criminals, temperance Christians insisted, alcohol created a culture of "moderate" drinkers and alcohol purveyors who could not see the causal relationship between alcohol and poverty—or, worse, were indifferent to it. It was as benevolent and godly to sway a moderate or indifferent drinker to the temperance cause as it was to reform a drunkard.[9]

Those who defined Christian moral righteousness in total temperance terms, however, were confronted with a problematic text: the Bible. Wine flows through both the Pentateuch and the Gospels. For temperance Christians, the stickiest theological inconsistency was Jesus's consumption of wine during Jewish religious rituals—most famously during the Last Supper, which occurred during Passover and has been described by biblical historians and scholars as a seder, an occasion where wine is copiously consumed. And how would they square the story of the wedding in Cana, where Jesus turned water into wine, with assertions that alcohol was a sinful substance? If the Bible were to be read and understood literally, as they believed it must, the presence of wine in the text would directly contradict the claims and block the goals of the Christian temperance movement.

Some temperance activists conceded that *yayin*, or intoxicating wine, was without a doubt present in the Bible, while pointing out that the ancient Israelites of the Hebrew Bible and the Jews of Roman Palestine lacked sufficient scientific information about the dangers of alcohol. One New York temperance leader suggested in 1839 that if Jesus had had access to the "better knowledge of our times," he would not have sanctioned the use of wine, much less made it himself.[10] Others, however, sought to do away with the contradiction altogether, by proving that the wine consumed by the early Jews, and therefore by Jesus, was in fact unfermented. Antebellum temperance clergy and lay Protestants pored over the Hebrew Bible in an effort to determine, through exhaustive biblical exegesis, whether the Israelites drank *yayin* or *tirosh* (unfermented grape or raisin juice). If it was just fruit juice, as anti-alcohol absolutists insisted, then there was no wine at the Last Supper. This would mean that unfermented wine, or "new" or "pure" wine as it was also known, could be used for Christian communion; more important, it would buttress temperance Christians' claims that total abstinence was consonant with Jesus's teachings and life.

Thus Jews were brought into early temperance discussions, although primarily as figures of symbolic and historical interest. When possible, evangelical temperance activists sought the expertise of contemporary Jews, under the assumption that current Jewish rituals paralleled those of the biblical era. They found a willing spokesman in the diplomat, playwright, and New York newspaper publisher Mordecai M. Noah. Noah was the best-known Jewish public figure in the antebellum United States, and his writings, both journalistic and dramaturgic, were widely cited as representations of Jewish opinion and tradition. In 1836, when the secretary of the New York State Temperance Society asked Noah about Jewish wine customs, Noah responded publicly in his newspaper, the *Evening Star*, that Jews commonly used unfermented raisin wine in their Passover rituals. This was true, as we have already seen. But what Noah did not say, and what he probably did not himself know—his knowledge of Jewish law and custom left much to be desired—was that this was primarily a practice of Diasporic expediency, a way for Jews far from Jewish population centers to have access to kosher wine.[11]

For Mordecai Noah, temperance activists' interest in Jewish alcohol consumption presented an opportunity to make a case for Jewish inclusion in American life. When he offered this Jewish practice to Christian solicitors, he intended for Judaism (and Jews) to be regarded as in alignment with a contemporary stream of American morality and politics. But for temperance Christians, Noah's "expertise" was primarily of value because it lent authority to their own theological claims and political demands. In fact, they ignored him when he later pointed to King Solomon's declaration that "wine maketh the heart glad" and criticized the temperance movement's absolutist position.[12] Noah's claims about Passover raisin wine seemed to confirm temperance Christians' theory that Jews did not drink fermented wine at Passover. In the end, that was the only thing his Protestant interlocutors wanted from him.

Noah's failed efforts highlighted a contradiction in Jews' status in the antebellum United States. As a religious minority accorded certain rights, they encountered relatively few barriers to full participation in American life. But according to the majoritarian politics of the nineteenth century, Jews were expected to accept that American culture and common law were Christian at their core. When confronted with attempts to align American legal and social practices with Protestant morality and theology, Jews responded variously. A radical few insisted that only the total separation of church and state could guarantee equality for Jews as a religious minority, and argued that the nation's founding documents guaranteed a high wall between the two. Others took the position that while the Bill of Rights guaranteed tolerance and equality for all peoples of all religions, the United States was still a *religious* (although not a sectarian) nation. Evocations of Christ in political and civic contexts, such as the opening of legislative sessions, were acceptable as long as a reference to Judaism could be included as well.

For much of the nineteenth century, the latter position prevailed. American Jews were usually satisfied when they were able to live as one religious community among many, without molestation or onerous impositions on their consciences or daily practices. When confronted with barriers to full equality and representation under the law, they responded inconsistently, arguing for the right to hold elected office in some cases and capitulating to statutes forbidding commerce on Sundays in others.[13]

But after the Civil War, temperance Christians gathered strength and escalated their demands. They extended their activities deeper into the civic realm, making religious arguments not just for individual abstinence, but also for the total legal prohibition of alcohol commerce. Further, they did so on religious grounds, calling for the overt infusion of Protestant theology into American political life. When Jews responded to this development during the late nineteenth century, they showed far less interest in accommodation than Mordecai Noah's actions had demonstrated. Instead of seeking to establish mutual understanding between themselves and the temperance movement, they openly and consistently denounced its imposition of evangelical morality on American politics.

Rabbi Isaac Mayer Wise led American Jewry in this ideological battle. When Wise founded his weekly newspaper, the *American Israelite*, in 1854, he intended his publication to unify and modernize American Jewry, and to act as armament in defense of Jewish civil liberties.[14] Wise editorialized about local and national political developments, and the temperance movement became one of his regular subjects. He was acerbically critical of temperance activists, expressing pointed irritation toward those who invoked religious ideology in their protests. "If religion and prayer are abused to wage war on liquor to-day," he wrote in 1880, "they may be abused to-morrow, on the same principle precisely, to persecute . . . Freemasons, Catholics, foreigners, infidels, or anyone who . . . does not conform to vulgar prejudices."[15]

Wise's accusation that the anti-alcohol movement "abused" religion indicates a shift in American Jewish political rhetoric. Beginning in the 1870s, and with greater force and frequency in the decades to come, rabbis and other Jewish communal leaders denounced erosions in the wall between religion and the state. American Jewish outspokenness was in part inspired by the growth of the American Jewish population itself, which by 1880 numbered approximately 250,000. Immigrant and native-born Jews were generally acculturated, economically stable, and as committed to the health of American institutions as they were to Jewish organizations.

Even as Jews as a group achieved both critical mass and middle-class status in the United States, the threat of marginalization (or possibly exclusion) emerged in the form of campaigns for a "Christian America." The unprecedented devastation of the Civil War led evangelical Christians, and some moderate Christians as well, to conclude that the nation had fallen from God's grace. Postwar spiritual anxieties were inflamed by many of the same economic and demographic changes that had spurred antebellum revivalism: industrialization, increased poverty and wealth disparity, and the growth of non-Protestant populations in American cities. Protestants from throughout the religious and political spectrum hoped to right the nation's spiritual wrongs by calling for legislative reform acknowledging Christ's moral authority over the government and the laws it created. They organized the National Reform Association, which set its sights on a constitutional amendment that would revise the preamble to include recognition of "the lord Jesus Christ as the Ruler among the nations, and His revealed will as of supreme authority." Others lobbied for the legal enforcement of Sunday Sabbath observation. While Sabbatarians found allies among a wide range of activists—especially labor organizers and workers' advocates seeking a guaranteed, government-sanctioned day of rest—those who oriented their politics around Protestantism hoped, first and foremost, that Sunday laws would strengthen the nation's devotion to God.[16]

American Jews responded with denunciations of the Christianization of the civic realm. Although there remained areas of Jewish life that some proved willing to compromise—a number of congregations, for instance, changed their Sabbath worship from Saturdays to Sundays in order to conform to mainstream American socioeconomic practices[17]—they regarded the imposition of Protestant theology or morality on politics, commerce, education, or the private lives of citizens as a direct threat to the nonsectarian state that guaranteed their equal status.

American Jews, it should be noted, did not contest the temperance movement's warnings against the dangers of excessive alcohol consumption. "It is undeniable that drunkards are degraded and degenerated persons," Wise wrote in 1868, "and drunkenness is an evil against which all good men should work." Rabbi Marcus Jastrow, of Philadelphia's Rodeph Shalom congregation, spoke of the "human misery" wrought by intemperance. And Gustav Gottheil, rabbi of Temple Emanu-El, the center of Reform Judaism in New York City, called intemperance a "disease" and a "scourge that slays sixty thousand otherwise healthy men and women annually in the country alone and brings ruin to a hundred thousand homes."[18]

Nor did they dispute the claim that American culture seemed to be newly awash in liquor and beer. Wartime military culture had given license to excessive drinking, which the American brewing and distilling industries heartily encouraged. Alcohol trade organizations and lobbying groups (in which Jewish alcohol entrepreneurs often played a role) stood ready to flex their considerable muscle against any legislation that threatened to hinder their business. As alcohol production grew, venues of public drinking proliferated—especially in cities, which were themselves undergoing dramatic growth because of both industrial concentration and immigration from Europe. The number of retail liquor dealers exploded during the late nineteenth century, from fewer than 90,000 in 1865, to 175,000 in 1880, to nearly 200,000 in 1900. These numbers only briefly, in the 1870s, represented an increase in the number of alcohol retailers in proportion to the national population.[19] Nevertheless, anti-alcohol activists shuddered in dismay and horror at the opening of new saloons, and even the creation of new saloon districts, in their cities and towns. They interpreted the sheer prevalence of alcohol and its widespread availability as a sign of social disorder, and regarded it as evidence of politicians' lack of interest in the common good.

American Jews sympathized with concerns that alcohol exacerbated poverty and other societal problems. But those who suggested approval of legislative remedy did so in inexact terms, offering a version of Jewish theological principles that made common cause with Protestant activists' demands for political reform and moral uplift. The 1885 Pittsburgh Platform, American Reform Judaism's founding institutional mission statement, announced Jews' commitment to "the great task of modern times, to solve on the basis of justice and righteousness the problems presented by the contrasts and evils of the present organization of society." These acculturated Jews promised to promote social justice and help the poor—not just the Jewish poor, but the gentile poor as well, who, they frequently pointed out, were most injured by alcohol consumption.[20]

Most Jews who weighed in on the relationship between alcohol consumption and social problems, however, remained vague about a cure. In the end, they were unwilling to lend their weight to any movement committed to the idea that righteous social reform could emerge only from Christian belief. Cooperation between Jewish institutions and the temperance movement proved impossible, since the movement received guidance and inspiration from evangelical Protestants who insisted that the political, economic, and spiritual state of the nation were inextricably intertwined. The social ills of the day could not be cured without Christ, temperance Christians argued.

These ideas, and the institutions that promoted them, determined the direction of the postbellum anti-alcohol movement. They also compelled Jews to keep their distance.[21]

Although temperance activists were not uniformly driven by religious faith—and, conversely, not all Christians favored temperance legislation—the movement benefited from preexisting church networks. Through these organizations, both formal and informal, they founded dozens of national, state, and municipal committees with hundreds of thousands of members. Christian institutions, including those comprising non-evangelicals, offered their support. In 1874, both the Seventh-Day Baptists and the National Conference of Unitarians declared themselves to be against all alcohol commerce, and in 1877 the General Council of the Reformed Episcopal Church and the General Assembly of United Presbyterians did the same. They were joined in 1880 by the General Conference of Methodists and by Quaker groups throughout that decade.[22]

Temperance organizations ranged widely in their missions, methods, and memberships, but they shared a commitment to the total eradication of alcohol commerce in the United States—by legislative action, ideally. Postwar anti-alcohol activists had reoriented their critique of the national alcohol question away from the issue of the individual drinker. They still promoted individual abstinence, but the movement now regarded the consumer as the victim of a wicked industry. The country's alcohol problem was a systemic problem, they insisted, and the system could be reformed only if the power of government were brought to bear on it. This was a major shift in strategy, credited by the prohibition activist Ernest Cherrington several decades later for "breaking down the ancient doctrine that the temperance movement and political activity should be kept separate," and ushering in a new (and more efficacious) era of anti-alcohol activism.[23]

None of the nineteenth-century efforts to restructure American law according to Protestant morality succeeded at the federal level. But anti-alcohol activists did accumulate significant victories in state legislative battles in the 1880s and 1890s. These achievements included local option laws, which gave counties and municipalities the ability to limit or ban the availability of alcohol by popular vote; taxes and high license fees imposed on producers and purveyors of liquor; and statewide prohibition legislation, although all but three states (Maine, Kansas, and North Dakota) saw these laws overturned by state courts or rejected at the polls by 1900.[24]

Prohibition legislation was just the sort of imposition of religion on politics that Isaac Mayer Wise abhorred. The movement's victories alluded, in concrete terms, to the growing activist presence of Protestantism in public life. More worryingly for Wise and his allies, the absolute and unconditional nature of their goal turned the debate over temperance into a zero-sum game, since Jewish religious practices were incompatible with temperance Christians' aspirations. Wise was not merely arguing against legislation that he regarded as ineffectual and unjust: he believed this to be a fight between religious tyrants and defenders of the rights and liberties guaranteed by the Constitution. If the tyrants won, Wise warned, the fundamental rights not only of Jews but also of all American religious minorities could be in danger. Indeed, democracy itself was imperiled. When religious passions of the moment can "override and defy the law and the Constitution," he wrote, "we stand at the brink of lawless despotism."[25]

Rabbi Marcus Jastrow also criticized the temperance movement on constitutional grounds, and warned against the impact that anti-liquor lobbyists could have on the rights of American citizens. Jastrow and Wise disagreed about much; both men advocated modifications of Jewish practice so that it fit the needs of contemporary American Jews, but Jastrow feared that Wise was moving American Judaism too far from its historical traditions and accused him of draining their religion of its fundamental meaning.[26] Wise and Jastrow agreed wholeheartedly, however, on the subject of the temperance movement. Jastrow condemned the temperance movement as "equal to tyrannical pressure," and in a later sermon pointed out the deleterious effects of prohibitory legislation on American property rights. Prohibition of the production and purveyance of alcohol, he insisted, amounted to "confiscation of property and proscription of persons," since hundreds of thousands of working Americans would be driven out of their livelihoods, and millions of dollars of property "reduced almost to worthlessness."

Economic oppression of just this sort, Jastrow insisted, had driven the colonists to proclaim independence from Great Britain's monarchical control. "Beware," he continued. "At some future day that many-headed tyrant may confiscate all your property. . . . This is a question of liberty as against tyranny, a question of the unwritten human rights as against the usurpation of power which assumes the name of right."[27] Mandatory temperance laws, for Jastrow, were akin to despotism. In his estimation, the temperance movement sought to enact unconstitutional intrusions of state power that would weaken Americans' fundamental protection from property confiscation by the government.

Jastrow's sermon underscored how debates over the alcohol trade, both before and after the Civil War, articulated wider-ranging concerns over the nature of American capitalism and the competing demands of individual rights and communal interests in a free market society. Was the alcohol industry to be valued as a force of capitalist dynamism and a source of economic growth? Was its presence in American cities and its popularity among many immigrant groups a benign symptom of cultural diversity? Were its potentially troubling effects on society tolerable and manageable? Anti-alcohol activists declared no, on all counts. When it came to alcohol, these activists insisted, the needs of the community required that the market be strictly regulated. The government was responsible for the morality of the community, and the law should reflect the community's definition of a moral environment. At the very least, they claimed, government should not stand in the way of the majority of voting citizens of a municipality, county, or state if they wished to limit or ban alcohol commerce within its boundaries.[28]

During the late nineteenth century, American Jews were among those whose disagreement with the anti-alcohol movement included a defense of the constitutional rights of the individual to accumulate and dispense with property as he or she saw fit. Wise and Jastrow evoked the nation's struggle at its founding to throw off England's restrictions on its colonists' civil liberties, which included, in their interpretation, the right to enjoy the fruits of their labor without undue government interference. In doing so, these Jews joined other Americans who extolled the virtues of the free market.[29]

This was not merely a matter of economic self-interest. Jews' memories of socioeconomic life in central Europe also affected their political and economic ideologies. Jews throughout Europe had long been restricted from owning land and barred from most occupations. Those who had witnessed and benefited from the progressive removal of political disabilities from central European Jewry in the nineteenth century, or who had emigrated to the United States to escape socioeconomic discrimination, regarded economic liberalism and open markets as inextricably intertwined with social and political tolerance. Any possible constrictions of economic and commercial markets—especially when championed by conservative and potentially exclusionary cultural forces—gave Jews cause for concern, as they regarded American socioeconomic environments as more meritocratic than any they had yet encountered. By defending unrestricted markets, which they saw as guaranteed by the liberal philosophies on which the nation was founded, they hoped to protect their own civic interests.[30]

When American Jews argued against temperance legislation and made their case for limiting the state's role in the marketplace, however, they were also looking beyond their own interests. They insisted that the anti-alcohol movement sought to undermine the constitutional rights of all Americans. Wise, Jastrow, and other Jewish critics of the postwar temperance movement believed themselves to be defending those prerogatives as Jews *and* as American citizens. Their Jewish identity, as they understood it, did not isolate them from the broader political culture; rather, it positioned them to defend the Constitution, and the national body as a whole.

These critics also proposed that Jewish particularism benefited the broader national community in their denunciations of the women of the temperance movement. In 1874, Rabbi Jastrow offered a stern rebuke to a group of local women who had asked him to circulate a petition to his female congregants. The petition, addressed to the city's mayor, expressed hope that municipal laws forbidding the sale of alcohol on Sundays would be more strictly enforced. As members of "the sex specially aggrieved by the traffic in alcoholic drinks and the consequent intemperance of husbands, fathers, brothers, and sons," the petitioners begged the mayor to ensure that "the Lord's Day may no longer be desecrated by the traffic in strong drink."[31]

The ladies of Rodeph Shalom were unlikely supporters of the petition, not least because it referred to Sunday as "the Lord's Day." Although a small number of Jewish congregations oriented toward religious reform had switched their Sabbath worship to Sundays or added a Sunday service, Rodeph Shalom had not (though it did adopt other reforms). Even within such congregations, Jewish participants rarely referred to Sunday in traditionally Christian theological terms, or parroted evangelical Protestant demands to ban alcohol commerce (or commerce altogether) on Sundays.

The fact that Jastrow received the petition in early 1874 suggests that its authors were participants in the Women's Crusade, a movement-transforming grassroots direct-action protest against the liquor trade that began in late 1873 and lasted through the following year. Even though women had been an important force in the antebellum temperance movement, they found themselves mostly excluded from formal membership in temperance groups such as the American Temperance Union and the Washingtonians. At best, they were relegated to women's auxiliaries, such as the Martha Washingtonians (also known as the Ladies Washingtonian Society). This marginalization frustrated many temperance women, who insisted that since members of the "gentler sex" were too often at the mercy of drunken men (usually their husbands), denying women the right to fully participate in the movement was not only unjust but also injurious to the cause.[32]

In December 1873, middle-class Protestant women in Ohio and western New York State began to orchestrate demonstrations against the American liquor industry. Armed with Bibles and church hymnals, and willing to put their own safety in jeopardy, groups of women preached and sang outside local saloons and liquor stores, stoically withstanding the humiliation—and occasional physical abuse—meted out to them by saloonkeepers and patrons. By the crusade's end in 1874, tens of thousands of women had participated in theatrical displays of civil disobedience in thirty states. They begged and shamed saloon patrons until the men promised never to set foot in a saloon again, and they even convinced some saloonkeepers, liquor dealers, and drugstore owners to destroy the offending stock.[33]

There is no record of Jewish women participating in the civil disobedience of the crusade, and considering the overtly Protestant nature of these demonstrations it is unlikely that any did. But some middle-class Jewish women witnessed their Protestant counterparts' engagement in the political sphere, and longed for a similarly bracing outlet through which to express their social and political points of view. They aspired to emulate their gentile neighbors, who organized or joined reform organizations that brought into the public realm what they saw as women's natural, motherly benevolence and single-minded passion for protecting home and family. The National Council of Jewish Women, founded in 1893 by middle-class women of central European birth and heritage, looked to the WCTU as the model for their organizational structure and admired its broad social agenda. And though they never took up the anti-alcohol cause themselves, the *American Jewess*'s affectionate and appreciative obituary of Frances Willard in 1898 suggests that acculturated Jewish women held this radical reform activist in high esteem.[34]

Even if groups like the WCTU sometimes served as models for Jewish organizations, Jewish women hesitated to join reform organizations that were directly affiliated with Protestant church associations. Some Christian social reformers openly sought to bring members into their religious fold, and Jewish women understandably shunned contact with those who expressed missionary objectives. Jewish women thus struggled to find a place for themselves within the larger context of American women's activism. The temperance movement was especially unlikely to attract Jewish women, both because of its open religious affiliations and because few American Jews, male or female, regarded it as relevant to their own experience.

As the Women's Crusade was winding down, Rabbi Jastrow presented his critique of the temperance movement. Among the movement's many repugnant qualities, he announced, was the behavior of the women within it. "There is no division of opinion among us," Jastrow declared, "as to the impropriety of the ostentatious manner in which those whose province is the domestic altar . . . allow themselves to be dragged into publicity and risk contact with such as ought forever to be excluded from the sight of the priestesses of decency and chastity." Regardless of their benevolent intentions, Jastrow implied, these women—members of "the sex whose power lies in its weakness"—had overstepped acceptable boundaries. In his estimation, their behavior was fundamentally un-Jewish. "Maybe we are a people too old-fashioned for the 'woman of the age,'" he quipped. "But it is sure that our hearts shudder at the idea of our wives, mothers, sisters, and daughters" venturing into the political arena and forsaking their dignity.[35]

Isaac Mayer Wise shared Jastrow's low opinion of women's political activism. Wise weighed in on the gender issue in March 1874, a few weeks before Jastrow's sermon. "Any Jewish lady," he wrote, "would consider it sacrilege and blasphemy to abuse prayer and benediction for purposes of public demonstrations." To make his case, he invoked two of the most celebrated women of the Pentateuch: "Miriam shouts and sings when liberty triumphs, Deborah rises when the country is in danger; but there were no whisky Amazons in the tents of Israel. Therefore our daughters cannot be misled into this piece of business."[36]

Wise's term of insult would have been familiar to his contemporaries. Some sympathetic observers evoked the image of the Amazon, the female warrior of Greek mythology, to convey respect and admiration for the movement. Amid the crusade, for instance, the New York Times reported that a gathering of "Amazons" in Ohio had "given no rest to the enemy," the local saloonkeepers. This movement led by "singing ladies," the Times continued, "enlists everywhere the full sympathy of the best people of every town and village . . . [with] a fixed purpose, based upon a principle."[37] According to this view, the bravery of the temperance "Amazons" echoed the fearlessness of their ancient and mythical namesakes.

But Wise did not invest the word with any positive connotations. In his opinion, temperance women radically transgressed their proper role and upended the natural order of gendered behavior—just as the Amazons of ancient myth had. Equally horrifying to Wise, they profaned religion by exploiting it in the service of political ideology. Where others saw noble warriors, Wise saw self-righteous fanatics and obstreperous harridans. Wise used the term as an insult to both their femininity and their politics. He was then able to present an idealized image of the Jewish woman, whom he regarded as the opposite of the temperance crusader: a politically astute yet ladylike, rational, and dignified defender of the nation.

A few weeks after Wise's piece appeared in the *Israelite*, Rabbi Samuel Freudenthal of Williamsport, Pennsylvania, also referred to the women of the temperance movement as "whisky Amazons." In response to yet another missive from a local temperance group (or perhaps the same group that had sent their petition to Rodeph Shalom) "urging him to appoint a committee of six Hebrew ladies to co-operate with it in a crusade," he declared that "it is impossible to fanaticize an Israelite" of any gender. Jewish women, Freudenthal insisted, would not deign to participate in the radical tactics of the Women's Crusade.[38] Freudenthal likely had read Wise's editorial in the *Israelite*, agreed with the sentiment, and when the occasion arose, found it useful to borrow his terminology.

As Jastrow's scolding sermon and Wise and Freudenthal's derisive comments suggest, many members of the American rabbinate had decided that temperance activism—and particularly women's temperance activism—had no place in Jewish life. So strong was their conviction, in fact, that they were sometimes willing to stifle the speech of Jewish women who expressed sympathy for the movement. In 1878, when a fourteen-year-old girl named Dora Rosenstein submitted an essay supportive of the temperance cause to Atlanta's *Jewish South*, the newspaper's publisher and editor, Rabbi Edward B. M. Browne, would not let it see the light of day. Browne, who also led the city's Hebrew Benevolent Congregation, noted in his publication that he would have published Dora's "very good" essay "but for the fact that we Israelites need no temperance literature as we are not intemperate. Try something else, Miss Dora."[39]

Rabbi Wise was correct in asserting that Jewish women would not be found among the "whisky Amazons," as he labeled them, since none engaged in the crusaders' very public form of civil disobedience that he and his colleagues found so repellant. Perhaps some would have expressed sympathy for the cause, if Dora Rosenstein's letter is any indication. We cannot know for sure, because communal leaders who either could not imagine or would not tolerate any Jewish alliance with the prohibition movement were disposed to silence them.[40] According to most of the Jews who spoke out on the issue of alcohol commerce, the only legitimate Jewish viewpoint was that the anti-alcohol movement's calls for sumptuary legislation were fanatical and intolerant. They insisted on a unified Jewish position on the matter; anything else would undermine their efforts.

Even more to the point, they insisted, sumptuary laws were unnecessary. As proof of prohibition's pointlessness, they pointed directly, and proudly, at themselves, as Rabbi Jastrow did when he chided the crusaders for their claim that women were "aggrieved" by the liquor traffic. "Our women," he wrote, "are not . . . specially aggrieved by the traffic in alcoholic drinks."[41] This was a reference to the long-standing assertion made by Jews and gentiles alike, as early as the eighteenth century, that the Jews were a sober and temperate people. The German Enlightenment philosopher Immanuel Kant explained Jews' aversion to heavy drinking as a reflex of communal self-defense. "Intoxication . . . deprives one of cautiousness," Kant wrote. Outsiders and marginalized populations who were regarded with suspicion and hostility, such as women and priests as well as Jews, were subjected to "the attention and criticism of the [larger] community and thus cannot relax in their self-control."[42]

American commentators also took note of Jews' reputation for moderate alcohol consumption throughout the late nineteenth century, and even those who viewed Jews in a negative light admitted that Jewish drinking habits were admirably restrained. In 1886, *Life* magazine partly attributed Jewish health and longevity to the fact that Jews "use alcoholic liquors very sparingly and thus keep up good digestion," even though they were a "holiday-loving people." Three years later, the temperance publication *Christian Advocate* pointed out, without apparent hostility, that "Jews who drink, but are seldom drunkards, are not as a class in favor of Prohibition." And in 1892, *Century Magazine* asserted that "the best proof of the moral standing of the Hebrews" was, among other factors, that "drunkenness is not a Jewish vice."[43]

In their arguments against prohibition legislation during the late nineteenth century, American Jews regularly highlighted their reputation for sobriety and moderate alcohol consumption, proposing themselves as living proof of the excessiveness of anti-alcohol legislation. They offered Jewish drinking habits as a model for non-Jews to follow, and some even used the inquiries of temperance Christians into the drinking practices of the ancient Israelites to further their case. Isaac Mayer Wise did so with particular vigor, regularly rebuking temperance theologians who tried to harness the Hebrew Bible in support of their cause. He insisted that there was no injunction against alcohol in Jewish history or theology. The leading figures of the Torah all drank fermented wine, he pointed out. Even though some, like Noah, drank to catastrophic excess, Moses "left no law regarding inebriation. . . . The Mosaic code knows of no punishment for the drunkard, not even for the habitual drunkard." The rabbis of the Talmud went one step further, including wine as a required component of Jewish domestic ritual. Some of them, he wrote, even considered it a sin to abstain from wine.[44]

Wise argued that temperance Christians who hoped to enlist a Jewish Jesus in their battle against alcohol were wasting their time and displaying an embarrassing ignorance of biblical history. If Christians were going to look to Jewish culture as a model or a guide, he suggested that they dispense with exegetical efforts and instead look to their Jewish neighbors. In 1872, Wise attempted to shift temperance activists' attentions away from the ancient past and toward the present. "Temperance men have often asked us," he wrote, why so few Jews developed excessive and unhealthy habits of alcohol consumption "although scarcely any of them abstain entirely from wine, beer and other fermented liquors." His answer was twofold: from childhood Jews drink alcohol at home, with their parents, as part of their religious ceremonies and learn to respect it; and the very teachings of Judaism created the sort of man who "controls his passions and bridles his appetites [and] has himself, more or less, under the control of reason."[45]

This explanation allowed Wise to make two claims: first, Jews' ability to drink in moderation proved that habitually excessive drinkers should blame themselves and not the substance; and second, American Jews could serve as a model of the rational, self-mastered citizen. When a British doctor and expert on heredity and dipsomania declared that Jews had somehow inherited a physiological insusceptibility to intemperance, Wise countered that it was not "racial" qualities, but rather "the liberated intelligence [which] is the motor of the will to domineer over the lower instincts."[46] Judaism, for Wise, was synonymous with reason and self-control—crucial traits for the modern and democratic citizenry envisioned by the most optimistic of the nation's founders.

Gustav Gottheil of New York City echoed Wise's arguments. In a sermon on Judaism and temperance delivered in the 1890s, Gottheil also dismissed exegetical claims: "We are sorry we cannot offer the temperance reformer the much-coveted comfort of the example of Jesus," since, as a Jew, he would have consumed fermented wine at the Last Supper. "We may render him more substantial aid . . . not as total abstainers or total prohibitionists, but as a sober people, who have been effectively taught by their religion to use every gift of God and not to abuse it."[47]

The role that the Jewish home and family played in inoculating Jews against excessive attitudes toward alcohol also figured largely in the anti-temperance rhetoric of the Philadelphia rabbi Joseph Krauskopf, a former student of Wise. Krauskopf beseeched American lawmakers to turn away from the temperance movement's demands and instead to look to the Jews, whose thousands of years of experience had led them to a sane and moderate approach to alcohol consumption. "Encourage the method pursued in Israel, a method that has almost freed them from drunkenness and its consequences," he declared in an 1889 sermon. "Encourage the free and open and unrestricted use of alcoholic stimulants within the sacred environments of the home." Acceptance of alcohol as a part of everyday life, according to Krauskopf, disinclined Jewish men from running off to the saloon; it kept them at home with their families, and "has contributed no small share to their . . . domestic purity and happiness." If all would follow the Jewish model, he concluded, "there will be *Temperance with all, Total Abstinence with none.*"[48] Jastrow, too, counseled his fellow citizens to "raise your children so as not to look with genuine or affected horror on a social gathering that is cheered up with so-called strong drinks, while you see its participants come forth unscathed in body and soul."[49] Jews, according to Jastrow, taught every upcoming generation to enjoy both nature's bounty and the company of others with equal measures of joyfulness and self-restraint.

All these rabbis presented American Jews as exemplars of voluntary moderation, even while they refused to allow Jewish history, or the Jewish body, to be used as weapons in the temperance arsenal. This strategy rendered real, flesh-and-blood Jews, rather than the ancient Jews of the evangelical imagination, as the temperance ideal: sober, industrious, and guided by reason. The Orthodox rabbi J. J. Peres of Memphis took it a step further, claiming that even while Jews drank on occasion (as they are instructed to do by Scripture), they "feel a patriotism too holy to prove themselves bad citizens by indulging in low debauchery." Love of country, Peres insisted, kept American Jews from drinking to excess and rendering themselves "unworthy of the protection of the laws, the equality of rights, and the love and esteem of their countrymen."[50]

That Jews regularly partook of drink and yet remained respectable American citizens proved, according to this argument, that total abstinence was unnecessary for a healthy, productive, and patriotic life. This argument also provided an opportunity to advocate for tolerant and unprejudiced political attitudes, and to imply that the nation would be ill served by the temperance movement's attempts to impose their extremist politics on an increasingly diverse population. Jews implied that they could be the models of such tolerance. Of course, they would also be its beneficiaries. As the New York *Jewish Gazette* editorialized in 1898, "Christian church workers" who advocated temperance "would accomplish more good by teaching the masses to imitate Jewish sobriety, industry, and general good behavior" than they would by legislative means. "As the world is surely progressing," the *Gazette* continued, "and as fairness and truthfulness are gaining ground, we may expect to have our virtues recognized and valued in the future."[51]

As the short piece in the *American Jewess* suggests, Jewish women also articulated their confidence that Americans might look to Jews as models of moderation in both consumption habits and political values. Esther Ruskay, an essayist on Jewish women's topics for both Jewish and secular publications, explored this issue in a 1902 essay that might have been based on her own experience. Ruskay described a discussion between four American women on some of the political and social movements of the day. Three of these women were Christian, and each was an advocate for a favorite fashionable cause: one a vegetarian, one a suffragist, and the third "a rabid disciple of Frances Willard." The fourth woman, and the only Jew among them, sat silent (and a little bored) until the temperance activist asked, "Is not drinking wines and liquors and stimulants a sin [and] a practice out of consonance with the highest conceptions of manhood?"[52]

Called on to defend Jewish religious practices, not to mention Jewish masculinity, Ruskay's Jewish character suddenly found her voice. She pointed out that "one of the Psalms refers to God . . . creating wine to make glad the heart of man." Therefore it could not be a sin. Besides, she tells her friends, "wine is a necessary adjunct of [Jewish] ceremonies, and yet intemperance has never been a prevalent vice among Hebrews."[53]

"As it all came to Number Four in a rush," Ruskay wrote, "she herself was struck by the practical tenor of the laws of her people." Jewish law, she suddenly understood, "enables the Jew to live a temperate, well-ordered life, with none of the evils and none of the fears of this modern age to puzzle or to threaten them." Temperance ladies, according to Ruskay, were so terrified of alcohol's effect on the modern world—so terrified of modernity itself—that they sought to have the substance banished altogether. Jews' moderate relationship with alcohol, on the other hand, proved a saner and infinitely more progressive model of "home protection." Jews, she implied, should be regarded as exemplars of calm rationality in the face of societal change and uncertainty.[54]

Ruskay's story presented Jewish women as uninterested in joining the temperance movement, and "Woman Number Four" offered a sharp corrective to the ideology and practice of the WCTU. Ruskay's critique of anti-alcohol activism reassured middle-class American Jewish men that their wives, sisters, mothers, and daughters did not aspire to enter the political realm, at least not in the style of women's politics most common at the time.

Jewish women's seeming disinterest in the temperance movement also reassured Jewish men that their female counterparts accepted the role of keeper of the home and intergenerational transmitter of Jewish domestic practices, which included the moderate consumption of alcohol in both social gatherings and religious rituals. That they embraced this role was, in a way, as important as the information transmitted. The possibility that Jewish women might independently follow Jewish men into the public realm, abandon their role as perpetuators of home- and family-based Jewish traditions, and develop social or even romantic relationships with gentiles imperiled the cohesiveness of American Jewish communities. The willingness of women to create and maintain a Jewish environment in the home, and to limit the purview of their organizational activities mainly to within the Jewish community, allowed Jewish men to avail themselves of the relative openness and fluidity of American political, economic, and social life.[55]

The vast majority of middle-class Jewish women eschewed the assertive activist role taken by temperance women, choosing instead the private world of home and insulation within Jewish community. Even so, the stance they took toward alcohol consumption still had significant political meaning. In a culture where middle-class Protestant women were encouraged to ban all alcohol from their homes, Jewish women continued to serve it. They also consumed alcohol as participants in Jewish religious ritual. One illustration accompanying the above-mentioned 1892 articles in *Century Magazine*, captioned "A Jewish Wedding," depicts a bride poised to take a sip from a goblet of wine. Other illustrations portray Jewish families around a seder table, in a sukkah, and at the havdalah ceremony that ends the Sabbath; in each scene, not only is wine consumed, but it is consumed in the presence of children. For Jewish critics of the Gilded Age temperance movement, this was a point of pride, for it showed Jewish mothers doing their part to create the next generation of temperate, rational, and politically tolerant Americans.[56]

Jews were not the only American ethnic group who were both openly critical of the anti-alcohol movement and happy to point to themselves as exemplars of moderation and rationality. German immigrants, most of whom were religiously moderate Lutheran Protestants, responded similarly. German Americans resented temperance activists' attempts to restrict American leisure activities, and denounced anti-alcohol activists for encouraging intolerant and antidemocratic impulses in American political culture. As did American Jews, Germans felt that temperance was at its core a battle between those who cherished the liberties guaranteed by the American Constitution and those who hoped to impose puritanical religious beliefs on American civic life.

Anti-alcohol activists had expressed suspicion of European immigrants since the 1830s, when a massive wave of newcomers—more than five million

6. "Feast of Tabernacles," *Century Magazine*, January 1892, 332. A middle-class Jewish family using wine in their celebration of Sukkot. This image challenged prohibitionist claims that alcohol undermined family stability.

men, women, and children, primarily from Ireland and German-speaking central Europe—swept onto American shores. These immigrants arrived with the very same drinking practices and attitudes toward alcohol that temperance advocates were determined to expel from American culture. From the perspective of those whose teetotalism was informed by anti-immigrant feeling, alcohol was a problem imposed on American society by alien and uncontrollable others. Of course, Americans had been drinking to excess well before the 1830s; it might be said that colonial settlers from the British Isles, from the seventeenth century onward, had pioneered European drinking habits in the New World. But temperance nativists either ignored or failed to recognize this continuity between "old" and "new" immigration. Instead, they displaced their anxieties about alcohol onto immigrants, accusing them of degrading American society with foreign habits. Alliances between the temperance movement and the anti-immigrant, anti-Catholic American Party, or "Know Nothing Party," in the 1850s testify to their shared concerns.[57]

Irish immigrants gave the temperance movement especial unease. Stereotypes of the drunken Irishman, a stock character of anti-Irish propaganda in both the United States and England, intensified nativist fears that Roman Catholics, such as nearly all Irish immigrants were after 1830, could never be made into republican citizens. "King Alcohol," temperance nativists insisted, was as ruthless a tyrant as the pope, and the Irish immigrant had declared his primary loyalties to both; such a man would only degrade and destroy democratic institutions.[58]

German immigrants had also acquired a reputation for enthusiastic alcohol consumption, but they were not stereotyped as dissolute bingers like the Irish. The image of German immigrants in the native-born mind was shaped by economic circumstances; as a group, Germans achieved middle-class status in the United States more quickly than the Irish did. Germans were regarded as law-abiding and fiscally responsible, and as inheritors of a culture that had produced some of the most enlightened political and philosophical theories and vibrant, progressive arts of the time. Their devotion to beer halls, however, and the ubiquity of Germans in the alcohol trade, led native-born Protestant temperance advocates to view Germans as corruptible and un-republican, and as responsible for a loosening of public morals.[59]

German immigrants and temperance reformers disagreed vigorously on the matter of Sunday leisure habits. As was the custom back home, German families in American cities enjoyed spending Sundays at the local beer garden, playing cards, discussing politics, and listening to the local German band play music from the old country. German Lutherans saw no sin in moderate alcohol consumption, so why would the Lord's Day be blemished by a glass of beer? But in the eyes of those who thought the day was most properly spent in contemplative worship and prayer, drinking (even in moderation) and card playing on the Sabbath was an impropriety of the highest order. Advocates of Sabbatarian laws aspired to put an end to "Continental Sunday" by outlawing all Sunday commerce, which they hoped would compel Christians to attend church instead.

German Americans regarded attempts to inhibit their leisure practices as fanatical and coercive, and as a threat to their civil liberties. They sensed nativism in the movement's occasional screeds against immigrants, and feared that the anti-alcohol initiative was, at its core, an attack on German culture and German American communities. They resisted temperance legislation via the ballot box, and editorialized against anyone who threatened to curtail the right to drink. "We are no defender of intemperateness," insisted a German American newspaper in Milwaukee, "but we hold fast to the basic principle that every person is independent and should be responsible for his own actions, and that those who arbitrarily transgress the laws of nature and damage their own bodies should alone bear the consequences." Naturally, the German American press, with few exceptions, stood against the women's suffrage movement and women's involvement in politics at any level. Temperance "witches" not only emasculated their fathers and husbands and dishonored their families, they insisted, but, if granted the franchise, could potentially tip the electoral balance toward prohibition.[60]

Clearly, American Jews and German Americans posited remarkably similar arguments against the temperance movement. This does not mean that all these Jewish immigrants thought of themselves as ethnically German, or that German gentiles regarded them as such. The degree to which central European Jews had been acculturated or legally emancipated in their homelands varied widely before German unification in 1871. Relations between Jewish and non-Jewish German immigrants in the United States also varied. The two groups generally enjoyed mutual admiration and cooperation, and even occasionally interacted in informal social settings where alcohol would be present, such as beer gardens, music halls, and private social clubs. But they more often than not remained separate, maintaining their own institutions and residential enclaves.[61]

But they did agree that prohibitory laws contradicted American values of liberty and individualism. Both groups expressed impatience with suggestions that drinking in moderation was deleterious, and both willingly pointed to themselves as examples that the opposite was true. Jews and Germans also shared the opinion that temperance women's political activism was unseemly. Some central European Jewish immigrants also expressed unease, and sometimes even downright hostility, toward the movement for women's suffrage; one Cincinnatian claimed that the German Jews of her city had steered clear of the suffrage movement because "they were afraid women would vote [for] prohibition."[62]

Shared antipathy to the anti-alcohol movement provided an opportunity for Jews to align themselves with German Americans, if they were so inclined. This connection would have served central European Jewish immigrants in three ways. First, it reflected positively on Jews to be associated with German Americans, who were regarded as among the more dynamic, organized, politically engaged, and well-respected immigrant groups in the United States. Second, it allowed Jews a feeling of inclusion and acceptance among non-Jews, an experience denied to all but a few elite of their background in Europe. And third, identifying with German Americans enabled those Jews who were ambivalent about assimilation to embrace a version of American identity that, while acculturated, remained distinct from the rest of American society.[63]

Although Jewish and gentile immigrants from central Europe generally stood shoulder to shoulder on this issue, their political activism often moved along parallel tracks, utilizing much of the same rhetoric in different settings and venues. One notable American Jewish figure did make an effort to align the two groups in their common efforts. The Bavaria-born lawyer Simon Wolf was a spokesman for both German and Jewish causes. He served on the executive committees of B'nai B'rith and the Union of America Hebrew Congregations, where he advocated for Jewish rights in the United States and abroad. He also worked as a lobbyist for the National German-American Alliance in the early twentieth century. Wolf fought against the anti-alcohol movement throughout his political career, often referring to both his Jewish and German heritages.[64]

One of Wolf's earliest forays into temperance politics coincided with the end of Ulysses S. Grant's presidential administration, in which he held a minor bureaucratic position. Grant's term in office had been marred by corruption and scandal—including a conspiracy between distillers and Internal Revenue officers to defraud the government of liquor taxes, a scheme that came to be known as the "Whiskey Ring." Hoping to keep his job through the next administration, Wolf wrote a letter to Rutherford B. Hayes, the Republican Party's candidate for the 1876 election. He advised Hayes that German American newspapers "charge you with being a strict temperance man," and that this would hurt Hayes with ethnic German voters. He stumped for Hayes as well, traveling to New York City to meet with more than a thousand potential supporters, whom he described as "merchants [and] bankers . . . mostly Israelites and Germans." Unfortunately for Wolf, Lucy Hayes, the candidate's wife, was an admirer of the Women's Crusade. Once in office, President Hayes asked Wolf for his resignation, a move Wolf suspected was the direct result of the first lady's pro-temperance politics.[65]

Several years after the Women's Crusade ended, the WCTU founder and former president Annie Wittenmyer published her *History of the Woman's Temperance Crusade*, an account of the uprisings that sparked the postbellum temperance movement. Wittenmyer's description of an especially stirring moment of anti-saloon direct action in Newark, Ohio—"a hand-to-hand fight with the powers of darkness"—ended with a pronouncement that good triumphed over evil that day. "The struggle was too intense to last long," she declared, "but victory turned on Israel's side, and many saloons were closed."[66] Of course, she was not evoking the ancient nation in the same way that Rabbi Wise had when he excluded "whisky Amazons" from their ranks. For Wittenmyer, the whisky Amazons *were* Israel. Throughout her book, she used language consistent with supersessionist claims that Christians had replaced Jews as God's chosen, and with temperance evangelicals' quest to eradicate sin and act as instruments of a divine plan for world redemption. Wittenmyer's reference to Israel's victory was, in fact, a triumphalist claim for temperance Christians.

Wittenmyer did mention a few actual Jewish people in her chronicle of the Crusade's advances. She scornfully described "a Jew's saloon" in Cleveland, where, presumably in an effort to unsettle the pious ladies, "a picture of Christ . . . was held up on a pole before the crowd, who [sic] were drinking beer and blaspheming." Yet she expressed appreciation for a Jewish saloonkeeper in Granville, Ohio, who "would not, on 'account of his religion,' allow the ladies to come into his saloon to pray," but nevertheless placed carpet and chairs out on the sidewalk so that the women could protest his establishment in some comfort.[67] Wittenmyer expressed both open-mindedness and ambivalence toward Jews, judged them depending on their behavior, and seemed to have no preconceived notion about their economic relationship to the alcohol trade. Several decades later, the hatchet-wielding prohibitionist Carry Nation—whose violent attacks on saloons in 1900/1901 gained her and her cause much notoriety—spoke of Jews with a mix of admiration and disdain. Despite her distaste for them as economic actors—"I know by experience that the Jews are tricksters," she wrote in her autobiography—the piety of Orthodox Jews prompted her to treat them with deference. When kosher-keeping Jewish peddlers stayed at the hotel she kept before she was a full-time prohibition activist, she recalled, "my other guests would often regard them with almost scorn, but when they were at their meals I would wait on them myself, showing them this preference, for I could not but respect their sacrifice for the sake of their religion."[68]

These prohibitionists' respect for Jews, however ambivalent, was not reciprocated, even in qualified terms. American Jews were at no loss for reasons to be hostile to Gilded Age anti-alcohol agitators. The movement's goals clashed with Jews' understanding of the United States as a nonsectarian, tolerant, multiethnic nation. Its most powerful and popular organization, the WCTU, was discordant with Jewish ideas of proper gendered behavior. And its success not only would have inhibited Jewish religious practices, but would also have forced scores of Jewish entrepreneurs to abandon a trade that had served American Jewish communities quite well.

To what extent was American Jews' anti-prohibition stance directly influenced by Jewish involvement in the American alcohol trade? While no record of communication between Jewish clergymen and Jewish alcohol producers specifically on the topic of temperance exists, rabbinic leaders' anti-prohibition stances were strengthened by their connections to congregants and supporters who made their living in the alcohol industry. Many of the institutions founded by Isaac Mayer Wise benefited from the generosity and cultural status of Jewish alcohol entrepreneurs. As mentioned above, the Louisville whiskey distiller Isaac Wolfe Bernheim funded the construction of the original library at Hebrew Union College, an edifice that today houses the American Jewish Archives and still bears his name. Members of Cincinnati's Freiberg family, along with other Jewish alcohol businessmen, played important lay roles in the organizations Wise created to unify American Jews and to standardize their religious practices. The mere fact that Wise lived and worked in Cincinnati, and that a significant number of his congregants were in the business, surely heightened his antipathy toward the prohibition movement.

Jewish disdain for the late nineteenth-century prohibition movement, then, was partly motivated by economic self-interest. To dismiss their stance as motivated *only* by economic self-interest, however, fails to take into account American Jewry's wider range of concerns about the implications of the growing prohibition movement. There was little to attract most post-bellum American Jews to the "dry" side of the wet/dry debate. The importance of the alcohol trade in Jewish life contributed to the development of Jews' anti-temperance politics. But Jews' relationship to alcohol consumption and production, which predated the temperance movement by centuries, was far more determinative, as was their fear that prohibition legislation would lead to further incursions of Protestant religious dogma into the civic realm. Any contemporary political development that might jeopardize Jews' civil liberties—as manifest by the possibility that politics, commerce, or other aspects of secular society would come under the control of sectarian religious forces—was a development of great concern, and, according to late nineteenth-century American Jews, one worth fighting against.

PART II

Alcohol and Anti-Semitism

3

Kosher Wine and Jewish Saloons

New Jewish Immigrants Enter the
American Alcohol Trade

In 1899, the Atlanta distiller Rufus M. Rose displayed a sign in his office window: "No Jew Trade Wanted," it declared. Rose's sign was visible to everyone passing by in the busy Five Points business district, including Aaron Bluthenthal and Monroe Bickart, whose liquor wholesaling firm was located in the same neighborhood. Rose was also a few blocks from one of the five pharmacies owned by Joseph Jacobs, who sold medicinal whiskey, rye, and sherry (and a new patent medicine called Coca-Cola) from his shops, and not far from the "whites only" drinking establishment of the saloonkeepers and theater owners Adolph and Sig Samuels. All these alcohol entrepreneurs were active members of the Temple, Atlanta's middle-class Jewish congregation, and some, such as Bluthenthal and Jacobs, were prominent in local civic life as well.

One might have expected an alarmed or dismayed reaction from Rose's Jewish colleagues and competitors. The only recorded response to the sign, however, came from Frank Cohen, the editor of the locally published *Jewish Sentiment and Echo*. Cohen reported the sign's appearance with little anxiety or umbrage. He criticized Rose's discriminatory trade practices as "un-American," and promised that "the Jews will never annoy [Rose] with their patronage in the future." Still, he seemed unperturbed. In fact, he made light of it. "There is a possibility of this being a case of 'sour grapes,'" he punned, "for two noteworthy facts present themselves in this connection: Rose's company has but little, if any trade from the Jews, and the Jews are excellent judges of good whiskey."[1]

Cohen's sanguine and unflappable response to Rose's anti-Semitism suggests that Atlanta's middle-class Jews felt confident about their standing in the city. When it came to their economic and entrepreneurial position, that confidence was well-founded. As the nineteenth century ended, Atlanta generally welcomed Jewish businessmen and manufacturers—that is, as long as they conformed to prevailing norms of middle-class white behavior. And despite social discrimination that often kept them from full integration, acculturated Jewish communities throughout the South eagerly styled themselves in a manner that rendered them indistinguishable from their white gentile neighbors. Cohen took this endeavor seriously; he had written in support of lynching in the past, and one of his editorials on the 1898 Wilmington Race Riot framed the massacre as a necessary defense of white supremacy. "The white man will rule by fair means or foul," he warned.[2] To be an astute evaluator of quality whiskey, for Cohen, was to possess a cultivated American palate, no less patriotic for being exquisitely refined.

But changes in the city's Jewish community, and in the nation's Jewish population, would soon undermine Cohen's efforts to ensure Jews' standing. Beginning in the 1880s, thousands of eastern European Jews arrived in American ports every year, and most of them came with limited economic resources. As had been true for their predecessors, alcohol commerce presented a historically and culturally familiar entrepreneurial choice. Indeed, this new group's historical involvement in alcohol commerce was particularly potent. They regarded trafficking in liquor, beer, and wine as a conventional way to make a living, and gravitated to it in hopes of establishing an economic footing in their new country.

This "third wave" of Jewish immigrants altered American Jewry's relation to alcohol. As a group, the eastern European Jews who came to the United States at the turn of the century had different commitments than did the central European Jews who at that time constituted an assimilated American Jewish elite. Their orientation toward traditional religious practices prompted them to create and support an emerging kosher wine industry, which both generated employment opportunities and helped to weave Jewish religious observance into the fabric of American consumer culture. In Atlanta and all over the country, however, eastern European Jewish immigrants' presence among the ranks of American saloonkeepers proved far more consequential. Although Rose undoubtedly intended for his middle-class Jewish competitors to feel the sting of his sign, he surely meant it for the city's rapidly growing cohort of Russian Jewish saloonkeepers as well.

Between 1880 and 1920, approximately two million Jews emigrated from the Russian empire to the United States. This constituted a massive reconfiguration of the Jewish Diaspora, since, in 1880, four million Jews—half of the world's total Jewish population—lived under Russian rule. The mass migration of eastern European Jewry was a response to anti-Semitism and poverty in the Pale of Settlement, the region of Russia where the majority of eastern European Jews resided. Both hardships were familiar to the Jews of the Pale, though both had escalated dramatically over these decades. In addition, Jews were being pushed out of the Russian liquor trade, an occupation that tens of thousands, perhaps hundreds of thousands, of Jews had come to rely on. The Russian government's attempts to exclude Jews from this economic pursuit played an important role in Russian Jews' mass emigration.

Jewish economic life in the Pale was severely circumscribed. The liquor trade, however, had long been open to them; to a great extent, it had been assigned to them, and they to it. In 1496, the Polish monarchy granted its noblemen an exclusive monopoly for the production and sale of alcohol. The noblemen leased the monopoly to Jews, with whom they had already established an economic relationship as *arenda* lessees. As exclusive holders of the right to tax and own land, nobles rented out these assets to Jews. Jews then collected taxes and rent on the nobility's behalf, or sublet portions of the concession to other Jews. When Russia took possession of Poland's eastern provinces, the liquor monopoly remained in aristocratic hands, and, as the historian Simon Dubnow wrote while Russian Jewish mass migration was still taking place, "the right of propination, exercised mostly by Jews on behalf of the nobles, proved a decisive factor in the economic and . . . social life of Russo-Polish Jewry."[3]

Alcohol production and purveyance was one of the few occupations available to Jews in the crowded and impoverished Pale. In nineteenth-century Belorussia, Jews owned anywhere between a third and two-thirds of the region's distilleries. For a few Jewish liquor merchants, this trade provided entrée to the Russian bourgeoisie.[4] But most Jewish alcohol entrepreneurs operated within the Russian liquor business as rural tavernkeepers and distillers. According to one estimate, 50,000 Jews managed taverns in the Russian Polish countryside at partition, and an 1870 census revealed that Jews operated 190,000 taverns, in addition to 89 percent of the distilleries and 74 percent of the breweries, in Kiev and provinces to the west.[5]

Rural tavernkeeping was rarely a lucrative endeavor. If he had connections and access to resources, a Jewish tavernkeeper might lease all of a region's venues of alcohol production and distribution, and then sublease each operation to individual Jews. For these low-level managers, however, rent, liquor licenses, and other costs of operation could be onerous. They often had to rely on multiple income streams, undertaking side occupations as moneylenders, pawnbrokers, peddlers, or dealers in other commodities besides liquor in order to turn even a marginal profit. On occasion, they participated in underground economies as dealers in fenced goods, or sold unlicensed or unreported liquor. Shady business though it sometimes was, Jewish-owned taverns were also an essential component in eastern European trade and transportation systems, since they regularly functioned as restaurants and boarding houses for travelers. They served as a crucial resource for the networks of Jewish peddlers who traveled far from home during the week and relied on the kosher food that tavernkeepers served.[6]

Relations with their non-Jewish customers were complex. The peasants who frequented Jewish-owned taverns had developed a culture of alcohol consumption so prodigious that it inspired a Yiddish folk song: "*Oy oy oy, shikker iz a goy, shikker iz er, trinken miz er, vayl er iz a goy*" (A gentile is drunk, he has no choice but to be drunk, because he is a gentile). When they were short of coin, they bought drinks on credit or pawned their belongings to the tavernkeeper, and their indebtedness exacerbated peasant hostility toward these Jewish tavernkeepers (and toward Jews in general). This ugly combination of alcohol consumption and anti-Semitic resentment, and the violence it aroused, heightened eastern European Jews' feelings of vulnerability. At the same time, peasants and rural Jews understood that they were mutually dependent on one another. Taverns became sites of interethnic cooperation; on the several occasions when Jews were banned from tavernkeeping by government decree, they often hired Christian peasants to bartend for them—an arrangement that allowed the tavernkeeper to maintain his business, and provided employment (and sometimes commission) for the gentile barkeep.[7]

While the nobility protected their Jewish taverners and relied on the revenue they produced, and peasants regarded them as an essential component of village life, czarist government officials believed that these entrepreneurs were a problem in need of reform. Jewish taverners, they insisted, economically exploited the peasants and rendered them unfit for productive labor. A report from Minsk to the czar in 1797 explained peasant poverty as caused not only by crop failure, but also by "landowners [who] keep Jews under leases in taverns in their villages. . . . By selling liquor to the peasants on credit . . . [the Jews] lead them into squalor and make them incapable of engaging in agriculture." This formulation placed a fair amount of blame on the nobility who leased propination rights to Jews, thereby sacrificing peasant well-being for their own financial gain. But the Jews who served the drinks were considered the more malevolent presence in this tragic scenario.[8]

Several times during the eighteenth and nineteenth centuries, both the Russian government and the Polish congress, which was permitted by Russia to maintain some self-governance and autonomy, attempted to remove Jews from the liquor trade. An 1804 czarist statute forbade Jews from holding leases on public drinking houses or selling liquor in rural areas. Contracts currently held by Jewish taverners in the countryside were deemed nonrenewable, and debts owed "to taverns run by Jews" declared "worthless and nonrecoverable." The goals of this statute were to protect the Russian peasantry from what reformers regarded as "Jewish exploitation" and to impel Jews toward other occupations that would incorporate them into the larger Russian economy. Jews were even granted the right to own land, in hopes that they would abandon the tavern and take up more "noble" agricultural pursuits.[9]

While some Jewish alcohol entrepreneurs probably made this shift (though exactly how many is impossible to know), these reforms generally failed to achieve their goals. Thousands of Jews found themselves without a livelihood, a calamitous development that rippled beyond Jewish communities. The dissolution of Jewish alcohol *arendas* drastically diminished the revenue coming into local treasuries. Further, though the writers of the 1804 statute used the word *arenda* to mean only propination leases, it was interpreted more broadly to forbid Jews from leasing any public revenues. This proved disastrous for provincial governments. By the 1820s, the law was generally disregarded, and in 1835 Czar Nicholas I once again granted Jews the right to lease taverns in the countryside. The government went back and forth about the rights of Jewish tavernkeepers for much of the rest of the nineteenth century—banishing them from the trade and then letting them back in—while Jews, as a group, remained firmly ensconced in the occupation.[10]

The Jewish tavernkeeper was so ubiquitous in the region that he became a recurring figure in local literature. In the Jewish-owned taverns of Polish fiction and theater, the innkeeper was often presented as a miscreant and a criminal, disfigured or otherwise physically repulsive, whose sole interest was his own enrichment and accumulation of power. In many nineteenth-century Polish poems, novels, and plays penned by gentiles, Jewish economic behavior in the tavern—not only their role in the liquor trade but also their practice of loaning money at interest—stood in symbolic opposition to Christian ethics and brotherly concern. (A notable exception, Adam Mickiewicz's epic poem *Pan Tadeusz*, features a sympathetic Jewish taverner and Polish patriot named Jankiel.)[11]

Cultural enmity against Jewish taverners influenced political policy in Russia in the last two decades of the nineteenth century, and eventually contributed to the conditions that led to Jews' mass emigration out of the Pale. The assassination of Czar Alexander II in 1881 ended a period of relatively liberal government policy toward Jews. Over the decades of Alexander II's reign, Jews had been increasingly incorporated into Russia's educational system and professional class, while industrialization and urbanization had afforded Jews new economic opportunities. In 1882, his heir, Alexander III, sought to slow Jewish integration by instituting the "May Laws," which included new educational quotas to reduce the number of Jews in Russian schools, as well as occupational and residential restrictions. As they became more culturally and economically marginalized, Russian Jews began to abandon their hopes for emancipation, and, in ever-greater numbers, to abandon Russia itself for points west.[12]

A surge of anti-Semitic violence acted as another "push" for potential Russian Jewish emigrants. Jewish participation in the Russian alcohol trade partly inspired this wave of pogroms, since the image of the Jewish tavernkeeper in the popular mind mirrored Russian presumptions about Jewish economic behavior. An 1881 government investigation into the earliest wave of anti-Jewish riots declared that the Jews were themselves to blame for the violence against them, since Jewish entrepreneurs had "exploit[ed]" the "native inhabitants." If the government was to root out this problem, the report concluded, it should "remove the abnormal conditions which now exist between Jews and natives, and protect the latter from that pernicious activity which . . . was responsible for the disturbances." An action committee formed in response to the report recommended that Jewish participation in the liquor trade be entirely forbidden in the countryside and severely restricted in cities and towns.[13]

Though the May Laws passed in 1882 did not specifically bar Jews from the Russian liquor trade, restrictions on rural land owning and land leasing forced some Jewish tavernkeepers out of their livelihood. Others evaded these laws the old-fashioned way: by hiring non-Jews to pose as the owners of their rural taverns. In the late 1890s, however, the Russian government imposed a national liquor monopoly in hopes of both placing a check on national alcohol consumption and increasing the revenue that went directly to the state. Under the new law, drinkers could legally purchase liquor only by the bottle at government-run stores. As proved true in the American case, however, illegal alcohol production spiked, and some Russian critics of the monopoly insisted that bootleggers outnumbered state-licensed liquor dealers in the Russian countryside.[14] Regardless, the new laws succeeded in reducing the number of Jewish alcohol entrepreneurs. Whereas Jews had owned 60 percent of the legal taverns in the Pale (and uncounted illegal taverns) in the 1880s, by the end of the 1890s they owned only 37 percent of such establishments—a figure that would continue to decrease as the government monopoly was consistently enforced.[15]

Some Russian and Polish Jews welcomed this development. As early as the seventeenth century, rabbinic authorities had expressed dismay at Jewish taverners' willingness to profane the Sabbath by producing and selling liquor during the hours when labor and economic exchanges were forbidden.[16] In the nineteenth century, urban middle-class Jews regarded the rural tavernkeeper as both symptom and symbol of Jewish degradation and oppression in the Pale. Simon Dubnow, too, lamented Jews' involvement in the Russian alcohol trade: "The Jews had been placed in the tragic position that thousands of them, in their search for a piece of bread, were forced to serve as a medium for promoting the pernicious Russian drunkenness." Jewish taverners, he insisted, sold liquor to peasants only because they had few other options, and would gladly have taken up other lines of work had they been granted greater economic opportunity. The Ukrainian-born Israeli poet Chaim Bialik articulated the misery of the Jewish tavernkeeper in "Avi" ("My Father"), from the autobiographical perspective of a taverner's child: "In a human swine cave, in the sacrilege of a tavern . . . my father's head appeared, the skull of a tortured martyr."[17]

Despite the ignominy suffered by many a Jewish tavernkeeper, the de facto closing of the alcohol trade to Jews made matters even worse by exacerbating Jewish poverty in the Pale. Estimates of the exact number of Jews deprived of their family's livelihood vary dramatically, from 12,000 to 200,000.[18] Whatever the number, there is little doubt that Russian restrictions on Jewish alcohol commerce acted as a significant factor in the late nineteenth-century growth of Jewish poverty in the Pale, and played a part in provoking mass Jewish emigration from eastern Europe. They left in droves: well more than two million by most scholarly approximations. Their diminished role in the Russian alcohol trade, of course, only partly accounts for their decision to leave. The crushing poverty of the Russian countryside, an autocratic and increasingly anti-Semitic political regime, and the upending of traditional Jewish socioeconomic life by industrial capitalism all had the effect of loosening Jewish communal bonds in the Pale and pushing Jews toward emigration.[19]

Eighty percent of the 2.5 million Jews who left Russia chose the United States as their destination. When they arrived, they were confronted by the challenges of an unfamiliar economic landscape. As had the central European Jews who preceded them—as all immigrants did, and continue to do—they negotiated between their experiences, religious traditions, and notions of expected or legitimate enterprise for workers in their group, and the opportunities and barriers they confronted in their new sites of settlement. If cultural continuity determined their occupational choices, Jews' experience and entrepreneurial history in eastern Europe prepared them well to seek a livelihood in the American alcohol trade. Even for Jews who had not worked in Russian and Polish taverns and distilleries, saloonkeeping and liquor production would have seemed conventional Jewish occupations.[20]

Alas, if we are seeking evidence of a direct relationship between individual immigrants' pre-migration and post-migration experiences in alcohol commerce, American immigration records can take us only so far. Passenger ships that docked at American ports recorded immigrant occupational data, and the U.S. Immigration Commission collected data on occupational continuity. But information on immigrants' involvement in the alcohol trade, both before and after they moved to the United States, is impressionistic and anecdotal rather than statistically precise. Further, such information was entirely self-reported, and immigrants of all backgrounds were known to obfuscate or embellish descriptions of their prior work experience in hopes that presenting themselves as economically useful would move customs officials and aid workers to ensure their entry or help them find work.[21] It is therefore nearly impossible to know whether individual Russian Jewish tavernkeepers consistently became American Jewish saloonkeepers, or how frequently Jewish distillers from the Pale transferred their skills into liquor production in the United States. Terminology, too, inhibits statistical knowledge of reported occupation. Many Jewish immigrants who reported their previous occupational experience claimed to have owned or managed a "store" or "grocery" or run a "restaurant" or "hotel" before they emigrated. But grocery stores sometimes sold liquor, and restaurants and inns served it by the glass. And readers will certainly recognize the maddening vagueness of the occupational category "merchant."[22]

If an eastern European taverner or distiller aspired to bring his skills and experiences to bear in the United States, he would have encountered some potential hindrances. First, immigrants who sought to apply their knowledge of production techniques (in alcohol or any other trade) could find their ambitions thwarted by rapid technological development or by differences between American and European production methods, both of which could render pre-migrational skills nearly obsolete.[23] This handicap kept at least one Jewish immigrant from resuming his previous occupation. In 1907, administrators of the Industrial Removal Office (IRO), a Jewish philanthropic organization that sought to reduce overcrowding in urban ghettos by relocating Jewish immigrants to smaller communities, steered a Russian newcomer away from American whiskey production. The IRO's general manager expressed skepticism that the man in their charge, who had made liquor in eastern Europe—vodka, most likely—was fit for similar employment in the United States. "The fact that he was engaged in the distilling business in Russia does not argue per se that he understands American methods of distilling," he insisted. "In fact I have yet to meet one Russian distiller who can take hold of similar work in this country and retain his position."[24]

A second barrier to eastern European Jewish immigrants who sought entrance into the alcohol production trade was the fact that the distilling industry was less hospitable to small entrepreneurs than it had been for much of the nineteenth century. The structure of the liquor trade was increasingly inclined toward larger producers and concentration of production. Between 1880 and 1900, the number of American distilleries increased only slightly, from 844 to 967, but the value of the product these distilleries produced more than doubled, jumping from $41 million to $96.8 million. Mass production had become the common practice, and small producers found it difficult to compete. In addition, after the 1897 passage of the "Bottled-in-Bond" Act, distillers were required by federal law to warehouse their liquor under government supervision for a set period, in order to guarantee that it was unadulterated and properly aged. Further, distillers had to pay excise taxes on "bonded" (warehoused) liquor even if it had not been sold, and those taxes were raised from 90 cents to $1.10 per gallon.[25] In sum, legal distilling on a profitable scale demanded substantial capital commitment, and most immigrants lacked such resources. Even those who had access to ethnic credit associations like the Hebrew Free Loan Society could not have borrowed enough to fund an endeavor as costly as building, purchasing, or running a distillery.[26]

For Jewish immigrant distillers who remained intent on practicing their craft in the United States but were without sufficient capital, another option remained open: moonshining. According to the *Los Angeles Times* in 1895, native-born whites in the mountainous areas of the Southeast produced most of the nation's illegal liquor, but they were not alone in this endeavor. "Polish Jews" in the "big cities of the North," especially New York and Philadelphia, the *Times* reported, ran unlicensed tenement stills that could produce hundreds of gallons of unreported and highly profitable whiskey a day. The paper provided a detailed sketch of a prototypical "Russian still used by

Jews in New York," clearly suggesting that these immigrants had learned how to distill liquor in eastern Europe.

Revenue agents (as collectors of liquor excise taxes were called) accused these tenement bootleggers of defrauding the government of significant income: "Uncle Sam is robbed of millions through moonshine whisky," the *Times* insisted. Newspapers in other cities gave similar accounts. Police raids in New York turned up illegal basement stills run by Russian and Polish Jewish immigrants, and detectives posted in Chicago's immigrant neighborhood claimed that several gangs of illicit Jewish distillers were waging a violent and "bitter warfare" to dominate and control the market.[27]

Illegal moonshining was precisely the kind of economic activity that Jewish immigrant advocacy organizations wanted the newcomers in their charge to avoid. Although organizations like the IRO did not have an official policy of directing Jewish immigrants away from the legal alcohol trade, they hoped that removing them from impoverished city slums would not only alleviate urban congestion and improve immigrant life, but also blunt American anti-Semitism. The Jewish Agricultural and Industrial Aid Society shared this mission (as well as a patron, the German Jewish railroad tycoon Baron Maurice de Hirsch), but they focused their efforts on organizing farming colonies for new Jewish immigrants. Working with the land, the society hoped, would diminish eastern European Jews' predilection toward urban life and mercantile occupations, and controvert stereotypes that "the Jewish immigrant in the United States objects to the hard manual labor involved in agricultural pursuits." The organization placed several self-identified former saloonkeepers and liquor merchants in farming colonies in Connecticut, downstate New York, and southern New Jersey. These new American farmers raised livestock and tended small farms, an outcome that Russia's czarist reformers of the previous century would surely have regarded as vindication of their own efforts.[28]

Among the crops grown by the Jewish agricultural colonies were Concord grapes, a native American varietal developed during the nineteenth century for heartiness and consistency and cultivated as both table and wine grapes.[29] Immigrant farmers, Italians and Slavs as well as Jews, used their crops to make "sour wine"; one observer of New Jersey's immigrant agriculturalists wrote that the homemade wine was their "staple beverage."[30] But most of their harvest went on the market, and the bulk of these grapes were sold to the Welch grape juice manufactory, first in Vineland, New Jersey, and then in upstate New York. It is perhaps ironic that the grapes produced by these Jewish farmers helped make the Welch family project possible: the evangelical Christian Welches

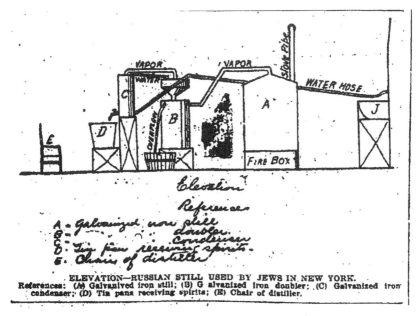

ELEVATION—RUSSIAN STILL USED BY JEWS IN NEW YORK.
References: (A) Galvanived iron still; (B) G alvanized iron doubler; (C) Galvanized iron condenser; (D) Tin pans receiving spirits; (E) Chair of distiller.

7. "Russian Still Used by Jews in New York," *Los Angeles Times*, July 28, 1895, 11. The U.S. Department of the Treasury confiscated this double-barreled still from a tenement in the urban Northeast. It was "of the sort used in Russia. . . . Such a still costs but a few dollars," the *Los Angeles Times* reported, and the bootleggers made profits of "400 to 500 per cent" of their production expenses.

advocated total temperance and promoted their juice as a non-fermented replacement for sacramental wine in Christian religious ceremonies.[31]

Legitimate winemakers also sought access to Concord harvests—especially New York vintners in search of crops that did not have to ship too far. One New York City winemaker became a prodigious consumer of Concord grapes. Sam Schapiro had immigrated to New York from Galicia (a region of Poland then under Austro-Hungarian rule) in 1899, and opened a restaurant in New York City's Jewish quarter. As a side project, he fermented sacramental kiddush wine in the cellar of the building and sold it to neighborhood customers. Over the next several years, Schapiro's wine business flourished, eventually outperforming the restaurant. By 1907, he had closed his restaurant and founded the business that would become Schapiro's House of Kosher Wine.

Schapiro's was the dominant commercial kosher wine producer on the Lower East Side during the early twentieth century. His enterprise occupied a building that spanned an entire block of Rivington Street, where the Concord grapes that he shipped from upstate New York were crushed, barreled, and fermented. These grapes made musky-tasting wine that would have been unpalatable if not for the sugar he added. Its flavor helped perpetuate the perception among American Jews that kosher wine must be cloyingly sweet. Its syrupy consistency, perhaps meant to evoke the experience of drinking homemade raisin wine, inspired the company's claim, and later their famous advertising slogan, that their product was so thick that "you can almost cut it with a knife."[32]

The success of his business required a large enough pool of potential customers to make mass production profitable. By 1907, he had them: the hundreds of thousands of Russian and Polish Jews pouring into downtown Manhattan were, by the late nineteenth century, more eager than their "uptown" German brethren to maintain adherence to rabbinic law, especially the laws of kashrut. Keeping kosher—even if they did so inconsistently—helped them remember and honor their old lives and served an indicator and daily manifestation of their religious and cultural identity as "a people apart."[33]

The development of a domestic kosher wine industry points to changes in the relationship between American Jews' religious practices and consumer habits. This shift mirrored the proliferation of kosher butchers and bakers in cities with a sizeable Jewish population during the early twentieth century. Larger concentrations of Jewish residents whose food and beverage consumption habits were influenced by communal custom and religious obligations fostered an economic environment where Jewish entrepreneurs could open businesses catering primarily to the specific consumer demands of Jewish customers.[34] Domestic kosher vintners such as Schapiro, in other words, owed their existence to the establishment of a vibrant and consistent Jewish ethnic consumer economy. Wine and liquor wholesalers and the proprietors of retail wine stores similarly offered merchandise that met the religious needs and consumer tastes of their Jewish customers. Advertising sections in New York City's turn of the century Yiddish newspapers included notices from local winemakers, wine and liquor retail shops, grocery stores, and wholesalers offering kosher grape wine from California, kosher raisin wine, and slivovitz (plum brandy) imported from Hungary, as well as vodka from Russia and whiskey from the American Midwest.[35]

But the American setting also played a crucial role in the development of kosher wine mass production. The emergence of a commercial kosher wine industry suggests an attraction among Jewish immigrants to modern American practices of production and consumption, even as they maintained traditional religious commitments. Mass-produced, store-bought kosher wine connoted modernity and convenience, and made sense in a consumer environment where food items were, with increasing frequency, mass-produced, prepackaged, and store-bought.[36] The increased availability of kosher wine also encouraged American Jews who no longer observed other Jewish dietary laws to purchase a bottle, especially in preparation for important Jewish holidays like Passover. In other words, once kosher wine was easier to procure, even Jews who never kept kosher under any other circumstances could buy it on occasion. Mass production augmented the kosher food market, even as the number of strictly observant Jewish consumers declined, and it enticed Jewish immigrants toward modern consumer practices at the same time that it encouraged Orthodox traditions.

Still, observant Jews could have kept the law without ever setting foot in a commercial establishment, just as their predecessors had. Rabbi Dov Behr Manischewitz, whose surname would become synonymous with kosher wine in the United States during the second half of the twentieth century, obtained Pesach wine in this way during his first few years in the country. In 1887, a year after he immigrated to Cincinnati and a year before he established his matzo bakery there, he wrote to his family in Russia of a neighbor and fellow immigrant, "a good man who fears G—d, and he made a little wine here, to sell, and I bought from him." This "wine from raisins," Manischewitz assured his family, enabled him to enjoy the holiday "in goodness and *kashruth*."[37] As did the maintenance of other traditional foodways, making and drinking homemade raisin wine yielded emotional and sentimental benefits by allowing immigrant Jews to maintain a connection between generations of tradition and life in the New World.

Jewish families could also procure kosher wine directly from rabbis seeking additional sources of income. While Jewish communities and congregations in the Pale economically supported their religious leaders and Talmudic scholars, rabbis who served immigrant congregations in the United States were often poorly paid—sometimes barely enough to survive. To lift themselves out of poverty, these rabbis were required to become, as the historian Arthur Goren wrote, "private entrepreneur[s] of religious skills subject to the laws of the marketplace."[38] Most rabbis in search of extra sources of income taught Hebrew to neighborhood boys. The kosher food industry was also a source of side work for rabbis who acted as *shochetim* (kosher slaughterers) or as inspectors of kosher goods and assured customers that the merchandise met rabbinic standards.

A few rabbis took up the wine retailing and manufacturing business as well, establishing relationships with vintners, buying their grapes, and borrowing their equipment. One rabbi who advertised in the Yiddish press offered his merchandise to peddlers and liquor dealers, as well as to private customers. "I went to California myself, and have my own wine press," he announced, promising that his kosher wines and brandies were both pure and affordable.[39] According to a California wine industry publication, another New York rabbi engaged the services of a Swiss winemaking family in Northern California. This rabbi traveled to the Varozza family vineyard near Santa Rosa in 1910 to personally oversee the production of seven thousand gallons of kosher wine for the coming spring's Passover holiday. This was at least his second such trip to the Varozza's winery; the article noted that this rabbi had worked with the vintner's father in the same capacity years before. The following November, a group of Orthodox rabbis visited a Fresno vineyard, where they "perform[ed] with their own hands the work of laborers in the vineyard and at the wine presses, taking care that no hands but their own in any way comes in contact with the fruit or the juice of the grape" in order to ensure that it could be used for Jewish ritual.[40]

A further source of kosher wine, which also straddled the religious and commercial realms and aroused deep spiritual and historical attachments, competed for consumer attention. Of the millions of Jews who fled eastern Europe, a small cadre of early Zionists had made their way to Ottoman Palestine, which they regarded as their ancestral homeland and hoped might eventually become an autonomous Jewish state. They organized farm settlements there, and stated their intention not only to sustain themselves economically but also to redirect Jewish occupational choices away from urban mercantile endeavors and toward agricultural production. Like Russia's reformers and American Jewry's immigrant aid organizations, these early Zionists and the acculturated European Jews who funded them saw farmwork as a path to both self-sufficiency and moral and spiritual improvement. They hoped to blend the Old World and the New; using modern scientific farming methods, they insisted, Jews would return to the métier of their origins.

Early Zionist agricultural settlements planted a variety of crops, for both local use and export. But these inexperienced farmers were starved for funds and teetered at the edge of financial failure. One of the benefactors who responded to the *Yishuv*'s pleas for support was Baron Edmond de Rothschild, a scion of the French branch of the international banking family. Although he was not ideologically allied with the early Zionist movement, he contributed prodigiously to the settlers, funding, among other projects, a massive vineyard-planting program in the 1880s and the construction of two wineries with large modern cellars and irrigation systems in the following decade. This choice of project reflected both the history of the region, which had been a center of wine production since biblical times, and Rothschild's personal enthusiasms: he owned Château Lafite, the renowned winery in the Bordeaux region of France. Rothschild transplanted French rootstock, as well as French viticultural technologies, to the Palestinian landscape, and heavily subsidized the wineries for more than a decade.[41]

Rothschild joined with European Zionists to form the Carmel Wine Company in 1896. Carmel exported Palestine wines to Jewish communities through company offices all over Europe and the Mediterranean. Carmel's management intended for their entrepreneurial mission to exceed mere trade and profit: they hoped that the Carmel brand would call attention to the efforts of the Palestinian colonies, give Diaspora Jews an opportunity to provide economic support for the *Yishuv*, and create emotional connections between the Zionist settlement and the Diaspora. Carmel wines were first introduced to American consumers in 1898, when K. T. Sarasohn, an Orthodox rabbi and publisher of several Yiddish-language weeklies, arranged to import and distribute a shipment for that year's Passover season. Carmel opened a New York City office in 1900. According to Simon Schama's history of Rothschild's Palestinian efforts, however, the American market for their product proved relatively small. Nonetheless, until Prohibition curtailed alcohol importation, the Carmel brand was regularly available to kosher wine drinkers who wished to participate in Zionist efforts through their consumer practices.[42]

Jews who bought kosher wine directly from a rabbi or chose the Carmel brand did so because of its spiritual and emotional connotations. But they had practical concerns as well: purchasing kosher wine from a religiously affiliated source, they hoped, would ensure its purity. American Jewry did not organize an agency to oversee kosher certification until 1923, and the Lower East Side was regularly rocked by scandals involving *shochetim* and kosher butchers who passed off impure meat as kosher. As with meat, a rabbi's imprimatur or a *hechsher* (the icon that denotes a food product's kosherness) on a bottle's label provided no guarantee. Fake kosher wine seeped into the marketplace. In 1907, Carmel successfully sued the New York wine-wholesaling firm of Solomon and Germansky for copyright infringement after the wholesalers had printed fake Carmel labels and affixed them to their own bottles. In 1914, the Pure Food and Drug Administration charged a Philadelphia man with falsely labeling twenty barrels of wine as "kosher l'Pesach," diluting the substance with other liquids to increase its volume and adding coloring agents.[43] These cases indicate that kosher wine had become a reliably saleable product, for if it had lacked a consumer market, it is unlikely that anyone—even the most economically desperate immigrant—would have gone to the trouble of counterfeiting it.[44]

While the emergence of the kosher wine industry played a role in the transformation of American Jewish consumption and household production practices, kosher wine as a commodity was only of concern to American Jews. Beyond the few participants in the wine industry who took note of collaborations between Orthodox rabbis and non-Jewish vintners, the kosher wine producers and retailers of the early twentieth century did not register in the national consciousness. But eventually they would: when federal Prohibition law granted special dispensation for the production and purveyance of sacramental wine, kosher wine producers and distributors came under intensified scrutiny. The "kosher wine scandals" of the 1920s will be elaborated on in later chapters. Meanwhile, as the century began, Americans who thought about Jews and the alcohol trade were far more likely to focus their attentions on the "saloon problem."

Several factors had caused the number of American saloons to mushroom, especially in cities. For one thing, consumer interest had risen: per capita consumption of alcohol rose from twelve to fifteen gallons of beer a year between 1890 and 1900, and peaked at nearly twenty gallons a year by 1913.[45] This can partly be attributed to the growth of the general population— millions of whom were new European immigrants, who brought alcohol-oriented leisure practices with them to the United States. Immigrant enclaves in American cities treasured their local saloonkeepers, who provided leisure space, news from the old country, and sometimes even financial services to their customers. For immigrants from cultures that encouraged recreational alcohol consumption—German, Irish, Slavic, and Scandinavian cultures, for example—saloonkeeping was an attractive way to make a living. It provided the proprietor some amount of independence, allowed him (or her, although only a small fraction of saloonkeepers were women) to cater to his neighborhood's consumer desires, and heightened his status within the community.[46]

Another reason behind the proliferation of saloons was the introduction of the "tied-house" system, which established a contract of mutual obligation between a saloonkeeper and a brewery. The brewery provided the saloonkeeper with fixtures, furniture, and sometimes even rent, license fees, and other forms of monetary payment. In exchange, the saloonkeeper bought and sold that brewer's beer exclusively. These arrangements made breaking into the saloon trade exceedingly easy, since the saloonkeeper needed little initial capital to open his business. Saloon districts expanded accordingly. But breweries, seeking reimbursement for their investment and hoping to make a profit besides, often charged their saloons exorbitant prices for their beer or levied an extra tax on each barrel supplied. Saloonkeepers were forced to ratchet up their competitive strategies in order to stay solvent, especially in areas where the number of saloons had increased drastically because of brewery support.[47]

Temperance and prohibition activists howled in protest at the expansion of the saloon industry and generally regarded all saloons as equally malignant. But there was no single type of saloon; they varied according to their location and their clientele, and a saloon's physical attributes usually reflected the economic class of its patrons. Drinking establishments that catered to middling or wealthy patrons could be quite elegant, even opulent. Saloons in working-class or impoverished neighborhoods might be outfitted with only a bar made of a plank of wood held up by sawhorses. The quality of the alcohol varied as well; rough saloons were known to serve cheap, adulterated liquor alongside the free, oversalted food that compelled patrons to drink more cheap liquor. Unfriendly observers of all saloons, regardless of the socioeconomic status of their clients, described the debauched behavior brought on by excessive alcohol consumption and the stench of vomit and urine that often wafted around the places.[48]

Prohibitionists demanded the shutdown of all saloons, and alcohol trade advocates fought to keep them legal. But the Committee of Fifty for the Investigation of the Liquor Problem sought a third path. A collective of prominent industrialists, clergy, intellectuals, and health professionals, the Committee of Fifty undertook a decadelong study of the effects of liquor on individual drinkers and the role the saloon played in American society. After reviewing the claims of the WCTU, and conducting some studies of their own, the committee concluded in 1903 that moderate alcohol consumption had little deleterious effect on most individuals, while admitting that excessive use "tends to produce disease and to shorten life."[49] The committee also refused to engage in absolutes when it came to the saloon question. They acknowledged aspects of saloon culture that anti-alcohol activists held to be the whole and only truths: too many saloons exploited their patrons' weaknesses in order to make a profit; criminal tendencies were amplified by alcohol, which saloons made abundantly available; saloons steered their patrons away from substitutes like churches, settlement houses, and libraries; and more of them were springing up at the turn of the century.

Yet the committee insisted that a greater number of saloons were "more worthy and more normal [of] motive" than critics of the saloon were willing to admit. Proletarian saloons acted as neighborhood gathering places, the committee reported, where workingmen could find "the society of other fellow-beings which the family alone cannot supply." Saloons often served their communities in the manner of banks, employment agencies, post offices, libraries, social clubs, and restaurants. In poorer neighborhoods, patrons gravitated toward saloons that were "more comfortable and cheery than their own so-called homes." In impoverished urban communities, the committee suggested, saloons provided services that the municipality failed to offer, creating a public space for men whose daily lives might otherwise be limited to the drudgery of industrial work and the cramped misery of a tenement apartment.[50]

Further, the committee pointed out, a saloon's character depended heavily on "the nationality and occupation if its patrons."[51] Each ethnic enclave created a public drinking culture that fit its consumer desires and leisure habits, they observed, pointing to the different kinds of ethnic saloons dotting the immigrant neighborhoods of New York City. The report briefly described differences between German, Italian, and Irish drinking establishments in New York, with particular attention to types of alcohol most plentifully consumed (beer, wine, and whiskey, respectively) and the behavior of their patrons (which was associated with the preferred beverage: the higher the alcohol content, the more depraved the consumers' behavior). As an example of a respectable saloon culture, the committee's report pointed to the "saloons [that] flourish among nationalities like the Jews in New York, which are noted for their moderation."[52]

Once again, the question of Jews' relation to alcohol was brought into the national debate. Here, however, discussions of Jewish drinking habits were couched within the larger and far more contentious issue of public alcohol consumption. Immigrants' drinking habits had long concerned the American anti-alcohol movement, and immigration restrictionists regularly referred to immigrants' drinking practices, and their predilection toward the saloon as a drinking environment, as a reason to shut the gates. As Jewish migration to the United States continued apace, Jews and gentiles both tried to explain how Jews fit into the larger picture. But no single answer emerged, and observers reached conflicting and inconsistent conclusions about the Jewish relationship to the American saloon.

Since the nineteenth century, American Jews had insisted that their religious and social practices kept Jews, as a group, away from saloons. The newer Jewish immigrants made similar claims. The *Yidishes Tageblat* newspaper declared that the traditional Jewish relationship to alcohol, which was oriented around family gatherings, religious rituals, and meals in the home, reduced public drunkenness in Jewish communities. "[The Jew] drinks when he feels so inclined, or when it seems to him the occasion warrants," the Yiddish daily noted, "but the drinking that is done on any of these occasions is done in the house." Observers of New York's Jewish quarter commented on the relationship between Jewish alcohol consumption and the celebration of special occasions: "The Jew does drink, but a little stimulant goes a great way with him," noted a reporter from *Harper's*. "He buys wine because at some of his religious merrymakings the feast would be no feast without wine."[53] Jewish convention, according to this analysis, rendered liquor and beer saloons unnecessary in Jewish neighborhoods, since Jews drank only at home or in celebration of the sacred.

Since saloonkeepers (and especially urban immigrant saloonkeepers) frequently catered to their own ethnic communities, some observers concluded that Jewish immigrants would unlikely be found among saloon proprietors. "The Jew is never found in the retail liquor business," noted one New York reporter in 1885. "Gin-mills and gin-slinging he gives the grand go-by, and allows our statesmen of Hibernian and German extraction to run the saloon. . . . There is not a bar, I am told, in Gotham, presided over by a Hebrew."[54] This remark wildly exaggerated the paucity of local Jewish saloonkeepers; "seldom" would have been more accurate than "never." Quantitative analyses confirmed that New York Jews did keep saloons, although their numbers were small—particularly in light of these immigrants' previous occupational choices. In 1907, Isaac M. Rubinow, an economist and himself a Russian Jewish immigrant, wrote that while 37 percent of taverners in the Pale of Settlement were Jewish, by his calculus Jews constituted only 2.77 percent of New York's saloonkeepers, in a city where Jews made up nearly 20 percent of the local population. Therefore, he concluded, "under conditions of freedom to enter the saloon keeper's trade the Russian Jews do not show any strong liking for this occupation."[55]

But they were there to be counted. An 1890 study of the occupations of Lower East Side Jews found 248 saloonkeepers among them.[56] A different study undertaken by an Episcopalian temperance organization a few years later found 237 saloons in the Jewish quarter (1 per 208 residents), as compared to 147 in the German quarter (1 per 111) and 179 in the Italian quarter (1 per 160). According to this report, the ratio of saloons to residents was lowest in the Jewish quarter—a claim that fit neatly with preconceptions that Jews did not drink very much. Yet the Lower East Side was still riddled with saloons and liquor shops, a phenomenon noted in the temperance report.

"Although the Jew is abstemious," their report stated, "the number of liquor dealers remains undiminished."[57]

How could a neighborhood populated by "abstemious" drinkers support so many alcohol entrepreneurs? Is it possible that some of the alcohol purveyors in the 1894 tally were Irish or German—members of the immigrant communities that had previously occupied these blocks? In his history of the Jewish Lower East Side, *World of Our Fathers*, Irving Howe noted that New York's saloonkeepers generally "regarded Jews as poor customers," since the only Jews who frequented saloons, he wrote, were "petty politicians, grifters, hangers-on . . . and gamblers"—in other words, "the bums," a category that Howe intended to refer to a tiny minority of New York's Jewish population. If most Jews did not frequent drinking establishments, saloonkeepers would not stay in the neighborhood. Such assumptions might be borne out by the claims of a German-born saloonkeeper in 1909 that Jews did not drink heavily and were therefore "N.G. [no good] for our trade."[58]

But these saloonkeepers (and Irving Howe) overlooked the heterogeneity of American saloon culture. When the Committee of Fifty posed the same question that the Episcopalian temperance organization had several years before, they asked how a neighborhood that consumed alcohol in relatively small quantities could sustain so many alcohol-serving businesses. They counted four saloons or more per block in the quarter, and mentioned that most of these businesses were Jewish owned and catered "exclusively to Jewish patronage; in fact without it scores would have to close their doors." Thus, the report continued, "we find saloon-keepers and saloon patrons of a most abstemious race. . . . [The Jews] drink, and the saloon is to them an important institution," even though as a group they did not drink to excess. The committee's crucial impression regarding Jewish saloon going was that the "thousands of Hebrews [who] are habitués of the saloon" frequented "exclusively their own saloons."[59] Rubinow's claims, while politically and culturally expedient, incorrectly implied that Jews had little relationship to New York's saloon culture. In fact, New York's eastern European Jewish immigrants patronized venues for public alcohol consumption, and these venues were often owned and run by Jews.

Many of these saloons differed from those that catered to other ethnic groups. Patrons of the "wine café" or the "coffee and cake parlor," the types of saloons frequented by most Jewish immigrants, did not belly up to the bar or rush the growler. Rather, café patrons sat around tables, restaurant-style. (This mode of saloon patronage was attributed to German immigrants as well.) Jewish saloon goers (if the term can be used to refer to café habitués) were as likely to order coffee or hot tea with lemon and a spoonful of jam as they were to drink a *schnaps* (Yiddish for a shot of liquor) or a glass of wine. Another important difference was that unlike the typical urban ethnic saloon, the Jewish saloon was rarely a homosocial environment. Jewish women frequented wine cafés and coffee saloons not as prostitutes but as customers and participants in the spirited political and cultural debates that characterized these "kibbitzarias." Even Talmud scholars sought out these social spaces: "They know they can here meet some of their brethren and argue to their hearts' content over the real meaning of some dictum of a learned rabbi many centuries in his grave," observed a reporter from the *New York Sun* in 1895.[60]

But not all of New York's Jewish saloons can be characterized as spheres of intellectual culture. Despite all the claims to the contrary, eastern European Jews did in fact have a cherished tradition of plentiful alcohol consumption. Some traditional Yiddish songs even extolled *mashke* (liquor) as a requirement for any enactment of communal joy:

> *Mir zenen nichter, mir zenen nichter* (We are sober, we are sober)
> *Trukn iz bay undz in halz!* (Our throats are parched!)
> *Git abisl mashke, git abisl mashke* (Get a little liquor, get a little liquor)
> *Veln mir zingen bald!* (And we'll soon begin to sing!)[61]

A notorious handful of Lower East Side saloons embraced this tradition. Even more horrifying to those who wanted to protect immigrant Jews from the dangers of the saloon, some of these Jewish-owned and -frequented saloons were as given over to vice and dissipation as those of other ethnic groups. The Jewish quarter of downtown Manhattan, after all, was an impoverished slum, and its poverty bred criminal activity. Some of the neighborhood saloons served as gathering places for the East Side Jewish criminals and seekers of illicit amusement. At 74 Rivington Street, for example, stood the University Saloon, which was owned by two Jews. According to a 1913 report commissioned by a collective of New York's Jewish leaders to investigate local Jewish criminal activity, this saloon catered to "the dregs of humanity dumped into New York City from Russia," and was assigned the dubious distinction of being "the worst hangout on the whole eastside for pickpockets, pimps, and thieves." Down the street, at 17 Rivington Street, stood a saloon co-owned by a Jew and an Italian that "catered to the underworld trade." Gambling and alcohol were featured at the Russian Casino on Eldridge Street, at Segal's on Second Avenue, and at the infamous Jake Wolf's saloon on First Avenue; Wolf's was a favorite spot not only for gamblers but also for corrupt policemen. At J. Cohen's restaurant on Forsyth Street, a disgusted reporter observed male and female patrons raucously and in unison singing "immoral Jewish songs." If a patron at the Oriental House Saloon on Grand and Ludlow was interested in a little "female companionship," the barkeeper sent for prostitutes from a nearby brothel on Eldridge Street.[62]

Within New York's Jewish neighborhood, saloon culture was, one might say, eclectic. But whether their patrons argued about political philosophy or formulated plans for illegal activities—and surely some hosted customers who did both—these saloons served a similar purpose, and fulfilled the same need as all immigrant saloons. The seedier joints, no less than the establishments that served more tea and cake than whiskey, created opportunities for Jewish immigrants to be among their own, to turn inward and nurture their own culture. Like any ethnic saloon or "workingman's club," they provided the solace of comradeship and shared leisure space, and fostered a sense of common experience and shared purpose among their Jewish patrons.

At the same time, these environments could also offer the possibility of interaction with non-Jews. Saloons co-owned by Jews and gentiles (like the one at 17 Rivington) likely attracted customers of both ethnic backgrounds. In addition, some eastern European Jewish immigrants visited the drinking establishments of New York's other ethnic groups. Jews who were drawn to radical political ideologies, for example, frequented the saloon owned by the German immigrant Justus Schwab on First Street, just north of the Lower East Side. In his history of Jewish immigrants and socialism in turn of the century New York, Tony Michels points out that "Schwab's saloon was for Russian Jews a congenial environment." Jewish immigrants like Abraham Cahan and Emma Goldman rubbed (and bent) elbows with German American socialists and anarchists at Schwab's, and established alliances and relationships with other leaders and thinkers of the radical Left.[63]

But eastern European Jewish immigrants were far more likely to interact with other ethnic groups in saloons in smaller cities and towns, where they lacked the insular and self-sufficient ethnic economies to which the Jews of New York had access. Differences between Jewish-owned and -patronized saloons were thus subject to regional and demographic determinants: in smaller settlements with fewer in-group breadwinners and entrepreneurs, Jews engaged in more economic interchange with their non-Jewish neighbors, and Jewish entrepreneurs needed to cater to both Jewish and non-Jewish customers.

Among the many differences between Jewish economic life in large cities with sizeable Jewish enclaves and in smaller cities or towns was the type of employment to which Jewish immigrants gravitated. New York, Chicago, and Philadelphia, the largest sites of Jewish settlement in 1900, were centers of American industrial production, and that sector employed a high concentration of Russian Jews. In smaller cities and towns, where such work was less plentiful, eastern European Jewish immigrants had to find other ways of making a living. As Ewa Morawska notes in her history of the Jews of Johnstown, Pennsylvania, the Jewish economy in a small town operated like its urban counterpart in that job seekers relied on in-group assistance; but in locations where industrial jobs were not as ubiquitous as they were in large cities, ethnic connections fed new immigrants into an entrepreneurial network of storekeepers, wholesalers, and skilled tradesmen who offered services to the general population. This system proved so effective that in some of these smaller commercial districts, observers concluded that Jews owned most, if not all, of the local businesses.[64]

In other words, while Jewish entrepreneurs in small and mid-sized cities might have been able to create and participate in an ethnic in-group of *sellers*, they were unlikely to have access to a homogenous community of *buyers*. Outside the most populous metropolitan areas, and away from the largest sites of Jewish settlement (since the two correlated more often than not at the turn of the century), the pool of potential Jewish customers could not sustain the businesses of all Jews with entrepreneurial aspirations. A businessman with ambitions to expand his trade would certainly have had to market his wares beyond the local Jewish community. Unless an immigrant taught Hebrew to Jewish boys, sold kosher meat or wine to the community, or in some other way provided goods and services that only Jews desired, it behooved Jewish entrepreneurs in smaller settlements to seek a clientele outside their own ethnic group.[65]

In a multiethnic business environment with a small population of Jewish customers, eastern European Jewish immigrants who entered the alcohol industry often opened saloons that catered to non-Jews. Jews in such environments were attracted to alcohol retail for the same reasons that other contemporary immigrants were: a saloon was a cheap and easy start-up, especially if a former saloonkeeper was liquidating his stock or had gone bankrupt; and customers were rarely hard to find (though competition might be intense). In addition, for eastern European Jewish immigrants accustomed to a culture where selling alcohol to gentiles was common, a saloon that catered to a gentile clientele was a reasonable entrepreneurial choice.

8. Max Lapides's Bauernschmidt Brewery Saloon, ca. 1900, Baltimore. Lapides (*center*) was proprietor of a tied-house saloon, which meant that he could serve beer only from the Bauernschmidt Brewery of Baltimore. The tied-house system was eventually outlawed, but for several decades it proved to be a boon to brewers and increased the number of American saloons. (Courtesy of the Jewish Museum of Maryland)

Deborah Weiner's study of Jewish life in Keystone, West Virginia—a small but booming and entrepreneurially "wide-open" coal-mining town with a regionally famous red-light district—points to this tendency. In 1898, five of Keystone's ten Jewish entrepreneurs were saloonkeepers.[66]

Another site where this phenomenon affected both the local liquor trade and Jewish entrepreneurial choice was Newark, which was in 1900 the sixteenth most populous city in the country.[67] Newark had long been known for its thriving alcohol industry and ethnic-oriented saloon culture, but central European Jewish immigrants to Newark had not taken to the liquor trade in significant numbers. In 1878, Newark's Jewish population stood at 3,500 (2 percent of the city's total), and most had emigrated from central Europe. Newark's Jews engaged in occupations that would have looked familiar to an observer of any German Jewish community at the time. Many sold groceries and dry goods, and their community included many tobacconists, butchers, tailors, and peddlers of junk and scrap metal, as well as a significant portion of industrial wage earners in the city's growing industries, such as trunk manufacturing and leather tanning. By 1880, around forty-five Jewish Newarkers were involved in the purveyance of alcohol in some capacity, usually as liquor storekeepers or wholesalers. This small cohort constituted just over 1 percent of the employed male Jewish population, and only 3 percent of the city's total alcohol industry.[68]

As was the case elsewhere in the United States, Newark's Jews did not gravitate toward brewing, even though the city's brewers were among the most prolific in the nation. In 1870, the manufacture of malt liquors was Newark's fifth-largest industry. In 1890, beer was the city's second most lucrative product, just behind leather goods. Between 1900 and 1910, the brewing industry's comparative economic output dropped from second to eleventh in local rank, but Newark remained one of the largest beer-producing centers in the Northeast.[69] As did German immigrants in other brewing cities, German Newarkers and their descendants dominated the local trade. Between 1870 and 1910, the percentage of Germans in the local population was between 11 and 15 percent, yet they consistently constituted at least three-quarters of the city's brewery owners and employees. Beer production, according to a local historian, was the "singular expression of German participation in the city's economic life," an overstatement that nevertheless suggests how large brewing loomed in the local business culture and how indispensable Germans were to it.[70]

The numbers and proportion of Jews engaged in Newark's alcohol trade increased during the last decade of the nineteenth century and the first decade of the twentieth. By 1900, fifteen thousand Jews lived in Newark.

Ten years later, that number had more than doubled, and Jews constituted 10 percent of the city's total population.[71] This influx of Jewish immigrants drastically changed the tenor of Newark's Jewish life. They created a residential and business enclave in the Third Ward, concentrated on Springfield Avenue, Broome Street, and Prince Street. To give some indication of the seismic shift in the Third Ward's ethnic makeup, consider the Morton Street School, which had educated the children of the Third Ward since the Civil War and served a predominantly German and Irish student body in 1886. In 1914, almost no German or Irish children were enrolled, and 97 percent of the school's students were Jews.[72]

But the Third Ward did not become homogenously Jewish. Instead, the area was a patchwork of ethnic neighborhoods: a small Slavic enclave butted up against a smaller Greek enclave, and both neighborhoods were surrounded by a concentration of Germans on one side and Russian Jews on the other. Living in tiny enclaves of several blocks at most were African Americans and Chinese immigrants, while much larger Irish and Italian settlements also called the Third Ward home.[73]

Businessmen from these diverse groups owned establishments in every section of the Third Ward, including those along the main thoroughfares of Springfield, Prince, and Broome. Among the businessmen operating on these streets were a number of saloonkeepers and liquor salesmen. Between 1890 and 1910, there were two changes in the makeup of alcohol entrepreneurship on these streets. First, the total number of these businesses declined, from eighty-nine in 1890 to seventy-four in 1910. Second, the number of Jewish alcohol businessmen on Springfield, Prince, and Broome Streets increased from seven to nineteen. This change was most drastic on Prince Street: in 1890 Jews owned only two of the twelve saloons there, and in 1910 they owned eight of the ten. These changes suggest that the increasingly concentrated Jewish settlement in the Third Ward precipitated some diminishment of interest in saloon entrepreneurship, although that reduction was relatively small. At the same time, even as a few saloons in the neighborhood closed, more Jews regarded saloonkeeping as an attractive and lucrative entrepreneurial choice.

Just east of downtown Newark stood Newark's other notable ethnic neighborhood, which, like any colorful character, had accumulated multiple nicknames: Down Neck (because of its placement on the curve of the Passaic River), the Ironbound (for the iron foundries and railroad tracks that surrounded it), and Beer Island (in honor of the many breweries there). Concentrations of Polish, Italian, German, and Irish immigrants lived side by side there, and mixed among them were small enclaves of Syrians, Portuguese, and Hungarians. A community of eastern European Jews, small but numerous enough to build a synagogue and maintain a congregation, also took up residence. The Ironbound was truly a polyglot immigrant neighborhood, and it had a vibrant ethnic saloon culture to match. According to one observer in 1912, for every seven residential buildings in the Ironbound, there was one saloon.[74] Jews were "less numerous" than the Irish, Polish, Italian, and German residents of the neighborhood, yet according to this 1912 observer, "the majority of the . . . saloon keepers on the Bowery [the district's main business thoroughfare] are Jews."[75]

This assertion is undermined by quantitative assessment of Newark's saloon owners, which shows that in 1910, Jews owned fewer than 20 percent of the saloons on Newark's Bowery, and fewer than 20 percent of the Ironbound's saloons in toto. How are we to account for this discrepancy? It is possible that Newark's city directories might not tell the whole story, if a significant number of Jews ran illegitimate saloons not listed there. Still, unless Jewish-owned "blind tigers" occupied nearly every storefront and backroom on the Bowery, saloonkeepers of other ethnicities would have outnumbered them.

A dramatic increase in the absolute number of Jewish alcohol purveyors citywide stands as a likelier cause of this misperception. Between 1890 and 1910, the number of Jews involved in Newark's retail liquor trade leaped from 42 entrepreneurs and employees (3.7 percent of all alcohol businessmen) to 178 (13.3 percent), although the percentage of Jews involved in the trade remained roughly proportionate to the percentage of Jews in the city's total population. That the number of Jewish dealers in wine, beer, and liquor nearly tripled in twenty years could have led to an overestimation of the proportion of Jews engaged in this occupation.

Another likely reason for this overestimation was the fact that the majority of Jewish-owned saloons and liquor stores were concentrated in Newark's immigrant neighborhoods. Even more than the Third Ward, the Ironbound raised concerns for those who worried about the effect of saloons and alcohol consumption on an immigrant's ability to become a productive American citizen and industrial worker. "For every one person who comes into the church, picture theatre, library or settlement" in the Ironbound, wrote the 1912 observer, "ten are entering the saloon. . . . For every one lesson taught in moral education or clean recreation, they are being given ten lessons in vice, wastefulness and indigence."[76] More than the overall number of Jewish alcohol purveyors, it was the precise location of Jewish saloonkeeping—the concentration of Jewish-owned saloons in immigrant neighborhoods—that brought this entrepreneurial tendency to the attention of reformers.

This concern about saloon clientele brings us back to Atlanta, where Rufus Rose hung his anti-Semitic sign in 1899. The eastern European Jewish saloonkeepers who established themselves in Atlanta found themselves in an environment that was entirely different from Newark's immigrant neighborhoods. Newark was an unequivocally industrial city; Atlanta was still in the process of becoming a regional manufacturing mecca. Local urban boosters had been calling Atlanta the "Gate City to the New South" since the end of Reconstruction, but at the turn of the century its economy still relied primarily on commerce and services rather than manufacturing.

Atlanta also differed from Newark in that the latter attracted huge numbers of immigrants, whose presence was simultaneously the result and the cause of the city's manufacturing power. In 1900, 71,363 Newark residents—nearly 30 percent of the city's total population—were foreign-born, and another 96,000 were of foreign parentage.[77] These immigrants and their progeny were certainly not the only patrons of Newark's saloons, but their leisure practices added significantly to the city's active retail trade in alcohol and fed into local temperance advocates' anxieties about immigration, alcohol consumption, and morality.

In Atlanta, on the other hand, the 2,531 foreign-born residents constituted less than 3 percent of the city's population.[78] This was fairly standard for southern cities; by 1910, immigrants made up merely 2 percent of the population in the South, as opposed to nearly 20 percent in both the North and West. The tiny state of New Hampshire, C. Vann Woodward has noted, received more European immigrants between 1899 and 1910 than did Georgia, North and South Carolina, Tennessee, Kentucky, and Mississippi combined. In no inland southern city would an intensely polyglot neighborhood like Newark's Ironbound—or even like those found in older, coastal southern cities like Charleston, Savannah, or New Orleans—have been remotely possible.[79]

Another important difference between the cities—one that would become a decisive difference for Atlanta's Jewish saloonkeepers—was race. In 1900, Newark's black population was small, only 2.7 percent of the total.[80] Atlanta's, by contrast, was nearly 40 percent: 35,727 of the total 89,872 residents. By 1900, Atlanta had instituted Jim Crow segregation both de facto and de jure, with especially rigid residential segregation. In the 1890s, the municipality enacted laws restricting black settlement, and at the turn of the century Atlanta's African American residents were allowed to live in only a limited selection of neighborhoods.[81]

One of those areas was the Decatur Street district. Decatur Street was one of Atlanta's main commercial avenues, and between its intersections with Pryor and Moore Streets, it ran through one of the city's more notorious red-light districts. The majority of the neighborhood's residents were black. But Decatur Street in no way resembled "Sweet Auburn," where the city's middle-class black community had settled just a few blocks away. Local reporters on the Decatur Street beat described the "long rows of dingy shops below and dingier dwellings above—markets where everything from eggs, overripe, to women's caresses, have their recognized price and alleged value." Black and white men from all over the city and the outlying countryside descended on Decatur Street on Saturday nights to visit the saloons, gaming tables, restaurants, dance halls, and brothels of "Rusty Row."[82]

As was the case in working-class black neighborhoods in other southern cities at the turn of the century, Decatur Street and the surrounding area also served as a magnet for immigrant settlement. It was the closest Atlanta came to a polyglot neighborhood. The neighborhood's low cost of living made Decatur Street and the blocks around it affordable for newcomers with few resources, and its active trade made the area an excellent one for an aspiring entrepreneur looking to set up shop. A small number of Chinese, Greek, Italian, and Syrian families had settled in Atlanta by 1900, and many opened storefront concerns in the Decatur Street area.

At the turn of the century, the majority of recent immigrants to Atlanta were eastern European Jews, nearly all of whom lived on or near Decatur Street. Like cities all over the United States, Atlanta saw a dramatic increase in its eastern European Jewish population. In 1880, when the Jewish population in Atlanta was approximately 600, only 14 individuals were of Russian birth or descent. By 1900, when approximately 2,000 Jews were living in Atlanta (constituting 2 percent of the total population), 493 were Russian by birth, and 890 American-born Jews claimed one or more Russian parent. Thus eastern Europeans and their descendants grew from about 2 percent of Atlanta's Jewish population to more than 50 percent within a mere twenty years.

Of the 220 businesses on Decatur Street between Pryor and Moore in 1905, seventy-six, or more than a third, were Jewish owned. Thirteen Jews owned shoe-repair stores, twelve ran clothing shops, and seven were pawnbrokers. A few Russian Jews set up shop as grocers, one as a barber, and another as a tobacconist. But the most common occupation for Jewish entrepreneurs on Decatur Street by far was saloonkeeper. In 1905, twenty-five Jewish immigrants ran or worked in Decatur Street's saloons, and Jewish immigrants constituted half of the saloonkeepers on the strip. Some of these saloons were designated "colored only," while others were open only to a white clientele.[83] For all these men, it was as plain as day that the street's business climate made opening a saloon an obvious choice. Saloonkeeping was an entrepreneurial opportunity they had grabbed because the product sold well in the neighborhood.

Many of these saloonkeepers attempted other kinds of businesses in Atlanta first, and took up alcohol purveyance after studying the local entrepreneurial environment for a year or two. In 1905, only four of Decatur Street's Jewish saloonkeepers had served liquor for a living in Atlanta for more than five years. Joel Bokritzky, for example, had immigrated to the United States from Russia in 1894. In 1900, he was a shoemaker living and working on Decatur Street. By 1905, another Jewish immigrant owned Bokritzky's shoe store and he had taken over a saloon formerly owned by two gentiles. Isaac Sinkovitz, who left Russia in 1886 and had been in Atlanta since 1890, was selling dry goods and groceries on Decatur in 1900. By 1905, he, too, had taken over a saloon previously operated by a non-Jew. Others took over saloons that had earlier been occupied by Jews. Samuel Kline owned a saloon at 110 Decatur Street in 1900; by 1905, Jacob Hirsowitz, a Russian immigrant and the leader of Atlanta's Orthodox Jewish community, worked out of that location. Kline, meanwhile, owned two saloons, one just up the street and another elsewhere in the neighborhood. Hyman Mendel, a Russian immigrant who in 1900 sold dry goods at 86 Decatur, had by 1905 converted his store into a saloon. He also co-owned with Louis Katzoff, another Jew from Russia, a saloon at 150 Decatur that had previously been kept by a gentile.[84]

Most of these Jewish saloonkeepers managed to keep a low profile and maintain their businesses without scandal or incident. There were exceptions, however, such as when Simon Marks's Decatur Street saloon went bankrupt in 1896. Marks was apparently not only serving drinks, but had also been acting as a banker for two Russian Jewish shoe dealers and an African American barber. Each had deposited several hundred dollars with him, and all claimed to have been ruined by Marks's bankruptcy. The saloonkeeper's scam became a matter of concern for Decatur Street's Jewish community, who, the *Atlanta Constitution* reported, "have been in a state of suppressed excitement since Marks's failure. . . . Indignation is rife on the street." In 1905, another Jewish saloonkeeper, Jake Feldman, was accused of perpetrating a "flim-flam." Two white, rural "countrymen" from Cobb County had come into Atlanta in search of alcohol, stopping a policeman to ask where

9. Mike Shurman's saloon, Atlanta, ca. 1905. The Russian Jewish immigrant Mike Shurman owned four saloons, several of which were in Atlanta's Decatur Street neighborhood. This photograph is likely of his "whites-only" establishment located in the city's business district. (Courtesy of the William Breman Jewish Heritage Museum)

they could find "a little Jew named Jake, who ran a saloon." Once they found him, they each purchased two bottles. Feldman also offered to "wrap up" the rest of the money they were carrying in a neatly tied roll. When they got home, they claimed to have discovered that all four bottles were empty and that Feldman had wrapped a few small bills around a wad of paper. Feldman denied that he had sold them empty bottles and stolen their money, but the police arrested him anyway.[85]

Yet such incidents were rare. For the first five years of the twentieth century, more Russian Jews opened saloons in Atlanta than closed them, and by 1905 a community that made up 2 percent of the city's total population constituted 50 percent of alcohol proprietors on the Decatur Street corridor. They contributed to a boom in Atlanta's retail alcohol trade at the turn of the century. In 1905, the Atlanta Chamber of Commerce reported that the city was licensing 550 alcohol retailers and had collected $124,562 in license fees—a substantial increase from the previous year. One assumes that the municipal authorities, or at least those responsible for the city budget, were glad to have these Jewish business owners in the city.[86]

By the end of the first decade of the twentieth century, the profile of the American Jewish alcohol entrepreneur had evolved in ways that paralleled demographic shifts in the American Jewish population overall. The earlier wave of central European Jewish immigrants had generally achieved middle-class status and acceptance in their local business communities. Eastern European Jews in the alcohol trade, on the other hand, were likelier to begin their careers in the socioeconomic margins and remain there. Perhaps this would have changed over the course of several decades in the business; maybe this newer immigrant group would have expanded their enterprises, or moved into more lucrative sectors of the alcohol traffic, and eventually joined German Jewish alcohol entrepreneurs in the middle class or even the elite. But they did not have several decades to accomplish this. Starting in 1908, prohibition became law in one state after another until 1920, when trafficking in beverage alcohol was made illegal in every state of the nation.

Social and economic differences between these two groups of Jewish alcohol entrepreneurs account for some of the disparities in the degree and depth of biographical detail offered in these pages. Chapter 1 described a cohort of businessmen who, as a group, achieved upward mobility in the alcohol trade over several decades. At the height of their success, they had attained the status and standing of industry and community leaders. Observers and colleagues wrote not only about their business endeavors, but also about their lives outside the alcohol trade, often in admiring and complementary terms. The written materials they left behind bear witness to the pride they took in their lifelong participation in the American alcohol trade, and show that they and their allies were able and eager to shape local and national debates about the role of alcohol commerce in national life. The present chapter has focused on a different sort of businessman. He entered a controversial sector of the alcohol trade just as national attitudes toward both alcohol and Jewish immigrants were deteriorating. If he kept a record of his commercial undertakings, those records rarely survived. Contemporaries who proposed to describe his experiences and explain his motivations were generally unsympathetic to him, often regarding him from a distance. Therefore analysis of this kind of entrepreneur must rely heavily on aggregate data.

Despite their differences, these entrepreneurs shared two important characteristics. One was the fact that they did not know, and could not have known, that they would soon be compelled to find another line of work. Recent immigrants who had not yet plugged into local political networks were at a disadvantage, since they were unlikely to be aware of the prohibition movement's growing power. But even savvy and politically connected businessmen remained confident that the federal government would never do something so radical, and in their opinion so foolish, as shut down the alcohol trade entirely.

They also soon came to share an ignominious place in the rhetoric and ideology of the anti-alcohol movement. As prohibitionists gained power and adherents during the early twentieth century, Jewish alcohol entrepreneurs—the established and acculturated distillers and wholesalers as well as the immigrant saloonkeepers—found themselves accused of posing a particularly fiendish economic and moral threat to American life.

4

An "Unscrupulous
Jewish Type of Mind"

Jewish Alcohol Entrepreneurs and Their Critics

Though observers occasionally noted Jews' presence in American alcohol commerce after the Civil War, American discourse about the Jewish relation to alcohol focused primarily on Jews' reputation for moderate drinking practices. An 1890 local color piece in *Harper's Weekly*, which remarked on the prevalence of alcohol entrepreneurs in downtown Manhattan's densely populated Jewish quarter, expressed admiration for Jewish habits of alcohol consumption. "Wine-shops and drinking places are common," he wrote, "though intemperance is rare. I see no tipsy man in the whole quarter."[1] Jews were engaged in the alcohol trade, in other words, but they did not drink very much: for this reporter, Jews' personal comportment overrode their economic behavior.

As the national movement to ban all traffic in beverage alcohol became a more powerful force in American politics, however, prohibitionists and their allies grew increasingly suspicious of Jewish alcohol entrepreneurs. Jews were intent on "domination" and "mastery" of the American liquor business, they warned. *McClure's* magazine suggested that the prospect of Jewish control over alcohol commerce posed a singular menace to American culture, calling readers' attention to "the acute and often unscrupulous Jewish type of mind which has taken charge of the wholesale liquor trade in this country." Journalists and politicians sympathetic to the prohibition movement declared that "Jews who were directly or indirectly interested in the liquor traffic" sought to obstruct sumptuary legislation, an insinuation that Jews undermined the democratic process and the well-being of the communities they lived in for the sake of their own enrichment.[2]

This development, it is important to note, was not engineered by the movement's establishment organizations, which maintained an open attitude toward Jews and hoped to bring them into the prohibition battle as allies. The Woman's Christian Temperance Union, whose lobbying and moral suasion efforts had a profound impact on American attitudes toward alcohol during the late nineteenth century, consistently extended themselves to Jewish sisterhoods and avoided anti-Semitic rhetoric. The Anti-Saloon League (ASL), which was founded in 1895, transformed the prohibition movement by taking a nonpartisan, single-issue approach to their lobbying efforts, and by insisting that the heart of the American liquor monster beat in by-the-drink retail establishments. Their focus on a single issue (articulated in their organization's name, as well as their motto "The Saloon Must Go"), their willingness to support any politician or official regardless of party affiliation as long as he advocated saloon suppression, and their meticulously hierarchical bureaucratic structure made them the most powerful and effective prohibitionist pressure group of the early twentieth century. Like the WCTU, the ASL welcomed and sought all potential allies, and while their rhetoric often invoked anti-immigrant sentiment, their early leadership eschewed direct criticism of Jews.

In order to understand why and how Jewish alcohol entrepreneurs came to be regarded as a problem, it is necessary to look beyond the organizations that constituted the prohibition establishment, and toward other political and social movements connected with prohibitionists. While these alliances were never politically formalized, each group that brought its own interests and concerns to the debate over alcohol commerce helped to shape the prohibition movement during the late nineteenth and early twentieth century. And where these concerns included suspicion of and hostility toward American Jews, prohibition and anti-Semitism became intertwined.

Anti-Semites and prohibitionists influenced American society in divergent ways in the early twentieth century; the former had an amorphous and mostly indirect effect on their object, while the latter spawned a political doctrine that gained the force of law. Despite the differences between them, they shared common concerns. Anti-Semitism and prohibitionism provided parallel ideological settings for Americans to express alarm about economic stratification and the increasingly commercial nature of the American economy, the growing presence of immigrants in American society, and challenges to the political and cultural dominance of white Protestants. The prohibition movement and anti-Semitic sentiment were both articulations of unease about the mutability of American culture, and each worldview offered a means to explain and protest against these changes. Together, they tendered a harsh critique of American Jewish economic activity, and intimated that Jews' presence in the alcohol trade proved their essential hostility to American values.

These allegations were not without precedent. An early incident transpired in Atlanta in 1885, after the voters of Fulton County narrowly passed a local option referendum severely restricting alcohol commerce in the city. In the month leading up to the vote, and through 1887 (when voters again went to the polls and this time rejected prohibition), city residents vigorously debated the wisdom and efficacy of the law. The referendum's champions, led by the Georgia branch of the WCTU in alliance with regional church leaders, declared that prohibition suppressed the "unmitigated evil" and "crime against the divine law" perpetrated by the liquor traffic.[3] A collective of the city's businessmen mobilized in opposition, arguing that destruction of the local alcohol trade would drive away visitors, drain the municipal budget of badly needed funds, put law-abiding entrepreneurs out of business, and undermine efforts to promote Atlanta as the South's most modern city. "Capital should rather be encouraged to come in than to be driven out," wrote a leading "Anti," as the referendum's adversaries were called. "This is a progressive age, and we must be up and doing if Atlanta is not to go backwards."[4]

After the referendum passed in 1885, several dozen Atlanta businessmen formed the Conservative Citizens Association to combat the law and promote "the freedom of individual conduct unvexed by sumptuary laws." When the local Methodist minister and outspoken prohibition advocate J. B. Hawthorne denounced the group and their efforts from his pulpit, he singled out the city's Jews, claiming that they were in league with this sinful and self-interested lot. "All Jerusalem responds to their call," he warned his audience in an 1886 sermon: "Stein, Goldstein, Bernstein, and all the other Steins" were working on behalf of prohibition's enemies.[5]

Hawthorne had noticed the handful of Jewish members in the Conservative Citizens Association, although they were a minority presence within the organization and unrepresented in its leadership. He might also have observed that a few of the city's most prominent Jewish businessmen did participate in anti-prohibition rallies.[6] But Hawthorne had wildly overstated his case. Even though Atlanta's Jews would more likely be found among prohibition's critics than its advocates, as a group they were not active or vocal on either side of the debates surrounding the referendum. The most vehement Jewish response to the Fulton County vote came from the New York City publication the *Jewish Messenger*, which described Atlanta's prohibitionists as "country yokels" and "religious fanatics."[7]

Hawthorne had fixed his attentions on Atlanta's Jewish community because he regarded them as economically suspect. Their anti-prohibitionist politics, he insinuated, were motivated by cupidity so powerful that they were willing to put aside their instinctive clannishness; Atlanta's Jews followed the gentile leaders of the Anti faction, "surrender[ing] their religious and racial prejudices," he wrote, because they feared that prohibition would hurt them financially. Several months later, the *Atlanta Journal* described a conversation between a "plain business man" and his neighbor, a "Hebrew citizen" who complained of "the financial injury done the city by prohibition." The writer suggested that it was the Jew's concern for his "own material prosperity" that blinded him to the law's positive effects on the city economy. When the "plain business man" quoted the Hebrew Bible as stating, "Cursed be he who putteth the bottle to his neighbor's mouth," his Jewish interlocutor refused to respond; the writer concluded that the "Hebrew citizen" was more interested in financial gain than in following the dictates of his own religion.[8]

Rather than regarding Jews as among the many Antis who disagreed with them about alcohol commerce, these Atlanta prohibitionists had surmised that Jews' economic interests differentiated them from other Americans and situated them as enemies of the public good. Such insinuations were not new to the American Jewish experience. European colonial settlers, many of whom came from religious and national cultures where Jews were regarded as economic parasites, had brought economic anti-Semitism to North American shores. American anti-Semitism grew during the nineteenth century, as central European Jewish immigrants became an especially visible commercial presence. But occasions where anti-Jewish policies officially curtailed Jewish economic activity (such as General Ulysses S. Grant's Order #11, which accused Jews of war profiteering and expelled them from the military district under his command in 1862) were uncommon. Compared to Jews' experience in Europe, American anti-Semitism, while alienating and upsetting, interfered only minimally with Jews' ability to conduct their businesses.[9]

Anti-Semitism was merely one component in Americans' myriad preconceptions about Jewish economic behavior. Attitudes toward Jewish businessmen were complex and sometimes contradictory; to a great degree, they mirrored American wariness toward an economic landscape undergoing radical growth and transformation. American Jewish commercial success garnered praise from some, resentment and suspicion from others, and, on occasion, a mix of positive and negative responses. "On the favorable side, the Jew commonly symbolized an admirable keenness and resourcefulness in trade," the historian John Higham has written. "In another mood, keenness might mean cunning; enterprise might shade into avarice."[10]

But ambivalence toward Jewish economic behavior tipped toward suspicion during the last two decades of the nineteenth century, as more Americans protested industrial capitalism's impact on their lives. Farmers, industrial workers, and small businessmen objected to industrialization and corporate consolidation, and demanded protection from legislation and monetary policy that favored the plutocrat and the non-producer. The organizations protesting these developments differed in their ideologies and prescriptions for reform, but they shared a suspicion that formidable political and economic interests sought to dominate American society.

The populist movement emerged from this challenge to modern capitalism.[11] Since the end of the Civil War, populists had formulated a critique of Gilded Age structures of business organization, such as monopolies, mergers, vertical and horizontal integration, and the dreaded "trust." Increased bureaucratization and centralization of the American economy, populists insisted, had concentrated manufacturing and monetary power into the hands of too few economic actors. They predicted that an industrial and banking aristocracy would soon control all American commerce, manipulating and eventually mobilizing the government so that it operated exclusively for the benefit of the rich. These powerful interests had already bought off politicians and newspaper editors, this theory continued; they owned the banks, the land, and the means of production, and now the citizenry was on the verge of enslavement. The People's Party, which was launched in 1892 to act as the populists' national political organization, raged against this state of affairs in their foundational Omaha Platform: "The fruits of toil of millions are boldly stolen to build up colossal fortunes for a few," they declared, "and the possessors of these, in turn, despise the republic and endanger liberty."[12]

Contemporary ideas about Jewish economic behavior fit within populism's vision of the struggle between the powerful and "the people." When Jews appeared in the populist narrative, they were often cast either as members of the economic plutocracy or as those who did the plutocracy's bidding. This was, in part, a response to Jewish immigrants' visibility as commercial intermediaries between agricultural producers and the market, which rendered them odious in the eyes of those who already regarded the middleman as the enemy of the American farmer. Among those populists whose politics were intertwined with their religious faith, Christian beliefs additionally reinforced distrust of Jews. For American Protestants—especially those who interacted with Jews only in commercial contexts—stereotypes of Jews as urban non-producers and price manipulators became entangled with the New Testament story of the money changers Jesus chased out of the Temple. Accusations that Jews were responsible for the Crucifixion, and Christian imagery of Judas's betrayal of Jesus for thirty pieces of silver, strengthened suspicions that Jews conspired to exploit gentiles and undermine the United States as a Christian nation.[13]

Though scholars who have studied the populist movement within the last several decades agree that the image of the Jewish economic actor in the American imagination placed Jews well outside the circles of populist sympathies, they have come to a range of conclusions about the pervasiveness and potency of populist anti-Semitism. Some historians insist that Jews barely registered in populist consciousness, and that the use of Crucifixion imagery and invocation of names like "Rothschild" and "Shylock" were "colloquialisms that had no real reference in their minds to the Hebrews."[14] Such assertions are undermined by the claims of historians who point to the unequivocally anti-Semitic rhetoric employed by the southern populists known as "whitecappers" during the 1890s, as well as by national movement leaders such as Ignatius Donnelly and William "Coin" Harvey. When Donnelly wrote, "In the evil conditions made by bad laws, the Jews alone thrive," he oriented populist thought toward Jew hatred.[15]

Taken as a whole, however, the populist movement cannot conclusively be described as either indifferent or hostile toward Jews. Populist anti-Semitism's precise measure, if such a thing can be ascertained at all, differed from place to place and varied depending on how local leaders regarded and talked about Jews, among other factors. The populists can best be described as ambivalent toward American Jewry, and in this respect they were like most Americans at the turn of the century. Even when anti-Jewish sentiment surfaced in populist rhetoric, it remained of minor consequence to their political platform.[16]

Nevertheless, as Richard Hofstadter wrote of populist anti-Semitism, "it is one thing . . . to say that this prejudice did not go beyond a certain symbolic usage, quite another to say that a people's choice of symbols is of no significance."[17] For populists who included Jews among the enemies of the American people, anti-Semitic assumptions that Jews were a foreign and exploitative element in American economic life mapped onto both populist suppositions about "money power" and Christian anti-Semitism's economic undercurrents. Claims of a Jewish conspiracy bespoke the broader concerns of those bewildered by modern capitalism's effect on their lives. The fact that most farmers and small-town residents knew Jews only as merchants and creditors (whom they likely resented) and as biblical figures (whom they regarded as rejecters of the Lord) deepened their suspicion that Jews were an alien and malevolent force in the American economy. Jews became a symbol, a stand-in for complex and discomfiting socioeconomic dynamics; characterizing these changes as a conspiracy hatched by Jewish capitalists and middlemen was a way to regain some amount of comprehension and control.[18]

This perception of Jewish economic behavior gained traction in the American prohibition movement as well. Populism nurtured a tendency among dry activists to see politically formidable business interests as the primary source of the nation's alcohol problem. The anti-alcohol movement absorbed and tapped into populist anxieties about the concentration of capital and the exploitation of labor and consumers, shifting its attentions away from its earlier concentration on the individual drinker or seller and toward the business itself. Prohibitionists insisted that the beer and liquor industry conspired against the public good for its own enrichment, pointing out that like the "robber barons" of other industries, American alcohol industrialists sought to minimize competition and control prices by consolidating production, monopolizing avenues of distribution (as breweries did with the tied-house system of saloon sponsorship), and employing any other instrument in their drive to increase profits.[19]

Like populists who accused politicians of acquiescing to the demands of railroad companies, prohibitionists decried lawmakers who befriended and accepted contributions from brewers, distillers, and alcohol trade advocates. When alcohol industrialists and trade-advocacy leagues agreed to cooperate with local regulations meant to limit the accessibility of alcohol, such as high license fees, hard-line prohibitionists dismissed such compromises as doubly unconscionable: a government that profited from the production and sale of beer and liquor was entirely complicit in the evil and misery it wrought. Both major political parties had fallen in line with the alcohol industry's demands, prohibitionists declared. A Boston activist denounced the Republican Party as "on its knees to the whiskey industry" in 1888; a Georgia minister described the Democratic Party in 1890 as "a straight-out opponent of all efforts that look to the annihilation of the traffic."[20] The "liquor evil," wrote the Georgian, had "obtained a place and power in politics never before secured or held by any one interest in our country."[21]

Prohibitionists were not entirely wrong in their analysis of the alcohol trade's postbellum power. Alcohol industrialists had gone to great lengths to increase their profit margin, including, on occasion, undermining elections and bribing newspaper editors. Brewing and distilling trade lobbyists regularly sought relationships with politicians who might protect their industries from onerous regulation. Prohibitionists were wrong, however, to assume that such relationships always signified a political conspiracy. It is true that plenty of elected officials were friendlier to alcohol tradesmen than they were to prohibitionists, and some were handsomely remunerated for their friendship. But avarice was not the only motivation that might inspire a politician to take the side of the wets. Their own and their constituents' ideological opposition to sumptuary legislation, as well as concern about lost jobs and revenue under prohibition law, also moved them to oppose the anti-alcohol movement. Further, although the alcohol industry did do its best—and sometimes its worst—to remain profitable, in the end neither the brewing nor the distilling business became the all-powerful cabal that so many prohibitionists feared them to be. Internecine rivalries between the brewing and distilling industries inhibited their ability to organize at the national level, and they viewed one another as competitors rather than confederates. Their ruthless battle for market share kept them from organizing to the extent that anti-alcohol agitators imagined they did.[22]

Prohibitionists who were influenced by populist interpretations of politics and economic power constructed a narrative that pitted the virtuous democratic citizen against the soulless corporate oligarch in a battle of good against evil. Prohibitionists had come to perceive the liquor and saloon interests in precisely these terms, insisting that their own efforts were squarely on the side of both God and the American people, while their opponents sought to undermine Christian and American values and subjugate citizens for economic gain.[23] "Like the Populists," the historian Michael Kazin has written, "foes of the saloon seemed convinced that Mammon was dominating man, and only their movement could right the balance."[24]

Throughout the 1880s and into the early 1890s, prohibitionists and populists recognized their shared ideological affinities and political concerns. Both movements drew significant support from rural areas and, to a lesser degree, small towns, although most prohibitionist leaders came from more densely populated regions.[25] Both movements flourished in places where Protestant church networks facilitated political activism, and both attracted Protestants whose politics were imbued with millennialist eschatology—a belief that political and social reform would help to bring about God's kingdom on earth.[26] Finally, both populism and late nineteenth-century prohibitionism responded to industrialization's effects on American life with horror and alarm, and insisted that the government should act on behalf of the people and not at the behest of powerful economic interests. Because of these kinships, agrarian radicals and state farmers' alliances generally supported temperance. In a few instances, the two groups cooperated politically, adopting each other's demands in their own party platforms; on occasion, leaders of one movement ran for office on the other's electoral ticket.[27]

But populists' and prohibitionists' commitments diverged as well, often because of class differences. Populism appealed most to small producers, farmers, and laborers who were critical of industrial capitalism, and their reform programs reflected their economic interests. Most prohibitionist leaders, on the other hand, were middle class, and uninterested in (or even hostile to) agrarian proposals for economic reform—especially the free coinage of silver, which they regarded as both a distraction to their cause and dubious economic policy. Even as populists remained unsympathetic to the alcohol traffic for both economic and religious reasons, movement leaders eventually disengaged from the formal anti-alcohol movement; once the national People's Party was established in 1892 and their movement seemed to be in ascendance, they feared losing "wet" voters, especially among the saloon-going urban industrial workers that the Knights of Labor had brought to the party.[28] They were therefore unwilling to sign on to an anti-liquor program as absolute as the prohibition forces demanded. A few populist leaders supported the idea of a state or national monopoly of the alcohol trade, a position that fit neatly within the populist economic program but which hard-line prohibitionists regarded as an intolerable compromise. By the mid-1890s, the two movements' attempts at "fusion" or "grand coalition" had come to nothing.[29]

Despite the failure of these groups to formalize their alliance, many prohibitionists continued to be profoundly influenced by populist thought—not only in their assignation of blame to the forces of "liquor power," but, for some, in their assumptions about the economic power of American Jews. All these tendencies can be seen in a pamphlet published in the early 1890s by Rezin B. Wasson, the treasurer of Wayne County, Ohio. Wasson was protesting a bond recently issued by the state to fund the building of an agricultural research institution in his county. He used the pamphlet as occasion to unleash a barrage of invective at Jews, whose involvement in the bond matter, he suggested, illustrated their general economic tendencies. "Upon a little reflection," Wasson stated, "the most casual observer will concede that the Jews have ruled the christian [sic] world since the beginning of its era by the use of gold and silver." (This was precisely the kind of language used by populists for whom Jewish economic behavior loomed large.) He tied Jewish corruption of politics and the economy to their controlling the beer and liquor industries. Jews "invested large sums of money in breweries," he wrote, and they strong-armed Secretary of State James G. Blaine (who had defended the rights of American Jews traveling in czarist Russia a decade before) "to drum up the beer trade" for themselves. Jews purchased local real estate through bond issuances, Wasson continued, and used it for the "beer brewery business" and "whiskey distiller[ies]." In addition, Jews "find little difficulty in getting good prohibition Editors [sic]" to tilt their newspapers' reporting so that it favored anti-prohibitionist politics.[30]

Wasson's anti-Semitic rage, at least as articulated in his pamphlet, had no discernibly specific object; he spoke primarily of "the Jew," rather than of any particular Jews, and if he had someone in mind he did not say so. Certainly, the prominence of Jews in the liquor industry throughout the region, in addition to Jews' animosity toward prohibition, could well have made a negative impression on him. Perhaps the presence of several of Peoria's Jewish distillers in what came to be known as the "Whiskey Trust"—an agreement among a collective of midwestern industrial distillers to control prices and production, for which John D. Rockefeller's Standard Oil served as a model—angered him as well, although the ethnic affiliation of these distillers, such as Joseph B. Greenhut and Adolph Woolner, was not publicly discussed until several decades later.[31] It is possible, too, that he was an acolyte of James Coxey, the Ohio populist leader and organizer of the 1894 "Coxey's Army," who founded the viciously anti-Semitic populist newspaper *Sound Money*.[32] Whether the connection between Jews, alcohol, and political power was, for Wasson, abstract and associative or concrete and responsive to specific events, his pamphlet demonstrates how populism's socioeconomic concerns—especially when it came to Jewish economic behavior—shaped anti-alcohol ideology and rhetoric, and shows how anxieties about economic power, the liquor industry, and Jewish influence became intertwined.

In 1885, the same year that the residents of Atlanta passed their short-lived countywide prohibition referendum, the *Chicago Daily Tribune* reported a courtroom appearance by an Irish immigrant who seemed to have been sent from central casting. Ellen Sullivan had turned up in that courtroom many times before, always as a defendant accused of drunken and disorderly behavior. But in this instance she was there, her "features bloated and distorted by excessive drinking," as a witness for the prosecution. According to the *Tribune*, the city had arrested two "Jews who keep saloons," and was charging them with the crime of "selling liquor to habitual drunkards." Sullivan testified that the saloon proprietor Bloom Harris had hired her to scrub his establishment's floor, paying her a nickel and five glasses of "vile five-cent whisky." Mark Rosenberg, who owned another saloon nearby, allowed Sullivan to barter her shoes for a drink. Both men were made to pay a fine, and Sullivan was returned to the prison where she had been incarcerated for public inebriation.[33]

The *Tribune* was generally sympathetic to the growing movement to restrict the liquor traffic in the United States, and their account of Harris and Rosenberg's trial voiced several of that movement's concerns. The article assigned Sullivan the stereotypical attributes of the pathetic and darkly comic Irish immigrant drunkard—a role frequently ascribed to the Irish in American discussions of the national "liquor question." That she was a member of the "gentler sex" made her inebriated condition even more shocking. Her dipsomania spoke to her own moral deficiency, but it was not her fault alone: as the charges against the saloonkeepers indicated, in the eyes of the court they had callously misused Sullivan and profited from her weakness. Further, just as the *Tribune* had associated Sullivan's drunkenness with her ethnic identity, the paper also connected Harris and Rosenberg's behavior to their ethno-religious affiliation. They were keepers of "Jew saloons," a category of drinking establishment where, according to the *Tribune*, "the most poisonous of vile liquor is retailed at cheap rates."[34]

Discussions of the "Jew saloon" and Jewish saloonkeepers first emerged during the 1880s. Quantitative developments offer a partial explanation: as Jewish immigrants took up saloonkeeping as an occupation, prohibitionists noted their presence with increased frequency. Earlier waves of temperance activists had little to say about Jewish saloonkeepers, one might suggest, because they encountered relatively few during the era of central European Jewish immigration. The more this ethnic occupational niche grew, the larger "Jew saloons" loomed in the prohibitionist mind.

Numbers partially explain why the "Jew saloon" began to attract prohibitionists' anxious attention. Another contemporary circumstance, prohibitionist anti-Semitism in Russia, might also have played a role. As we have already seen, Jewish involvement in the Pale of Settlement's alcohol trade had animated anti-Semitic sentiment and oppressive state policy in Russia for centuries, and did so with invigorated intensity after 1881. Among the commentators who exported these ideas to the English-speaking world was Charles Dickens, Jr., who published an essay describing Russian Jews' relation to alcohol in *All the Year Round*, the British literary journal his father had founded. "It is a Jew distiller who brews the vile corn-brandy . . . which poisons and maddens the Russian peasant," it read. "It is a Hebrew who retails it, and whom sullen drunkards accuse of adding unduly to the score of honest topers, while, with Semitic obstinacy, he keeps sober in their midst." Dispatches from Russia's own prohibition movement, several of which were published in American newspapers and magazines, blamed the Jewish taverner for his "demoralizing" control of the Russian peasantry. Luckily for these peasants, according to one such account, "these old publicans, with their adulterated drinks and their usury, were swept away" by laws barring Jews from participating in the alcohol trade.[35]

In addition, Polish Catholic and Russian Orthodox immigrants likely brought their homelands' antipathies to Jewish tavernkeepers with them to the United States. But their influence on the American anti-alcohol movement would have been minimal, since these groups took up saloonkeeping themselves stateside and thus were regarded by prohibitionists as part of the problem.[36] This dynamic points to the generally antagonistic relationship between immigrants and the American anti-alcohol movement. Enmity between immigrants and prohibitionists, of course, dated back decades. When antebellum temperance activists first blamed the nation's growing alcohol consumption on foreigners, their accusations reflected contemporary political and cultural anxieties about the expansion of Irish Catholic and German immigrant communities in the United States. But their claims also revealed genuine cultural differences between the two groups: immigrants from continental Europe were more permissive in their alcohol consumption habits, and less likely to be sententious about drinking, than were native-born Anglo-American Protestants.[37]

In the late nineteenth and early twentieth centuries, as millions of Europeans migrated to the United States, anti-immigrant sentiment reemerged as a powerful force in American society. Nativists of the 1880s and 1890s denounced immigrants as agents of radicalism and violence, immorality and social dissolution, and racial degeneration; this "scum and offal of Europe," xenophobic editorialists insisted, were nothing but "a danger that threatens the destruction of our national edifice by the erosion of its moral foundations."[38] Nativists insisted that all immigrants must learn to live according to "American" values, and any perpetuation of pre-migration religious identities, political ideologies, and cultural practices should be considered reasonable cause for exclusion or deportation. National political organizations such as the Immigration Restriction League pushed for the reduction of immigration and the outright denial of entry to those deemed "undesirable for citizenship or injurious to our national character."[39]

European attitudes toward alcohol stood foremost among immigrants' undesirable attitudes and practices. At the turn of the century, as immigrant populations and the liquor industry ballooned simultaneously, the nativist program once again provided prohibitionists with a compelling explanation for the growth of the trade. Many American prohibitionists feared that immigrants were entirely resistant to efforts toward curtailing alcohol commerce, and regarded the urban immigrant saloon to be an especially troubling and contemptible presence in American culture.

As had been true of populism's informal yet powerful influence, however, prohibitionists did not unilaterally embrace nativism in its most exclusionary form. Prohibitionists, like Americans in general, expressed a range of opinion about how thoroughly newcomers could be assimilated, and some anti-alcohol activists hoped that immigrants would join the fight against the liquor trade and its attendant evils. A reformed and efficiently run city free of corruption, crime, and immorality, they reasoned, would benefit the foreign-born poor as well as the native-born middle class. These reforming impulses inspired and motivated the American progressive movement, whose adherents hoped to transform both government structure and individual behavior so that American society would operate in more modern, rational, and productive ways. Progressives who held compassionate rather than intolerant attitudes toward immigrants—as did the progressive activists of the settlement house movement—were determined to modify immigrant behaviors so that they did not clash or conflict with American mainstream ideals.[40]

According to prohibition's more progressively minded advocates, alcohol kept immigrants from becoming productive and assimilated Americans, and saloons capitalized on this dynamic. Prohibitionists pointed to saloons in immigrant neighborhoods as the public spaces where disjunctures between Old World and New World ways were most acutely manifest. "The saloon fosters an un-American spirit among the foreign-born population of our country," claimed the sociologist John Barker in his 1905 polemic *The Saloon Problem and Social Reform*. "The influx of foreigners into our urban centres, many of whom have liquor habits, is a menace to good government," since urban saloons often acted as sites of political organization. Saloonkeepers were known to rally their patrons to vote for specific political causes or candidates. Wet politicians then relied on saloonkeepers to bring voters to the polls, which gave the taverner political power. But whereas an exclusionary nativist might suggest that ethnic saloons stood as concrete proof of the dangers immigrants posed to American society, Barker insisted that closing all saloons and prohibiting all liquor traffic would end the problem of municipal corruption. Further, he insisted, prohibition would curb immigrants' alcohol consumption, teach them "self-restraint," and help them to "assimilate

American ideals" of thrift, hard work, and proper moral comportment.[41] Prohibition, in other words, would remake immigrants into Americans by compelling them to behave according to Anglo-American, Protestant, middle-class norms.

Prohibitionist organizations ranged in their commitment to this project, sometimes even internally. In 1888, the Prohibition Party conveyed their ambivalence toward immigrants by approaching the issue from both directions simultaneously: even as they printed pamphlets in German and Scandinavian languages and subsidized the distribution of a Catholic newspaper, they stated their approval of restrictive immigration legislation. The WCTU and the ASL also played both sides, utilizing nativist rhetoric while they sought to establish connections with groups that represented the interests of immigrant ethnic communities. They published educational and political materials in foreign languages and distributed them in urban ethnic neighborhoods, and sought alliances with religious associations that attracted an immigrant membership.[42]

Some leaders of immigrant and ethnic associations responded to this outreach positively and supported the anti-alcohol movement, usually in the spirit of assimilation and community uplift. According to Irving Howe, one Lower East Side *landsmanshaft* (Jewish immigrant fraternal association) refused membership to saloonkeepers, a move likely inspired by the Knights of Labor's similar restriction.[43] But immigrants as a group remained ill disposed toward the prohibitionist agenda, and prohibitionists' efforts at cross-cultural cooperation met with little success. Immigrants generally regarded alcohol as morally neutral—a substance some might abuse, but one that also fostered communal good cheer—and the saloon as an important community resource. In 1894, when New York City's monsignor followed the lead of Columbus, Ohio's prelate and denounced the liquor traffic—even going so far as to suggest that Catholic priests should refuse Communion to liquor dealers—New York Catholics of a multitude of ethnic backgrounds responded angrily. Catholic liquor dealers, unsurprisingly, spoke out with particular venom. "I was born a Catholic, and I expect to die a Catholic," avowed one downtown saloonkeeper, "but I would give up my religion before I would give up my business." Another Catholic liquor dealer employed his own version of nativist logic, pointing out that the monsignor was himself an immigrant from Italy. "He knows nothing about our country," the saloonkeeper said, "and he should be the last man to set himself up as a censor of our customs."[44]

Nativist turnabout may well have been fair play, but immigrant saloonkeepers rarely had the opportunity to utilize it. Prohibitionists' rage against the alcohol industry influenced their attitude toward the immigrants within it, especially since the number of immigrant-owned saloons climbed precipitously during these decades. The growth of the American alcohol industry, and the number of immigrants employed within it, led prohibitionists to conclude, as did John Barker, that "the majority of saloon-keepers are foreigners."

If anyone had looked at the census and done the math, however, they would have noticed that Barker's conclusion was incorrect. Of 127,000 total saloonkeepers and bartenders counted by the U.S. census in 1890, 59,000 were foreign-born.[45] Simple arithmetic demonstrates that the majority of men and women who served alcohol by the glass were born on American soil. This discrepancy between perception and reality was likely heightened by the presence of first-generation Americans among those who served alcohol to their own ethnic communities. Yet the perception only grew more intense over the next several decades. According to the 1910 census, 67,000 of the total 169,000 men and women behind the bar were immigrants—a reduction in the ratio of immigrant to native-born saloonkeepers. At that moment, anxiety about the influence of immigrant purveyors of alcohol was approaching its zenith.[46]

Accusations of alien dominance of the saloon trade (and of the alcohol trade in general) had purchase in American culture because such claims offered a simple and straightforward explanation to a complex and vexing national concern. Many of Pittsburgh's saloons, wrote a local prohibitionist, were owned by immigrants who "from the day they first set foot on American soil, engaged in no business but liquor selling."[47] And when the WCTU founder Annie Wittenmyer described the liquor trade as an oligarchy "largely made up of foreigners [who] had the government by the throat," and described these immigrants as "enemies open and defiant to American institutions," she expressed a commonly held perception about the provenance of the American "liquor problem."[48] According to anti-alcohol reformers who drew on nativist ideology, foreign-born liquor dealers participated in commercial behavior that betrayed their failure to conform to American values of thrift, sobriety, and hard work.

Alcohol commerce and consumption, according to those who held this point of view, was entirely at variance with American politics and morality, and the only way it could have developed into a thriving industry was if it had been imposed, even forced, on the nation by outsiders. Nativism's influence on the anti-alcohol movement was similar to that of populism: it allowed prohibitionists to ascribe the practices they despised and feared to an external and sinister force—in this case, immigrants and ethnic Americans—and to divide social and economic practices into those that were properly "American" and those that were not.

The "Jew saloon," as assessed by its detractors, thus represented an element within the broader category of immigrant-owned drinking establishment, albeit one with specific qualities associated with its proprietor. In the urban North, views of Jewish alcohol entrepreneurs dovetailed with assertions that eastern European Jews were racially and culturally predisposed toward vice and crime. Jewish immigrants' involvement in urban prostitution rings amplified these claims, not only because sex trafficking was regarded as a terrible threat to morality, the family, and public health, but also because it seemed to confirm Jews' eagerness to derive commercial gain by even the most vile means.[49]

The fact that prostitutes often procured or even attended to customers in saloons exacerbated anxieties about Jewish saloonkeepers. "The criminal instincts that are so often found naturally in Russian and Polish Jews" were reflected in both their economic behavior and their leisure activities, wrote the urban reformer Frank Moss in 1898. Moss pointed to the Jewish quarter of the Lower East Side as proof, describing the neighborhood as "dotted with disreputable saloons and disorderly houses" where drunken behavior and prostitution "were carried on without concealment and in open defiance of law and decency." Jewish immigrants were the primary perpetrators of vice in New York, he concluded, and Jewish "dive-keepers," in his estimation, facilitated much of the area's criminal and morally reprehensible behavior.[50] These concerns seemed to be vindicated in 1908, when Theodore Bingham, New York City's police commissioner, released a report claiming that the overwhelming majority of the city's criminals were immigrants, mostly Polish and Russian Jews and southern Italians.[51]

Assertions of Jewish criminal tendencies, and of Jews' eagerness to capitalize on vice, were not limited to New York. The "Jew saloons" of Chicago, according to the *Daily Tribune*, selfishly capitalized on deprivation in the city's immigrant slum, accumulating profits where "the crowded tenements empty forth their horde of night-prowlers and thieves" and "drunkards and outcasts go staggering along the sidewalk."[52] Prohibitionists and other moral reformers who referred to a Jewish presence in saloon districts were not merely responding to a rising number of Jewish saloonkeepers. The "Jew saloon" was a seen as a symptom of mass immigration. Anxious and angry accusations against immigrant saloonkeepers, Jewish or otherwise, were expressions of worry about the relationship between immigration, alcohol, and crime in American cities.

During the first decade of the twentieth century, concerns about alcohol, crime, and the presence of Jews in the American economy combined with yet another anxiety: the resilience of the color line. With growing frequency, alcohol's enemies mentioned Jews not as admirably moderate in their alcohol consumption, but as suspect in their commercial practices—especially when they sold alcohol to African American men.

This version of prohibitionist anti-Semitism emerged as a response to events in the South, where the twentieth-century prohibition movement had its first string of significant victories. The passage of several statewide prohibition laws in the South inspired the Anti-Saloon League to reconfigure its national strategy, which moved anti-alcohol activists closer to their ultimate goal: an amendment to the U.S. Constitution that prohibited the manufacture and sale of beverage alcohol. The event that set these developments in motion—a 1906 race riot in Atlanta—became a subject of national discussion and inquiry. Several of the journalists investigating the causes of the riot declared that Jewish alcohol retailers were partly to blame. Understanding how Jews found themselves subject to such accusations—first in Atlanta, and soon throughout the South—requires examination of the development of southern ideologies about both race and alcohol during the early twentieth century.

By 1900, all the counties that surrounded Atlanta had gone dry. A wet island suspended in a legislatively bone-dry sea, the city—and especially its Decatur Street district—attracted significant traffic from miles around. The area was turning into a tourist attraction for "slummers," middle-class whites who, as the historian Chad Heap has written, wanted to visit and observe "socially marginalized urban neighborhoods and the diverse populations that inhabited them." Some city boosters promoted Decatur Street as a site where visitors could observe and enjoy the local culture. Northerners of "wealth and refinement" visited the dance halls and drinking establishments on the street, claimed the *Constitution*, "being desirous of getting a correct insight of the negro in all his social phases"—which, apparently, included watching them dance "the quadrille, the buck and the hoochee coochee."[53] But a growing number of middle-class Atlantans denounced the "Decatur dives." Despite the fact that white middle-class businessmen, journalists, and politicians enjoyed the street's less-reputable offerings on occasion—including Mayor James Woodward, whose public intoxication and patronage of brothels scandalized the city[54]—local newspapers focused on the street as the city's locus of lower-class depravity. The forms of leisure that Decatur Street made available to unemployed and underemployed "loafers," they insisted, inhibited productivity, kept the city from reaching its full economic potential, and acted as a drag on Atlanta's collective moral standards.

Decatur Street also posed a threat to the color line. The saloons, restaurants, gambling rooms, and dance halls of "Rusty Row" drew black and white men from all over the city and the outlying countryside every Saturday night. These establishments were segregated by race, but when the "white only" and "colored only" businesses disgorged their patrons, the neighborhood provided space—from public streets to back-alley brothels—for blacks and whites, women as well as men, to engage in a spectrum of unsavory and illicit activities. Moral reformers denounced the interracial drinking, gambling, and other forms of depravity available in the district, declaring that Decatur Street's recreations muddied the racial boundaries that divided and defined every aspect of southern life.

By 1900, concerns about race and the color line most differentiated the southern prohibition movement from its northern and western variants. Middle-class southerners, both black and white, had concluded that liquor provoked racial conflict. Working-class men were more vulnerable to the demoralizations of liquor, prohibitionists argued, and had a greater tendency to get at each other's throats than did "respectable folk." Prohibitionists and other progressive reformers all over the New South confidently asserted that limiting the availability of alcohol and saloon settings to black and white men of the "lower levels" would reduce the number of race riots and lynchings in the region.[55]

Racial mixing and conflict among the lower classes was only regarded as part of the problem, however. Middle-class southern whites feared, above all else, the availability of alcohol to African American men. Class-based arguments for the abolition of the liquor traffic were drowned out by white claims that black men were incapable of controlling their desire for alcohol. Just as northern prohibitionists of the previous century had said of Irish immigrants, southern progressives insisted that a black man's unquenchable thirst rendered him a helpless pawn of the liquor industry. Gaining access to the franchise, by this analysis, had done the freedman no favors, since his vote was easily corrupted by an industry that debased him and used him for its own self-interested purposes. Southern prohibitionists suggested that one way to end liquor commerce was to disfranchise black men and purge the electorate of liquor power's instrument. Disfranchisement would serve the general good, and, one southern prohibitionist insisted, was intended "in consideration of the true welfare of the negro race."[56]

But southern whites who called for a ban on alcohol commerce were actually not interested in protecting black men from "liquor power" or from their own worst impulses. In the imagination of the white southerner, a drunken black man was always a rapist in the making, and the object of his lust was invariably a white woman. Limiting black men's access to alcohol, prohibitionists argued, would not only protect southern white womanhood, but would also diminish the incidence of lynchings and race riots, since it would eliminate what white middle-class reformers saw as their root cause: black men's lust, fueled by liquor.[57] Northern leaders of the mainstream prohibition movement agreed: Francis Willard, president of the WCTU, understood southern race conflict in similar terms. "The colored race multiplies like the locusts of Egypt," she proclaimed in an 1890 interview. "The grog-shop is its center of power [and] the safety of woman, of childhood, of the home, is menaced."[58]

These anxieties about race, sex, and alcohol came to a crescendo in Atlanta in September 1906, after several months of incendiary reportage from the local papers. Lurid and hysterical articles about "black brutes" assaulting white women filled the *Journal*, the *Constitution*, and the *Evening News*. Reporters and editors shamelessly exaggerated their dispatches; an incident in which a white woman looked out her window and saw a black man standing on her lawn, for example, was reported as an assault.[59] All summer and into the fall, the press and local reformers blamed Decatur Street dives for fueling the epidemic of sexual violence. "These clubs and dives are hot-beds of crime," the *Journal* insisted. "Much of the recent outlawry on the part of the negroes is attributable directly to the influence of the places." As if the availability of limitless amounts of liquor was not bad enough, according to news reports, there was also the matter of the "pictures of nude white women that for some time have adorned the walls of negro dives." Images of lovely and voluptuous ladies—lily-white and in various states of disrobe—in fact adorned the walls of all kinds of saloons and drinking clubs across the nation; then as now, marketers of alcoholic beverages relied heavily on feminine flesh to sell their product.

When these racy advertisements appeared in drinking establishments catering to white men of means, only anti-alcohol activists expressed outrage. When used to sell liquor to black men in the South, they inspired a consensus among whites that such images, when consumed along with the merchandise being advertised, directly inspired black men to rape white women.

On September 22, the day's newspapers blared headline after headline: "third assault"; "angry citizens in pursuit of black brute"; "clean out the dives." Atlanta city officials harassed "colored" saloons in particular: five black men

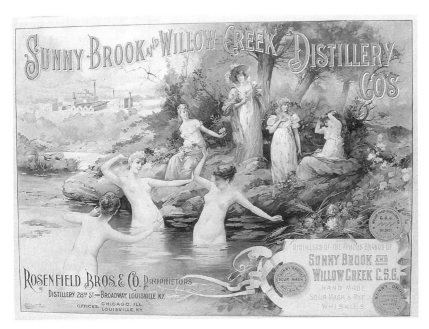

10. Bar sign advertising the Sunny Brook and Willow Creek Distillery, Louisville, date unknown. The Rosenfield brothers of Chicago had been rectifying and wholesaling Kentucky whiskey for a year when they founded their distilling company in 1892. Alcohol manufacturers' use of nudes to sell their product infuriated reformers—especially in the South, where whites feared that such images inflamed the lust of the "black beast rapist." (Courtesy of Showtime Auction Services)

were arrested for working in black-only saloons decorated with portraits of nude white women, and the city's police chief requested that the city council refuse liquor licenses to twenty-six saloons and restaurants that catered to an African American clientele. A Methodist minister and official for the Georgia branch of the Anti-Saloon League, which had been organized in 1904, insisted that the connection between Decatur Street's saloons, black men, and rape was as clear as could be. "Tank him up on booze," he warned, "and the black brute makes toward a white woman." As a case in point, the *Constitution* recounted a black man's defense for assaulting a white woman: "Judge I don't remember a thing that happened last night. . . . I got drunk with another negro and the last thing I remember was when I was in a barroom on Decatur Street."[60]

That evening, a mob of several thousand white men stormed the Decatur Street neighborhood and brutally attacked its black denizens. The rioters smashed saloon windows, drank what they found inside, and then spread throughout the city in a spree of random assaults on black people and black-owned businesses. By the time calm was restored two days later, dozens of black Atlantans had been murdered and scores more injured.[61]

Georgia prohibitionists responded to the riot by redoubling their efforts. Liquor had caused the violence, they insisted; drunken blacks had committed the "unspeakable" crime, and drunken whites had exacted vengeance. The only solution was to outlaw alcohol, for the sake of citizen safety, economic progress, and national reputation. In the summer of 1907, after less than a year of postriot prohibitionist agitation, the Georgia House of Representatives easily passed a statewide prohibition measure and Governor Hoke Smith signed it into law.[62]

Georgia's newfound consensus on the need to restrict alcohol consumption and regulate behavior—a significant shift from long-standing southern inclinations against government regulation of white men's personal liberties—had a monumental impact on the state's African Americans. State legislators were convinced that limiting the availability of alcohol would protect and purify politics; since voters would no longer be able to vote "under the influence," they would no longer be under the influence of the liquor trade. The next step, which the state legislature took the following year, was to remove those voters understood to be irreparably unstable and easily corruptible from the rolls—namely, black men, whose lack of self-control had already been agreed on during the prohibition debate. By 1900, several southern states had already taken this step, through voter restriction methods such as the poll tax or implementation of party primaries that excluded black voters. In 1908, Georgia joined North and South Carolina, Louisiana, Alabama, and Virginia by writing black disfranchisement into their state constitution.[63]

But the prohibition law had impact far beyond the state's borders. Georgia's outlawing of the sale or production of alcohol signaled the beginning of a series of prohibitionist successes in the South. By the end of the decade, Alabama, Tennessee, Mississippi, and North Carolina had passed similar legislation; by 1915, West Virginia, Arkansas, and South Carolina were dry as well.[64] Prohibition had come to be embraced by white southerners who regarded it as a crucial progressive reform.

As the regional debate over prohibition geared up, and as northern observers traveled to the city to investigate the riot and opined in print on its causes, the presence of Jewish immigrants in Decatur Street's alcohol trade entered public consciousness. These journalists combined older accusations that Jewish entrepreneurs were economically unscrupulous with more current discussions of Jewish involvement in prostitution rings and other forms of female exploitation. Some of the same writers who warned against Jewish alcohol entrepreneurs had also published investigatory essays on Jewish "white slavers."[65]

Southern concerns that Jewish men would betray white concerns by failing to protect white women mirrored and fed into national uncertainty about Jews' racial status. Eugenicists and others who claimed scientific expertise on the topic of racial identity and human heredity suggested that Jews from the Pale of Settlement, as well as other recent European immigrants such as Italians and Slavs, were of lower racial status than northern Europeans. Race theorists of the day gave precedence to phenotypic characteristics, such as hair texture or skin color, and suggested an ancestral link between Jews as a "Semitic" people and Africans.

In the turn of the century South, where the black/white divide was most assiduously policed, regional attitudes toward Jews depended on which side of the divide Jews were seen as standing on. Jewish storekeepers' seeming indifference to Jim Crow customs heightened white southern skepticism about Jews' capacity to assimilate into the region's white culture. Since the nineteenth century, Jewish immigrant peddlers and storeowners had acquired a reputation for interacting more intimately with black customers than native white entrepreneurs would, even using honorifics like "Mister" in conversation with black customers—transgressive behavior, by white supremacist standards. Whether Jews treated blacks in this manner because of their own experiences with oppression or out of ignorance of (or indifference to) southern social norms, their willingness to treat black customers with deference and respect gave southern whites cause to worry that Jewish economic practices blurred the racial divide in potentially dangerous ways.[66]

In the wake of the riot, the leaders of Atlanta's acculturated Jewish community expressed opinions that resembled those of the city's white middle class—the sector of the population of which they felt themselves to be a part. Very few Jews spoke about the riot publicly, and when they did, they insisted that maintenance of law and order should be the highest priority. Whether they genuinely supported this position or feared the repercussions of criticizing white city leaders' response to the violence is difficult to ascertain; the historical archives offer too few clues. The recorded minutes of the Temple's executive board meetings, for instance, make no mention whatever of the riot in the weeks or months that followed. Perhaps they felt that it was a matter that did not concern them, and the less they said about it, the better.

But they reacted to the postriot swell of support for prohibition as American Jews had for decades: they defended the alcohol trade, although in this case their defense was cautious and conditional. Dr. David Marx, rabbi of the Temple, served on the citizen's committee that had recommended the closing of "colored only" barrooms but had allowed bars that catered to whites to reopen.[67] When asked to make a public statement, the liquor wholesalers Aaron Bluthenthal and Monroe Bickart insisted that it was not liquor itself but rather a small group of immoral and irresponsible purveyors who had caused all the problems. "If there was a man in the city selling whisky who was not a fit person to engage in the business," a representative of the firm asserted, referring not so obliquely to the saloonkeepers of Decatur Street, "he should have been pointed out and his license revoked."[68] A few days after the riot, the city alderman Joseph Hirsch, then the only Jewish elected official in Atlanta, suggested that the city council consider liquor licenses for negro saloons and restaurants on a case-by-case basis rather than revoke them all in a single edict. His suggestion was unanimously opposed.[69]

If Decatur Street's immigrant saloonkeepers resented Bluthenthal and Bickart's insinuation against them or appreciated Hirsch's attempts to protect their businesses, there is no public record of it. In a memoir he wrote many years later, the Atlanta resident and former peddler David Yampolsky described the riot as a "pogrom on the blacks," expressing empathy for those who were beset upon so mercilessly and in a manner that Jewish immigrants would find familiar.[70] At the time, however, Atlanta's more recent Jewish immigrants reacted to September's riot with silence. Although Decatur Street's Jewish-owned saloons surely suffered some damage, there is no evidence that either they or any other Jewish-owned businesses were singled out by the mob for destruction. But the city council's decision to revoke all "colored only" liquor licenses threatened their livelihoods. By October 1906, the number of whiskey saloons in Atlanta had contracted from 110 to 77. That number included several dozen Jewish-owned saloons on and around Decatur Street.[71]

Concerns about Jewish alcohol purveyance in the South first emerged during Georgia's debate over statewide prohibition legislation. These accusations were initially oblique. But within a day of the riot's conclusion, the editorial board of the *Journal* made clear that they abhorred the white saloonkeepers who sold alcohol to black men. "Let it be understood," they wrote, "that the white man who sells or gives away liquor to a negro is an enemy of his own race, an enemy of society, an enemy of law and order." An article in the *Constitution* a week after the riot angrily described the blurring of the color line in Decatur Street's drinking establishments. "Some of the saloon men allow the negroes to curse them, applying the vilest epithets," this journalist wrote, "while they in turn call the negroes 'mister' and speak of them as gentlemen."[72] Although both remarks made use of older accusations often made against Jewish salesmen in southern shops, neither was directed at Jews specifically.

The first public mention of Decatur Street's Jewish saloonkeepers occurred not in the local press but in national publications, when two of the most widely read national muckraking magazines of the progressive era printed essays on the riot. Both essayists pointedly mentioned the presence of Jewish saloonkeepers in the Decatur Street district. *Harper's Weekly* described the neighborhood as "the very worst part of Atlanta" and "the hatching-place of negro criminals." The author, Thomas Gibson, noted that "white men—mostly foreigners, Russian Jews and Greeks—run many of the saloons, pawn shops, and restaurants which cater to the negro trade." Like the *Journal*, Gibson had nothing but contempt for such businessmen. "As to white foreigners who cater to negro trade and negro vice in this locality," he contended, "it is left to the judgment of the reader which is of higher grade in the social scale, the proprietors or their customers."[73]

An essay on the riot and its aftermath in the *American Magazine* followed in April 1907. The journalist Ray Stannard Baker also described Decatur Street as "the worst section of the city," and he offered photos of two Atlanta saloons: Abram Abelsky's and Michael Cohen's. "Many of the saloons for negroes were kept by foreigners, usually Jews," read the caption.[74] While Baker's mention of Jewish saloonkeepers on Decatur Street was less vitriolic and accusatory than Gibson's, their shared observations suggested that Jews were among the riot's causes.

These two articles precipitated a stream of portrayals of Jews who sold alcohol to black men as a dangerous presence throughout the South. Of all the Jewish alcohol entrepreneurs whose commercial relationship to blacks inspired alarm, Lee Levy received the most attention. Levy was born in New York City to central European Jewish immigrants, had moved to Gainesville, Texas, and established a liquor wholesale business there by 1900. Within a few years, he moved to St. Louis, where he and his business partner, a German Jewish immigrant named Adolph Asher, established a wholesaling concern that distributed liquor throughout the Mississippi Delta region.

Levy became nationally known in 1908, after a series of articles by Will Irwin in *Collier's* described a terrible crime in Shreveport: a young white girl named Margaret Lear had been murdered, allegedly by a black man

COMPANION PICTURES

Showing how the colour line was drawn by the saloons at Atlanta, Georgia.
Many of the saloons for Negroes were kept by foreigners, usually Jews

11. Assessing the causes of the 1906 race riot in Atlanta. Photographs from Ray Stannard Baker, *Following the Color Line* (New York: Doubleday, Page & Co., 1908), 26.

Lee Levy of Lee Levy & Co., makers of a vile, obscenely labeled gin largely sold to negroes

A type of the Louisiana field hands, who are the principal buyers of such gin as Levy sells

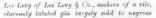

"Is it plain now—the secret of many and many a lynching and burning in the South? The primitive negro field hand, a web of strong, sudden impulses, good and bad, comes into town or settlement on Saturday afternoon and pays his fifty cents for a pint of Mr. Levy's gin. He absorbs not only its toxic heat, but absorbs also the suggestion, subtly conveyed, that it contains aphrodisiacs. He sits in the road or in the alley at the height of his debauch, looking at that obscene picture of a white woman on the label, drinking in the invitation which it carries. And then comes—opportunity. There follows the hideous episode of the rope or the stake"

12. Pictures of Lee Levy of St. Louis, maker of a "vile" brand of gin "largely sold to negroes," and an unnamed black "field hand," envisioned by Irwin as one of "the principal buyers of such gin as Levy sells." This customer "pays his fifty cents for a pint of Mr. Levy's gin. . . . He sits in the road or in the alley at the height of his debauch, looking at that obscene picture of a white woman on the label, drinking in the invitation which it carries. And then comes—opportunity," in the form of a vulnerable white woman. Photographs from Will Irwin, "Who Killed Margaret Lear?," Collier's, May 16 1908, 10.

named Charles Coleman. But "the real murderer of Margaret Lear" had gone unpunished, Irwin insisted. "What if he wears a white face instead of a black," he asked his readers. "Would you grease a rope for him?" The true villain, according to Irwin, was not Coleman, but Lee Levy, since Coleman had been supposedly had been drinking Levy's "nigger gin" (as Irwin called it) when he assaulted Lear. There was no way for Irwin to know precisely what Coleman had been drinking, or whether he had been drinking at all. But Levy's gin was cheap, popular, and available in "every low Negro dive in the South." As if the product was not already scandalous enough, its brand name—"Black Cock Vigor Gin"—was brazenly suggestive, and its packaging featured an illustration so racy that in 1908 Levy and Asher were convicted of sending obscene materials through the mail. Irwin's inclusion of Levy in the story shifted attention away from the alleged perpetrator, and even away from the attack itself. In Irwin's estimation, Levy held primary responsibility for the violence done to young Miss Lear, since his liquor, and its obscene packaging, had inspired the assault.[75]

Irwin's series on race and alcohol in the South had far-reaching impact. Tennessee prohibitionists picked up the story of Levy's gin as that state was fighting over sumptuary legislation. "The liquor dealers of Tennessee at this very time are selling to negroes Lee Levy and Co.'s gin," Nashville's dry newspaper insisted. "They are selling it in Chattanooga. They are selling it in Memphis. They are selling it in Nashville." Prohibition activists exhibited bottles of Levy's gin all over the state, displaying its risqué label to scandalized audiences. Within the year, Tennessee had passed a statewide prohibition law of its own.[76]

Irwin identified two other liquor wholesaling and manufacturing concerns: Bluthenthal and Bickart of Atlanta, and Dreyfuss and Weil of Paducah. The latter company claimed in their own advertising to be "the most widely sold brand in the South," and Irwin took them at their word.[77] All four of these men were Jewish, and although he did not mention their religion or ethnicity, he clearly intended for their names to identify them as such. He was far more explicit about the Jewish relationship to alcohol commerce in a piece on the liquor industry's propaganda methods, where he profiled the editors of a Jewish weekly magazine in St. Louis called the *Modern View*. This small magazine also published the *Caddo Adviser*, a circular underwritten by the city's brewing industry and distributed in Louisiana during the battle for statewide prohibition. When asked whether it was odd for a Jewish publishing firm to be so closely tied to the beer trade, one editor (whose "pockets bulged with anti-prohibition propaganda," according to Irwin) took a staunchly pro-alcohol position on the matter. "We are a Jewish religious weekly," said the editor, "and the Jews are opposed on moral grounds to prohibition." Irwin quoted another employee of the *Modern View*: "We are anxious to press its sale in every town of the South where the prohibitionists are contesting the ground."[78]

Irwin presented Jews who advocated against prohibition in the region as a danger to the well-being of the South, and as acting on behalf of their own self-interest and benefit. They were a defensive guard for distillers, saloonkeepers, and liquor wholesalers, at just the moment when the South most desperately needed this flow of liquor to be stanched. As national magazine readers absorbed this image of the immoral and self-interested Jewish alcohol entrepreneur, similar accusations surfaced in Georgia's statewide prohibition debate when a prohibitionist from Columbus declared in a local board of trade meeting that "Jews and whiskey men" were responsible for blocking efforts to pass statewide anti-liquor legislation. When the Jewish businessman serving as president of the Columbus board of trade protested this "attack upon the Jews as a people," the prohibitionist responded that the president was unqualified to lead that organization, since he "was not a representative of the Christian people of the city, as he was a Jew."[79]

Such demands for Jewish exclusion from the southern mainstream emerged several times during the state's prohibition battle. The itinerant minister John Cawhern articulated this perspective with particular viciousness in 1908, not long after Georgia's prohibition law went into effect. Cawhern celebrated the victory over liquor power by publishing a poster praising the politicians and activists who fought for the cause, and condemning the enemies of the prohibition movement. Among those he singled out for vilification were the "flat heeled, flat nosed, course [sic] haired, cross eyed slew footed Russian Jew whiskey venders [sic] whom the old Georgia politicions [sic] have licened [sic] to poison our boys."

Cawhern's description of Russian Jewish saloonkeepers as physically misshapen and hideous suggests that these immigrants were a racially alien and politically corrupting presence. In the Jim Crow South, such intimations were dangerous indeed. It is unclear whether he used the term "our boys" to refer to black or white men. Regardless, as had the populists of several decades previous, Cawhern suspected that Jews and crooked politicians collaborated in their efforts to degrade and ravage the community. Even if Jews were not alone in profiting from the liquor trade, according to Cawhern, they certainly benefited from its traffic and from government corruption. While the "Seed of Abraham" maintained their special covenant with God, he wrote, their economic behavior undermined both their status as chosen people and their claims to be loyal Americans: "Commercialism Controlled by these Pagan Devils called Jews Has wrought its curse to American Patriots," and left them with "no Christ, no conscience, no hope of Heaven nor care for Christian manhood and Civilization."[80]

Georgia's prohibitionist triumph was astoundingly short-lived. The year that the state's prohibition law went into effect, the Jewish leader and anti-prohibition activist Simon Wolf traveled from Washington, D.C., to Atlanta to visit friends. During his time in the city, he wrote, "I found every home amply supplied with dozen [sic] cases of beer, wine, and whiskey." His hosts, it seems, had prepared for the new law by stocking up on alcohol. Meanwhile, Wolf reported, drinkers who had not thought ahead or could not afford to stockpile could still import whatever beverage they wanted from other states; Atlanta's newspapers, Wolf noted, "had whole page advertisements of liquor houses residing in Cincinnati, St. Louis and other cities of the west and southwest advertising their wares and giving inducements to purchase in bulk."[81]

Much to the dismay of its champions, Georgia's prohibition law would prove largely ineffectual, especially in Atlanta. Observers on both sides of the debate declared it an unmitigated failure. Thousands of gallons of liquor washed into Atlanta from cities just across the Georgia border, as local residents imported cases of whiskey, beer, and wine from taverners and wholesalers who had moved so that they could stay in business and continue to supply their customers. "White lightning" was also plentiful, and increasingly so, as moonshiners in the state's mountain region ramped up production to meet escalating demand. By early 1909, "near beer"—which was supposed to be nonintoxicating, although most everyone knew it to be otherwise—was widely available at hundreds of saloons, clubs, beverage stands, and illegal "blind tigers" throughout the city. No one could deny that the city was soaking wet.[82]

With few exceptions, Atlanta's middle-class alcohol entrepreneurs, Jewish and gentile alike, scrambled to unload their inventory and find new livelihoods. This worked to the benefit of at least one Jewish wholesaler in Chattanooga, who advertised in *Der Southern Veg-Vayzer* (The southern guide), a local Yiddish-language newspaper, that he had acquired his inventory from an Atlanta liquor dealer right after the passage of Georgia's prohibition law.[83] (One cannot help but wonder what the fellow did with *his* stock after Tennessee went dry a year later.) Perhaps he bought the stock of Harry Silverman or Israel Oppenheim, café proprietors who both transformed their liquor businesses into restaurants and launched cigar-manufacturing shops. The Lowenstein family, who had run a wholesale liquor establishment and a saloon, reconfigured their operations and started an extract manufacturing concern. The drugstore chain owner and liquor dealer Joseph Jacobs leased the whiskey department of one of his pharmacies to a shoe company. Others left town altogether: the wholesalers Bluthenthal and Bickart announced that they would be quitting Atlanta within the year, and soon relocated their operations to Baltimore.[84]

Generally speaking, acculturated Jews demonstrated their willingness to embrace the new law—even if, as Simon Wolf's observations suggest, they continued to drink in the privacy of their own homes. When Henry Alexander, a young lawyer and descendant of Atlanta's oldest Jewish family, declared his candidacy for the state legislature in the fall of 1907, he included in his announcement a brief statement in favor of the new law. "The recently enacted prohibition law is the expression of a noble aspiration on the part of the Georgia people," he stated. "It will promote decency, good order, and the general prosperity. . . . It shall at all times receive my unqualified support."[85]

Working-class Jews, on the other hand, had fewer resources and fewer options, and were less likely to be sensitive to the surrounding culture's disapproval. A few Decatur Street saloonkeepers were able to repurpose their businesses as dry goods stores, butcher shops, clothing stores, and lunchrooms. Others turned, or returned, to peddling.[86] The saloonkeeper and leader of Atlanta's Orthodox Jewish community Jacob Hirsowitz reconfigured his Decatur Street bar into a pawnshop, but in February 1908 he was shot and killed by robbers who, according to newspaper reports, had come to his store to steal a gun.[87]

At first, it seemed as if prohibition would reduce Jewish immigrants' employment opportunities and hamper the work of Jewish immigrant aid organizations (e.g., the Industrial Removal Office) when they tried to send newcomers to Georgia. In November 1907, when the IRO dispatched a Russian immigrant who had experience as a distiller to Atlanta, the local officer pointed out to the New York headquarters that liquor distillation "in Georgia at present is no trade." "Perhaps Louisville might have been a better selection," came the reply from New York.[88] But if this immigrant was willing to work in a marginalized entrepreneurial sector, he might well have found himself gainfully employed within a few years. In 1910, at least fifteen Jewish-owned near-beer saloons and poolrooms operated on Decatur Street, and fifteen more were scattered throughout the city.[89] The Jewish presence among Atlanta's saloonkeeping cohort had been radically reduced, but not altogether obliterated.

A few Jewish Atlantans engaged the growing illegal alcohol trade in the city and around the state, as well. The Russian immigrant Morris Cohen was arraigned for selling liquor and beer from his soft drink shop several times in 1908. In February of the following year, a few days before his daughter's wedding, police searched Cohen's Decatur Street store and found a stunning cache of alcohol: a thousand bottles of beer, five cases of whiskey, and several cases of wine. Cohen insisted that it was all for the wedding, and that he only kept it at his store since he had no space to store it at home. His supporters petitioned the court in his defense: "We are familiar with the customs of Orthodox Jews as to their weddings," they wrote, "and respectfully submit that the temporary storing of the articles to be used at the wedding of his daughter in his place of business on Decatur Street was certainly not an intentional violation of the law." The judge was not convinced that Jewish wedding rituals demanded vast quantities of beer and whiskey, and Cohen was sentenced to a $1,000 fine or twelve months on the chain gang.[90]

Longtime liquor dealers found themselves on the wrong side of the new prohibition law as well. The German Jewish immigrant David Loeb had been in the local liquor trade for more than two decades with his brother Jonas, as both a saloonkeeper and a wholesaler. One of his customers, a black sharecropper named Martin Wyatt, was arrested for selling alcohol in Morgan County, a dry area sixty miles east of Atlanta. Prosecutors offered to reduce the charges against Wyatt if he gave them the name of his supplier, and Wyatt named Loeb's Lomax Distilling Company. The state accused Loeb of using Wyatt as an agent for Lomax; Loeb maintained that he had sold the liquor to Wyatt before the state prohibition law went into effect, and had no idea what Wyatt did with the whiskey. Further, said Loeb, Wyatt was a "low grade roustabout negro" and convicted felon whose testimony could not be trusted. Loeb was pronounced guilty of all charges, and his appeal for clemency was denied in 1909. The judge agreed with a witness for the prosecution that Loeb "deliberately employed an utterly disreputable, criminal negro to distribute whiskey and other kinds of intoxicating liquors," and "put it in the power of that negro to seriously interfere with the farming operations of the good people of the community."[91]

A Jewish businessman was accused of using a local black man "of the criminal sort" to do his nefarious business, and then trying to lay the blame for the crime entirely on the black man: the stage was set for Leo Frank's ordeal a few years later. A Texas-born, Brooklyn-raised Jew, Frank was the superintendent of Atlanta's National Pencil Company in 1913, when local police accused arrested him for sexually assaulting and murdering Mary Phagan, a white girl in his employ. Frank's lawyers argued during his murder trial that Jim Conley, a black man employed as the pencil factory's janitor, had committed the crime. Despite significant evidence pointing to Conley's guilt, and inconsistencies in Conley's testimony, hostilities against the northern Jewish industrialist—which were openly expressed by the crowd chanting "Hang the Jew!" outside the courtroom during jury deliberations—led to a guilty conviction and a death sentence. Governor John Slaton commuted Frank's sentence to life imprisonment in June of 1915; in August, a mob of armed men kidnapped Frank from prison, drove him to Mary Phagan's home town, and lynched him from a tree near her family's property.[92]

The accusation that Frank, as a Jewish man, posed a threat to the sexual purity of southern white women came as a shock to many observers, both

Jewish and gentile. But similar accusations had in fact been present in both southern culture and in national press coverage of the South for nearly a decade. Such insinuations first emerged in Atlanta in 1906, spread throughout the South in the years that followed, and revolved specifically around the presence of Jews in the southern alcohol trade.

In 1910, Isaac Wolfe Bernheim published his memoir, recounting his journey from Jewish immigrant rags to Kentucky bourbon riches. He had arrived in the United States at the age of eighteen with a few dollars in his pocket, and became one of the wealthiest men in Louisville—an internationally renowned whiskey distiller, as well as a local civic leader and an important figure in national Jewish organizations. Life in the liquor industry had served Bernheim spectacularly well. Yet he had come to rue his choice of livelihood. "If I had to choose my occupation over again," he mused, "I should prefer to engage in some other line of trade, but we are all creatures of circumstance."[93]

Bernheim's emerging ambivalence toward the liquor business should come as no surprise: his industry was under siege. The "anti-liquor craze," as Bernheim called it, showed no signs of abating anytime soon, and the growing "hysteria" had "left a costly scar on our business." But the industry itself was not without fault. "The low dive, catering to the wants of the vicious and depraved classes, should be suppressed," he wrote. With efficient and appropriate reform that limited alcohol purveyance to "responsible, law-abiding, and temperate people," Bernheim concluded, "we may safely look forward to a period when the manufacture and sale of liquors will again become a legitimate and respected occupation."[94]

And who, one might ask, might qualify as properly responsible and temperate? "It is one of the most striking characteristics of the Jew," Bernheim reminded his readers, "that he is temperate in his habits, and especially in the use of intoxicants."[95] But Bernheim's efforts to evoke Jews' reputation for moderate alcohol consumption as a defense for Jewish involvement in the alcohol business had little effect. The discourse was shifting: for the next several decades, the Jewish relation to alcohol would be regarded less as a solution to the nation's "liquor problem" than as itself part of the problem.

Even as American Jewish leaders sought to defend their community against accusations that their attachment to the trade was stronger than their attachment to the country, some American Jews started to quietly express their own concerns about Jews' relation to alcohol. During the thirteen years that Prohibition was national law, American Jews were increasingly divided and at odds with one another on the question of alcohol, and these divisions would make navigating the Prohibition era exceedingly difficult.

PART III

Jews and the Prohibition Era

5

Rabbis and Other Bootleggers

Jews as Prohibition-Era Alcohol Entrepreneurs

By 1916, prohibitionists had good reason to expect total victory, and sooner rather than later. Since Georgia adopted its dry law in 1907, nineteen states had done the same, either through voter referendum or by legislative action. In 1913, Congress passed the Webb-Kenyon Act (over President Taft's veto), which forbade the shipment of intoxicating liquors into any state that had outlawed alcohol traffic within its borders. The states had also ratified the Sixteenth Amendment that year, empowering the federal government to levy direct a income tax; considering that liquor excise taxes accounted for nearly a third of federal revenue, drys could now refute wet assertions that the national budget would shrivel without alcohol commerce.[1] The number of Anti-Saloon League–approved members of the House of Representatives had risen in the most recent election, and the prohibition lobby predicted that the federal government was moving toward passage of a constitutional amendment that would eventually destroy the American liquor trade once and for all.

But Joseph, Hyman, and Edward Jacobs, brothers and wholesale beer and liquor dealers, were determined both to keep their business profitable and to maintain the appearance of legality. Both were entirely possible, despite the prohibitionist sweep: although Webb-Kenyon had given states the legal means to achieve absolute aridity, most statewide dry laws permitted some amount of liquor to be purchased for "personal consumption." Even Georgia's recent revision of their law, which a state legislator hoped would make "the smell of liquor illegal," allowed state residents to purchase two quarts of distilled liquor, one gallon of wine, and forty-eight pints of beer through the mail each month.[2] The law was set to go into effect on the first of May, 1916, so the brothers positioned themselves in their company's branch offices—one in Atlanta and one each in Chattanooga, Tennessee, and Girard, Alabama, both just over the Georgia state border—and spent April trying to locate Georgians who wanted to place large orders. "You will probably want a few cases of assorted whiskies for your-self and friends," the Jacobs brothers wrote to one potential customer, "before the new two quart law goes into effect."[3]

Jewish connections proved central to their strategies. Edward sent Joe out "drumming" for new customers to small Georgia towns like Athens and Elberton, and counseled him to find "some Jewish merchant" to ask "who controls the business and who does the most buying, then follow up that lead." It is not clear whether Edward expected those small-town liquor deal-ers to be Jewish, too. But even though their lists of contacts included mostly gentiles, the majority of the Jacobs brothers' closer relationships were with Jews. "Hyman is dealing with Isaac Sinkovitz," wrote Edward, "and would not consider any other deal unless Morris Lichtenstein could be a partner in it." Elsewhere, he mentions "that young fellow Goldberg" as an informal employee, and tells Joe to "ask Max Goldstein" for assistance navigating offi-cial state liquor policy. Non-Jewish liquor dealers were discussed as competi-tors (though sometimes also as collaborators who offered useful business ideas), and more often as customers—but never as partners.[4]

Jews and Jewishness figured in the Jacobs' more illicit business dealings as well. At one point, Edward discusses splitting Atlanta's "tiger custom-ers" (the illegal saloon proprietors) with another Jewish whiskey whole-saler, and letting a third take "the Jews and white folks business [sic]" in expensive liquors and "high price beer." Ed later suggests that if Joe needed to write down a customer's order for whiskey, he should write in Yiddish; that way, prohibition enforcement officials would not be able to tell when he had broken the law.[5]

The Jacobs brothers' interactions with and attitudes toward the alcohol trade reveal two dynamics that repeated themselves all over the country, and for years to come. First, dry legislation was never as solid and impenetrable as staunch anti-alcohol activists hoped it would be. First at the state and then at the national level, prohibition laws were perforated at their creation by loopholes and special dispensations (such as Georgia's two-quart rule for private consumption) that allowed enterprising entrepreneurs to continue to supply alcohol to interested customers. Many were able to do so by acting within the letter, if not the spirit, of the law. But illegal production and com-merce, which proved common throughout the Prohibition era, was often made possible by exceptions written into the rules.

Second, as the Jacobs' entrepreneurial networks and business methods suggest, American Jews who continued to engage in the alcohol trade after it had been regulated into the margins or made illegal often did so within a

Jewish milieu. For both recent immigrants and longtime residents—even for native-born Jews like the Jacobs brothers—commerce in alcohol was usually an in-group affair. As had been true in the United States since the late nineteenth century, Jews in the American alcohol trade continued to rely on their ethnic socioeconomic networks, even after beer, liquor, and wine became contraband merchandise.

Other ethnic groups—urban Italians and rural whites from the Appalachian Mountains, to name just two—behaved similarly. In fact, bootlegging was a decidedly pluralistic pursuit, a law broken by purveyors and consumers as diverse as the nation itself. But Jewish alcohol entrepreneurship during national Prohibition had a particularly consequential attribute. The special dispensation granted by Prohibition regulation that gave American Jews access to sacramental wine for religious purposes, and established procedures by which Jews could buy and sell it, emerged early in the Prohibition era as a massive breach through which hundreds of thousands of illegal alcohol flowed. The fact that Jewish alcohol production, purveyance, and consumption was actually built into federal Prohibition law had a profound effect on Jewish attitudes toward Prohibition, and on prohibitionists' attitudes toward Jews.

Though the prohibitionists of the early twentieth century employed scientific, political, and economic arguments in their fight against "liquor power," Prohibition did not achieve its ultimate triumph in the spirit of progressive reform. Instead, a swell of xenophobic patriotism, in the form of a wartime call for "100 percent Americanism," pushed it to victory. As war paralyzed Europe, and with even greater fervor once American forces were deployed overseas, prohibitionists argued that intoxicating beverages impeded the nation's military effort against Germany. Grains that should be baked into loaves of bread and fed to American soldiers and war refugees, they insisted, were instead brewed and distilled into substances that undermined soldiers' ability to fight and left the war's innocent victims to starve. A congressionally appointed defense advisory panel recommended, as a strategy for mobilizing national resources, that the use of foodstuffs in the production of brewed or distilled alcohol be banned until the end of the war. Between 1917's Food and Fuel Control Act (which followed the recommendation) and the Wartime Prohibition Act the following year (which restricted the domestic sale of intoxicating beverages), the country's alcohol trade was brought to a screeching halt. Meanwhile, Congress outlawed saloons in Washington, D.C., and at the end of 1917 approved the ASL's proposed prohibition amendment to the Constitution. The amendment then started to make its way around state legislatures for ratification.[6]

Prohibitionists had momentum on their side, and they knew it. They worked another wartime development—nationalistic anti-German sentiment—to their advantage as well. The nation was wracked by a nativist spasm that inspired the banning of the German language in Iowa and music composed by Germans in Boston, and led to the lynching of a German immigrant in Missouri. Anti-alcohol activists and their allies pointed a collective accusatory finger at German Americans, and publicized the prevalence of Germans in the American beer and liquor industries. The "Kaiser-loving brewer" was a seditious and powerful presence in American politics and culture, they warned. ASL president Wayne Wheeler declared that "the liquor traffic aids those forces in our country whose loyalty is called into question at this hour," and *American Issue*, the ASL's monthly magazine, denounced American brewers as "the chief hope of the Kaiser in his plot to enslave and Prussianize this land." "No Germans in the war are conspiring against the piece and happiness of the United States," a Wisconsin politician claimed in 1918, "more than Pabst, Schlitz, Blatz, Miller, and others of their kind."[7]

The brewing industry was unable to defend itself against this onslaught— a disorienting and unfamiliar experience for men who until then had no doubt that they could continue to keep prohibitionists leashed. One strategy that the United States Brewers' Association (USBA) had favored for decades was to declare that its purpose was to promote responsible alcohol consumption and purveyance. USBA leaders presented themselves, and probably genuinely regarded themselves, as moderates doing righteous battle against both the "excesses and improprieties of all kinds connected with or growing out of the traffic," according to USBA president Julius Liebmann, as well as the "destructive tendencies [and] utter lack of fairness" of the Anti-Saloon League's anti–free market policies.[8] They would protect the public, they insisted, even as they protected the rights of responsible brewers, wholesalers, and saloonkeepers.

But most of the brewers' political strategies had a backroom, cloak-and-dagger quality, and this, in the end, worked to their resounding disadvantage. For instance, their long-standing battle against woman suffrage, fought under the assumption that women would vote the alcohol trade out of existence, utilized covert propaganda operations and the creation of counterfeit anti-prohibition activist groups. (The *Caddo* circular, whose anti-prohibition work had been made public by Will Irwin, was just such an "Astroturf" endeavor, to use an anachronistic phrase.) They funded extravagant election-day campaigns to bring alcohol industry workers to the polls. The brewers usually achieved their immediate goals of defeating sumptuary and regulatory legislation; but when muckraking journalists exposed their schemes to the public, it seemed to confirm all the terrible things prohibitionists had long been saying about the alcohol trade.

Their fatal move, in hindsight, was to undertake a clandestine partnership with the National German-American Alliance (NGAA). The NGAA was founded in 1901 to promote German language, culture, and ethnic pride in the United States, and had participated in wet politics since its inception. After the brewers' group funded a 1911 NGAA anti-prohibition campaign, leaders of both organizations expressed concern that any direct and obvious connection between them could raise suspicions of a conspiracy and damage their common cause. So in 1913, in response to the Webb-Kenyon bill, the USBA created the National Association of Commerce and Labor (NACL), which would serve as an "independent" lobbying organization and have access to the NGAA's network.[9]

Despite efforts to keep their collaboration covert, the NACL came under government scrutiny during the war, thanks primarily to the lobbying efforts of Wayne Wheeler. In 1918, the U.S. Senate opened investigatory hearings on potential connections between the alcohol industry and pro-German subversion in the United States. The organization's surreptitious anti-prohibition activity through the NACL especially damaged the German Americans' case, and on the Senate's recommendation, President Wilson revoked the NGAA's charter at the end of that year.[10]

The former B'nai B'rith president Simon Wolf played a part in the events that led to the NGAA's downfall, and his ethnic identity was crucial to his involvement. Among the documents brought to light during the Senate investigation were a series of letters between Wolf and the leadership of the NACL. Since his dismissal by the Hayes administration in 1877, Simon Wolf had become a prominent lawyer, diplomat, and activist in Washington, D.C., with friends in high places. (He would soon write a book, *The Presidents I Have Known from 1860 to 1918*, to prove it.)[11] He was a vigorous lobbyist for both German and Jewish causes in the United States, and one of the few Jews active in the NGAA.

In 1913, Wolf accepted a prominent position in the NACL, for which he was paid $50 a month. His assignment was to meet with and lobby his friends and colleagues on Capitol Hill, as well as coordinate the efforts of other wet allies, such as Jewish and Catholic groups and labor unions. This arrangement would turn out to be a problem for Wolf, and for the NACL. In 1914, when Wolf testified before the Senate Judiciary Committee during a congressional debate over prohibition legislation, he had claimed that he represented himself solely, and had no connection to brewing or liquor interests. This turned out not to be true. One of the letters showed that at the time of his testimony, Wolf was enthusiastically in the employ of the NACL. "I am in constant touch with our friends in Congress," he had assured John Hexamer, president of the NGAA, when he was first brought on board, "and shall watch their every step."[12] The NGAA and the Brewers' Association considered Wolf to be a powerful weapon in their fight, precisely because he was a leader of American Jews. "Mr. Wolf is not only one of the most respectable citizens of Washington," wrote Hexamer, "but he is also—which is very important for our purposes—one of, if not the most influential of Jews in the United States. He will therefore bring in a vigorous and persistent element of our population to work for us."[13]

Alas for the brewers, neither Wolf's influence on lawmakers nor his ability to organize Jews against prohibition sentiment proved effectual. Distillers' trade organizations had also failed to halt the prohibitionists' impetus. "Spirits men" from the Midwest formed the National Model License League in 1908; their founder was T. M. Gilmore, editor of *Bonfort's Wine and Spirits Circular*, and the Louisville Jewish community leader Isaac Wolfe Bernheim served as the director of the organization's executive committee. The league (and their regional affiliates) spent the following decade trying to convince voters and legislators that the continued presence of alcohol commerce in states that had passed dry laws proved that "prohibition did not prohibit." More could be gained, they insisted, from regulation of saloons and liquor retail than by banning alcohol entirely. They promised to expunge the dive saloon from the American landscape, and hoped to prove their dedication to reform by self-policing their own—even going so far as to expel Lee Levy from their organization and send back his contribution after Will Irwin's series of articles about him in *Collier's*. But whatever successes they achieved fighting prohibition legislation were undone by the ASL's victories after 1917.[14]

By then, Americans viewed any anti-prohibition organization as a self-interested agent of the alcohol trade, or as a subversive fifth column in a moment of national crisis. As of the first day of 1919, sixteen states had already ratified the proposed Eighteenth Amendment to the Constitution; by the middle of the month, twenty more had followed suit and ratification was complete. On January 16, 1920, according to the amendment, the manufacture or sale of "intoxicating liquors" and its transportation into or out of the United States and its territories would be illegal.

Would Prohibition achieve its goals? In some places it seemed as if it might. "The closer one lived to the middle of the country," writes the historian Daniel Okrent, "especially in towns and cities inhabited by Protestants of northern European extraction, the more likely it was that drinking was down."[15] In other words, wherever the population was already enthusiastic about personal temperance and viewed legal prohibition as legitimate— where Americans approved of anti-alcohol laws *and* were also willing to observe those laws themselves—Prohibition had the intended effect. Cities, longtime bastions of wet sentiment, also showed signs of drying up a bit— at least at first, as saloons and liquor stores closed their doors. Some urban denizens who were ambivalent about legally mandated abstinence noted a decrease in public drunkenness, and even they welcomed the development. Overall, according to recent scholarly estimates (based largely on records from hospitals, insane asylums, and arrest reports), alcohol consumption did decrease by about a third.[16]

But alcohol was still available, and plentiful. Some of it came from the cellars of drinkers who had stocked up in advance. The National Prohibition Act, which was written by the Minnesota congressman Andrew Volstead (based on recommendations from the ASL's Wayne Wheeler) and usually referred to as the Volstead Act, allowed individuals to legally consume alcohol in their own homes as long as it had been purchased before the law went into effect. Forward-thinking drinkers of means bought out saloon inventories, club stockrooms, and liquor retailer and wholesaler wares, and proceeded to spend the next several years behaving as if the Eighteenth Amendment had never been ratified. The Baltimore writer and vehement anti-prohibitionist H. L. Mencken famously collected a private stash reputed to be of breathtaking size and variety, and which reportedly enabled him to ride out the Prohibition era with little inconvenience. Lawmakers, even at the highest level, did the same; President Warren G. Harding moved his considerable stock into the White House in 1921 after his inauguration, and outgoing president Woodrow Wilson moved his own supply back to his private home in Washington.[17]

But private stockpiles were not accumulated so that they could be sold. Strictly speaking, home consumers acted within the parameters of the law, even when they tippled with self-consciously law-flouting élan. In any event, this privileged few constituted a minority of dry-era drinkers. By far, most of those who drank during Prohibition broke the law, and there was no shortage of opportunities to do so. A stunning variety of contraband alcohol remained available to anyone who wanted to buy it. Canadian whiskey, Caribbean rum, and scotch from the British Isles arrived stateside in cars and boats specially outfitted for speed and concealment. It was sold by the bottle and by the case out of trucks, warehouses, basements, and stockrooms.

Speakeasies popped up everywhere, generating an enticingly sophisticated and heterosocial underground drinking culture. All economic classes regularly consumed homemade beer, wine, and "bathtub gin." Countryside stills pumped out moonshine and "white lightning." "Needle beer" (near beer spiked with a syringe of ethyl alcohol) became a lucrative product to produce and distribute. And for desperate drinkers, the fact that consuming modified industrial alcohol might be fatal proved to be an insufficient deterrent. "All that is certain about the consumption of alcohol during the dry era," observed Herbert Asbury, "is that anybody who wanted it, and was able to pay for it, could get it." Bootlegging provided a vital source of income for Americans of every stripe, in every region, in big cities, small towns, and rural areas. Instead of reducing illegal activity, as its proponents had promised it would, Prohibition inspired a crime wave so substantial that it overwhelmed both the courts and the prisons.[18]

Bootlegged alcohol came from all directions; a contemporary social scientist studying the demographics of bootlegging asserted that "native and foreign born alike are in the grip of the Profit-Making Frankenstein." But a great deal of bootlegging took place in cities, and compliance with the law among urban immigrants was notoriously spotty. Immigrants and immigrant communities had resisted the temperance and prohibition movements for decades, and formed a crucial caucus in urban wet politics. They did not suddenly change their attitude, or their behavior, once the law was passed. "Prohibition," the social scientist concluded, "has effected no important or widespread changes in the drinking habits of the foreign born."[19]

Jews participated in this diverse underground economy as both purveyors and customers. The question of how much bootlegged alcohol Jews were responsible for is impossible to answer definitively. Bootlegging, like all criminal practices, required a low profile. An accurate assessment of this kind of business is lost to the historian, since bootleggers did not advertise, and illegal distillers' workplaces were not listed in the city directory. Still, some historians have attempted an estimate. Jenna Weissman Joselit, for example, found that nearly 12 percent of all persons accused of violating Prohibition law in New York City between 1924 and 1932 were Jews. This serves as a reminder that while New York's Jews were common within the trade, they represented only a fraction of the bootlegging business. Indeed, Joselit writes, "relative to their proportion of the population, Jews were slightly underrepresented."[20]

But records of arraignment before a court of law do not tell the whole story. First, whether the accused were pronounced guilty of any charges remains unknown. Second, some of the accused were probably not involved in any alcohol-related commerce. "Most foreign born do not intend to violate the prohibition law," observed the above-mentioned researcher. "In *general*, they manufacture light wine and beer primarily for home consumption and not for sale."[21] Third, and most important, for every bootlegger who got caught, innumerable others did not.

Among those who did not get caught, or who managed to move massive quantities of alcohol before they did, were Alphonse Capone, Dion O'Banion, and Meyer Lansky—young men from urban immigrant communities who created multiregional, tactically agile, and monstrously lucrative bootlegging enterprises. They were the most visible of bootleggers, operating on the largest scale and in the grandest style.

Class and environment played a significant role in their choice of occupation. The greatest number of these most notorious and successful bootleggers came from the rough ethnic ghettos of New York, Newark, Philadelphia, Detroit, and Chicago; they emerged from urban quarters that still teemed with struggling working-class immigrants, many of whom were desperately in need of economic resources. (Dutch Schultz, born Arthur Flegenheimer to "uptown" German Jewish parents, serves as a notable exception.) Some were themselves immigrants, others first-generation Americans; all were young (between twenty and thirty years old) and ambitious "upstarts," as one historian has called them. Few had been involved in large-scale criminal activity before Prohibition, but a significant number had been members of ethnically homogenous urban gangs. Because of class and ethnic discrimination, they viewed traditional paths of economic opportunity as closed to them, and rejected slower, societally approved routes to upward mobility. They were criminals, but they were also entrepreneurs. They saw that the pre-Prohibition alcohol industry had folded almost entirely, and realized that pre-1920 criminal networks failed to recognize that Prohibition presented an unparalleled opportunity to make fantastic sums of money.[22]

And that they did. Successful bootleggers accumulated great wealth, which granted these men entrée into "high society." Urban ethnic criminal occupations of the past, like arson, pimping, and robbery, carried an ugly social stigma for all but those most desperate for a ghetto-based model of ethnic self-esteem. Prohibition-era bootleggers, on the other hand, were often glorified rather than marginalized in urban society. The glamorization of their profession made gangster culture seem chic and attractive to other young and ambitious urban ethnics. Gangster slang and style became a subject of fascination and emulation in popular culture, a development that obscured distinctions between moral and immoral behavior.[23]

Mark Haller's study of the socioeconomic and ethnic structure of the Prohibition era's illicit alcohol trade, which concentrates on seventy-three members of this "gangster" class, found that 50 percent of these bootleggers were Jewish, 25 percent Italian, and around 10 percent Irish; the rest were of Polish heritage, native-born WASPs, or of unknown background.[24] Jewish gangster bootleggers operated, to some degree, within a Jewish ethnic economy that looked like a violent, underworld version of other Jewish economic networks. Here, too, established Jews funded Jewish newcomers to the trade, and businessmen sought out their coreligionist colleagues in other cities to further extend their market share. The Lower East Sider Waxey Gordon, for instance, received an initial capital investment from the underworld business manager and gambling baron Arnold Rothstein. He then started a smuggling operation with Jewish associates from other cities, such as Maxie Greenberg of St. Louis and Max Hassell of Philadelphia. Gordon then hired the Newarkers Abner "Longy" Zwillman and Joseph Reinfeld, who had already garnered reputations as hijackers of other bootleggers' shipments, to protect his own stock while it was in transport. Although few of these men were religious in any conventional sense, they appreciated the opportunity to work with fellow businessmen from a similar cultural background to their own.[25]

Most of these bootleggers relied, in part if not entirely, on one of the Prohibition era's mightiest sources of production: the Bronfman family of Montreal, via Saskatchewan and, before that, Bessarabia. Whether the Bronfmans made or sold liquor before they migrated from eastern Europe to Canada in 1889 remains a matter of speculation; their name, which means "liquor man" in Yiddish, suggests that distillation could well have been part of their family's past. The family patriarch, Yechiel, a man devoted to traditional Jewish practice, tried his hand as a wheat farmer, fish peddler, and lumber middleman before he purchased his first tavern and inn. By 1910, Yechiel (now Ekiel) and his sons Harry, Abe, and Sam owned several successful hotels in western Canada. Inspired by the profitability of the hotels' bars, and by the wave of prohibitionist sentiment sweeping over Canada, in 1916 Sam took up the mail-order liquor business, which was unregulated by Canadian federal law, as American interstate liquor commerce had been before Webb-Kenyon. Two years later, when Canada passed its own wartime prohibition legislation, the Bronfmans were able to take advantage of a loophole in the law that allowed liquor to be sold for "medicinal purposes." (A similar exception created a gap in the Volstead Act as well.) Sam became, nominally, a wholesale druggist and pharmaceutical dealer; in fact, he was organizing a string of liquor warehouses along Canada's southern border.[26]

When Prohibition went into effect in the United States, Bronfman and his brothers began buying American liquor, rectifying it, and selling it in Canada. Then they purchased a Kentucky distillery, dismantled it, sent the pieces north, reassembled it at home, and took up distilling whiskey themselves. Soon they were exporting millions of dollars worth of alcohol south, often working with American Jewish bootleggers such as Zwillman and Reinfeld in Newark, Solly Weissman in Kansas City, Nig Rosen in Philadelphia, and Moe Dalitz in Cleveland. The Jewish bootleggers he supplied ran so much Canadian alcohol across Lake Erie that locals referred to it as "the Jewish Lake."[27]

American Prohibition-era liquor runners also pioneered interethnic criminal business activity. In the past, urban gangs were strictly divided by ethnicity, and motivated in part by animosity toward other ethnic groups. Prohibition-era bootleggers, on the other hand, developed ethnically heterogeneous criminal collectives. The Russian-Jewish Meyer Lansky and the Italian "Lucky" Luciano established the "Big Seven" syndicate, the most famous and productive of the interethnic bootlegging networks. Following the lead of the men they admired, smaller gangs of petty criminals and bootleggers in other cities also began to establish alliances outside their own ethnic group during the Prohibition era. Interethnic cooperation represented a profound change in underworld behavior, and suggested that the imagined boundaries between urban ethnic neighborhoods, which had been defended and enforced for decades, had the potential to become porous.[28]

Such cooperation was required by bootlegging's division of labor into manufacturing, accounting, armed protection of stock, and transport of goods to speakeasies and warehouses. Bootlegging on the most substantial scale needed lots of manpower, as well as a wide variety of skill sets. Overcoming their ethnocentricity, they understood, would help them realize their goals. Or, as one Italian gangster glibly said of the Prohibition-era affinities between Jews and Italians: "It was a marriage of the three M's: moxie, muscle, money. The Jews put up the moxie, the Italians supplied the muscle, and together they split the money." Anecdotes about these gangs suggest that labor often conformed to ethnic stereotype—the Jews were the accountants and the Italians the toughs. Still, there is ample evidence that Jews, too, could perform acts of brutal violence: Detroit's "Purple Gang," murderous Jewish gangsters who specialized in hijacking other rumrunners' shipments, and Brooklyn's "Murder Inc.," an interethnic collective of hit men, made that clear.[29]

Today, gangsters like Lansky, Zwillman, and Reinfeld have come to represent the Jewish contribution to the Prohibition era, and their chroniclers have celebrated their careers and their chutzpah. For those who came of age after the Holocaust and during the mass bourgeoisification of American Jewry, these gangsters have served as models of rough, devil-may-care Jewish masculinity.[30] Some writers have positioned Jewish gangsters as active foes of anti-Semitism, and at least one has suggested that Jewish bootleggers performed a brave and subversive act of ethnic protest. In one literary flight of fancy, Albert Fried, in his *Rise and Fall of the Jewish Gangster in America*, imagines a Jew-friendly personification of Prohibition speaking to the young cohort of up-and-coming Jewish bootleggers: "There is a crusade under way in this land to reduce your people to second-class citizens," intones this disembodied spirit of Fried's imagination. "You represent the advance guard of a counter-crusade and deserve the gratitude of all who participate in it."[31]

It is, to be sure, highly problematic that criminals, many of them murderers, might be granted the status of heroes. It is even more awkward to present these men as defenders of American Jews considering that they regularly exploited Jewish merchants through extortion.[32] Another problem with this view of Jewish alcohol entrepreneurship during Prohibition, and one that more directly affects historical interpretations of the phenomenon, is that these gangsters were entirely atypical. The scale and success of their criminal activity was only matched by that of other leading bootleggers. For everyone else interested in making a profit from Prohibition, bootlegging was a fairly modest endeavor. The majority of those who violated the law did so on a small scale, producing batches of alcohol at home or buying a few cases or a truckload to retail by the bottle. It lacked the frisson of gangster-style bootlegging exploits, but it could augment a family's income. For immigrants in urban ghettos, it might signify the difference between making rent and getting evicted; for moonshiners in the Appalachian Mountains, bootlegged corn liquor sometimes made the difference between feeding one's family and going hungry.

The prevalence of Jewish and Italian involvement in illicit liquor commerce during Prohibition, and the constant attention these ethnic bootleggers received in the press, led some Americans to believe that bootlegging was primarily, or even only, an immigrant endeavor. But this was not the case. Even American-born WASPs, the demographic most likely to approve of the law, got involved in illicit alcohol manufacture. Locally produced, locally purveyed, and locally sold liquor was in high demand in rural and small-town America, where few Jews had settled. "Stills were everywhere," wrote Herbert Asbury, "in the mountains, on the farms, [and] in the small towns and villages." After traveling through a small town in western Pennsylvania, he estimated that liquor was manufactured in "practically every other home," and local residents drank and sold their product in equal measure. Of the 51,368 stills seized by the federal government in 1923 and 1924, most were located in rural areas of southern states, especially Georgia, Tennessee, Virginia, North Carolina, and Alabama.[33]

The Appalachian Mountains famously hosted generations of native-born, Scots-Irish-descended moonshiners, who put their mastery to use throughout the 1920s. These men and women had developed not only their distilling skills, but also an expertise in camouflaging their operations and eluding (or co-opting) revenue officials. Some of Prohibition's defenders regarded these Appalachian distillers and bootleggers with something like admiration, despite their chosen line of work. "These resisters are not city foreigners," wrote a reporter for the Committee on Prohibition in 1927. "In all other respects than moonshining he is a solid, lanky citizen, cherishing Nordic prides, patriotic to frenzy when the demand is made upon him. These moonshiners are Americans with an ancestry as straight back to early days as the Emersons of Boston." This reporter obviously meant for her readers to judge Appalachian moonshiners and immigrant bootleggers differently; even though their occupations were essentially identical, the former were, at least, of respectable heritage.[34]

Much of the bootlegged liquor consumed by southerners was produced by these mountain moonshiners. But Jews did participate in southern bootlegging as well. A mill worker in Atlanta recalled a "Jewish fellow" who sold peanuts on Decatur Street during Prohibition; under the peanuts "he had some schnapps and a little glass" for customers who wanted a shot. In Durham, North Carolina, in 1926, police seized nearly fifty gallons of moonshine from the residence and business of Mose Levy, although Levy insisted, as had the Atlanta resident Morris Cohen in 1909, that he kept the liquor for a "Hebrew celebration." And a bon vivant known as "Jew Joe" garnered a reputation for supplying the nightclubs of Charleston with whiskey from Florida—"as close to a gangster as we ever got in Charleston," according to a local resident.[35]

In general, however, southern Jews were not as deeply involved in the region's illegal alcohol trade as were Jews in the Northeast and Midwest. One reason was that most southern states had already been suppressing their local alcohol traffic for a decade, and the majority of Jews who had been in the business previously had settled into new occupations. (The Jacobs brothers, for instance, had left the alcohol trade for the linen industry before national Prohibition became law.) In addition, southern bootlegging networks and syndicates were often organized around rural producers, since farm and mountain stills provided much of the alcohol distributed throughout the region. As an urban population, few southern Jews would have had access to these sources.

Finally, whereas anti-Prohibition sentiment was openly expressed in cities of the Northeast and Midwest, southerners generally proclaimed wholesale support of the law—even when they broke it. Rabbi Harry Merfeld of Fort Worth stated in 1926 that the local group most strongly in favor of Prohibition was "Southern Democrats," all of whom "drink in the cellar"—that is, in the privacy of their own homes. Rabbi George Solomon of Savannah, Georgia, agreed. "There is lip service to the law," he wrote, but he found "pretty general violation." Or, as Rabbi Isaac Marcuson of Macon, Georgia, described local feelings toward Prohibition, "everybody favors it, and everybody drinks."[36] Under these circumstances, men and women on the cultural and economic margins, who needed the income more than they cared about government-imposed moral standards, were most likely to take up illegal alcohol commerce. By the 1920s, southern Jews had found some level of economic stability and comfort. They did so, in part, by internalizing local standards of behavior, which dictated that respectable white folks did not openly engage in criminal activity. Or, perhaps, with Leo Frank's horrifying murder fresh in their memories, southern Jews had not internalized local standards as much as they feared the repercussions if they failed to uphold them.

After the Volstead Act went into effect in January 1920, there did remain a few ways to access alcohol while adhering to both the letter and spirit of the law. While the legislation was, in many ways, as strict as the most extreme wing of the prohibitionist movement had hoped for, it enumerated several situations in which alcohol commerce and consumption were allowed. In addition to permitting the storage and consumption of intoxicating beverages acquired before 1920 so long as it took place in a "private dwelling," the Volstead Act also allowed for beverage alcohol to be made and sold for two purposes. The first was medicinal: doctors were permitted to prescribe one quart of wine or one pint of whiskey per patient every ten days. The other exception was in the case of religious rituals. Section 6 of the Volstead Act, which articulated this special religious dispensation, was meant to ensure that the Eighteenth Amendment did not compromise the integrity of the First Amendment.[37]

Between ratification and the date a year later when the law was set to go into effect, religious and secular American Jewish leaders of all three denominations consulted with the Bureau of Internal Revenue, which had been assigned the task of administering the new law. The home-centered nature of Jewish ritual wine consumption complicated these negotiations. For other religious groups that used wine in religious ritual, such as Catholics and Episcopalians, consumption took place exclusively in their houses of worship. Ideally, wine would never leave their churches, and violations of the law would be relatively easy to trace. Observant Jews, on the other hand, required wine every week in Sabbath rituals that took place at their dinner table. It was widely understood that distributing wine for home use would present many temptations and opportunities to violate the law.

Perhaps hoping to redeem himself after the NACL debacle, Simon Wolf offered his services as a legal mediator between the American government and the Union of American Hebrew Congregations, the organization founded by Isaac Mayer Wise fifty years before to coordinate and promote American Jewish religious and cultural life. His first communication with the organization expressed doubt that Jews would be granted access to sacramental wine at all, even if they argued that the First Amendment superseded prohibition law. "It is a religious *rite* and not a civil *right*," he wrote to the union's executive board in March 1919; they should not expect the government to protect religious customs that American law deemed outside the parameters of civic prerogative. After meeting with the assistant attorney general, he presented the organization with some bad news. "Use of wine in the household," he wrote, "is a matter which the government's attorneys cannot pass upon." He advised that Jews who wanted to bring wine into their homes should only do so after consulting with a lawyer. Wolf had gone from defending, both publicly and surreptitiously, the right to drink, to encouraging the union to avoid the matter entirely.[38]

A few months later, Commissioner of Internal Revenue Daniel Roper wrote directly to J. Walter Freiberg of the Cincinnati distilling family—not in his capacity as a liquor industrialist, but as the president of the UAHC. Roper asked Freiberg for help in constructing the regulations that would allow American Jews "to secure wines for use in their ceremonies and festivals as heretofore," but would also "render it difficult or impossible for imposters to secure wine for illegal purposes."[39] There is no record of Freiberg's reaction to this painfully ironic request: his assistance was required in writing the law that would destroy his own family's business.

In consultation with Freiberg, several leading clergymen from the Central Conference of American Rabbis (CCAR), and Congressman Julius Kahn of California, Roper constructed a method that, for the moment, satisfied both the Jewish representatives and the Bureau of Internal Revenue. A member of a synagogue congregation would place an order with his rabbi, who was required by the law to be "recognized as the head of an ecclesiastical jurisdiction" and a member of one of three rabbinical organizations: the Reform CCAR, the Conservative Rabbinical Assembly, or the Union of Orthodox Rabbis. The next steps in the process were described by the manager of the Brooklyn office of the Carmel Wine Company, which imported kosher wine from Palestine, to a rabbi in Cleveland: "You will fill in five copies of the enclosed form #1412 which you are to sign in the presence of a Notary Public. The five copies are then to be presented to the Prohibition Director in your locality. . . . His whereabouts can be ascertained from the Internal Revenue Office. After receiving the approval, the five copies are to be forwarded to us together with your order. We are not permitted to ship less than five gallons at any one time according to the Government regulations."

The rabbi, if he had not by now thrown his hands up in defeat in the face of these torturous bureaucratic requirements, would then distribute the wine to his congregants for home use. Through this complicated and labor-intensive process, every American Jewish family would have legal access to ten gallons of wine per year.[40]

Jewish leaders had intended that section 6 would nip a potential problem in the bud. They shared the Department of the Treasury's desire that Prohibition law be widely obeyed, and that its enforcement be as transparent and consistent as possible. At the same time, their involvement in the composition of section 6 was a direct effort to lessen the possibility of Jewish malfeasance, specifically. Jewish leaders feared that section 6 would create opportunities too tempting to forego. By working with Prohibition officials, they hoped to keep Jews within the law—not only out of a sense of community responsibility, but also to protect Jews in general from any anti-Semitism incurred by the criminality of a few.[41]

That hope turned out to be desperately naïve. Congressman Volstead, Commissioner Roper, and, it seems, the Reform Jews of the CCAR had failed to take the nonstructured, nonhierarchical nature of traditional Jewish rabbinic ordination into account. Compared to Christian religious institutions, the American rabbinate was loosely organized and minimally supervised. No bureaucracy existed that could be given the task of overseeing and regulating how kosher wine was being dispensed or used. Further, while Reform and Conservative rabbinic schools in the United States provided evidence of their graduates' credentials, Orthodox rabbis who had emigrated from eastern Europe were often ordained outside formal religious or scholarly institutions. Forging Orthodox rabbinic certification was thus relatively easy; or, conversely, it rendered the absolute authentication of Orthodox rabbinic

13. Storefront shop selling sacramental kosher wine during Prohibition, ca. 1920s. The Volstead Act allowed Jews to purchase kosher wine for use in religious rituals, and sacramental wine stores were established in Jewish neighborhoods all over the country as the 1920s began. These stores also served as wellsprings of bootlegged alcohol. (Courtesy of Underwood Archives Inc.)

credentials nearly impossible. Lincoln Andrews, the assistant secretary of the Bureau of Prohibition, stated in 1926, years after the "sacramental wine scandals" of the 1920s unfolded, that "the Jewish faith is not organized as our hierarchal churches are. There is no discipline and no control. Anybody can become a rabbi . . . and the bootlegger has taken advantage of it."[42]

They had also failed to consider the poverty in which many immigrant rabbis lived. Orthodox rabbis who served immigrant communities generally earned far more modest wages than did their counterparts in acculturated denominations. Before Prohibition, immigrant rabbis had done side work within their areas of expertise—performing circumcisions, preparing boys for bar mitzvah, and, as we have seen, producing kosher wine. When prohibition became law, rabbinic access to alcohol became a means to escape destitution and, for a few, to achieve genuine financial comfort. Of course, not all Orthodox rabbis participated in bootlegging networks, and quite a few were as horrified and angered by the scandals as were their more assimilated colleagues. But men on the margins, those alienated from American culture and unfamiliar with American law, were less likely to be concerned about communal ignominy or to think of selling their rabbinic services as a *Chillul Hashem* (desecration of God's name).[43]

By 1925, the Bureau of Prohibition had determined that rabbinic authorization and sacramental wine stores were "the chief sources of the illicit liquor supply." The bureau approved the distribution of 2,138,909 gallons of sacramental wine in 1922, 2,543,491 gallons in 1923, and 2,944,764 gallons in 1924. "If these figures were a true index of Jewish devotion to the historical customs of their forefathers," the *American Hebrew* peevishly noted, "it would indicate a rapid growth of Judaism." But everybody understood that American Jews were not suddenly returning to traditional religious practice. In 1925, the *American Hebrew* asserted that the Prohibition Unit had recorded only one violation of the sacramental wine exemption by Catholic clergy, as opposed to the "scores" of cases involving rabbis (though the breakneck growth of Georges de Latour's sacramental wine production for Catholic, Lutheran, and Russian Orthodox denominations suggests that his product was enjoyed beyond sanctuary walls as well).[44]

Violation of section 6 was often as flagrant and egregious as could be. "Rabbis" (some of whom were not in fact Jewish) claimed new and enormous congregations filled with members named Houlihan and Maguire. Rabbis requested wine on behalf of fictitious or long-dead congregants, or sold their legitimately acquired wine permits to bootleggers. The sacramental dispensation also made available a far wider variety of alcoholic beverages than is traditionally present in Jewish practice. The Prohibition agent Izzy Einstein claimed to have busted numerous rabbis (and "rabbis") dispensing "sacramental" sherry, vermouth, and champagne. Rabbi Jerome Mark of Knoxville, Tennessee, complained that a local Jew had "assumed my name as an aid to peddling 'corn' and 'mountain-juice.'"[45]

Federally designated sacramental wine sources got in on the act as well, by honoring obviously fake rabbinical wine permits or selling their wares independent of any rabbinic request. Schapiro's kosher winery on the Lower East Side, which operated throughout the Prohibition era as an official sacramental wine dealer, filled local rabbis' orders out of the front office in accordance with section 6. But the company did not limit itself to such transactions. "In the back," claimed a descendant of Schapiro's founder, "he had the juice." Even while Schapiro's complied with (and benefited from) the Volstead Act, the company was also bootlegging its product, and possibly other kinds of alcohol, on the sly.[46] But the "sacramental wine scandals" of the early 1920s plagued Jewish communities far from New York, as well. The *New York Times* reported from Buffalo that a local rabbi's wife was caught selling sacramental wine out of their home for a dollar a bottle. An Omaha rabbi complained to a leader of New York's Orthodox community that local wine dealers were "conducting a free-for-all and selling their sacramental wine to Jews and Gentiles alike." In Alameda, California, according to Rabbi Rudolph Coffee in nearby Oakland, the local Jewish population of fifty families had organized a "paper" congregation of more than five hundred names. Even in his own city, Coffee noted, three new congregations had formed since Prohibition had become law, and he estimated that "ninety percent of the wine withdrawn—if not ninety-nine—has been used for any but religious purposes."[47]

While some American Jews participated in this illegal practice without regret or reservation, others were infuriated by Jewish bootlegging and frightened by the damage it did to the community's standing. In 1923, a Jewish Baltimorean read that the city jail was currently incarcerating thirty-five Jewish bootleggers, and wrote a panicked letter to his city's *Jewish Times* about the potential fallout. The actions of these few criminals tainted the reputation of the city's entire Jewish community, he insisted. Jewish bootleggers' malfeasances would "prove a ready and dangerous weapon for anti-Semites," who would "seize any opportunity" to present evidence that "a Jew is a lawbreaker and one who does not care where he gets his money as long as he gets it."[48]

But it was too late: what he feared had already happened. By the time he wrote his letter, the reputation of American Jewry had been besmirched. Assertions that Jews were foremost among illicit alcohol purveyors were heard from all stations of American society. It came from church pulpits: Jews were "doing everything to upset the Eighteenth Amendment," according to a Presbyterian clergyman in Newark. "The majority of the Hebrew race are engaged in the liquor business for money." (The reverend later claimed that he had been misquoted, having actually said that the majority of those in the illicit liquor traffic were Jewish rather than that the majority of Jews were bootleggers—although it is hard to imagine that the city's Jewish community found any consolation in his correction.) It came from the popular press, as when Imogen Oakley of the General Federation of Women's Clubs wrote in *Outlook* magazine that as many as three-fourths of American bootleggers were foreigners, mostly Jews and Italians. Both of these public figures warned that Jewish violation of the law suggested not only Jews' lack of patriotism, but also their desire to dominate American society for their own gain. The Prohibition law "has come to mean much more than the regulation of the liquor trade," Oakley insisted. "It is the answer to the question, which race and which racial traditions shall control America?"[49]

When the popular magazine *World's Work* published a series of articles on the history of American Jewry, the author Burton J. Hendrick mentioned the prevalence of eastern European Jews in the American alcohol trade, and pointed out that this occupational proclivity had pre-migrational precedent. "For centuries," he wrote in 1923, "the Polish Jews had been active in the liquor trade, and again in this country their energies found an outlet in the same direction." In the United States, they had made their mark as wholesalers and middlemen in wine and whiskey commerce. In the decade prior to national Prohibition, he continued, Jews profited from state Prohibition by developing a mail-order business in alcohol, "shipping this indispensable beverage from alcoholic into non-alcoholic states," sometimes in violation of the Webb-Kenyon Act of 1913. "At present," he concluded, "they furnish more than their just proportion of 'bootleggers.'"[50] All that Hendrick had written was absolutely and undeniably true. But in the context of his article, which made the overall contention that eastern European Jews were an unassimilable presence in the American population, Hendrick's claims about Jews' historical relationship to alcohol rang a malevolent note.

One of Jewry's most influential Prohibition-era accusers was Henry Ford. Ford is best known as a car manufacturer and industrial titan, but during the 1920s he also expended his energy and resources promulgating his belief that Jews controlled American finance, exploited American farmers, fomented Bolshevik revolution and world war, and dragged American morality through the mud. In order to publicize these and other views, he purchased a failing newspaper, the *Dearborn (Mich.) Independent*, in 1919. Starting in 1920 and continuing for five years, Ford printed a series of anti-Jewish essays and published the anti-Semitic forgery *The Protocols of the Elders of Zion* in serialized form. The *Independent*'s anti-Semitic essays were then reprinted and distributed as individual booklets, which were later compiled into four volumes titled *The International Jew: The World's Foremost Problem.*[51]

In 1921, Ford angrily itemized a wide range of Jewish alcohol-related transgressions. "The Jew is on the side of liquor," he declared, "and always has been." Again, as was the case for Hendrick's brief chronicle of eastern European Jewry's engagement in alcohol commerce, the truth of Ford's statement was irrefutable. If to be "on the side" of alcohol meant to participate in its production and purveyance and to defend its presence in the commercial marketplace, Jews were among those Americans who fit Ford's description.

But his intent was not to disinterestedly point out the historical background of Jewish alcohol entrepreneurship. In addition to being the nation's most prolific anti-Semitic propagandist, Ford was also a stalwart defender of Prohibition. Being both dry as a bone and suspicious of Jews as economic actors, it was nearly inevitable that Ford would not only see Jews everywhere in the history of American alcohol commerce, but also that he would see that history as part of a larger Jewish conspiracy.

That "the bulk of the organized bootlegging . . . is in the hands of Jews," by his estimation, was only part of the problem. Ford also claimed that Jews had destroyed the liquor industry when it was legal, through industrial consolidation and low-quality manufacturing. "Distilling," he wrote, "is one of the long list of businesses which has been ruined by Jewish monopoly." In Louisville and Cincinnati, he continued, distilling had once been an art, and the whiskey of the purest quality—an odd lament from a prohibitionist, to be sure. But when Cincinnati became "a thoroughly Judaized city" and Louisville a place of "Judaic complexion," the distilling trade in both cities followed suit.[52]

After Jews took over the trade, Ford claimed, American whiskey "ceased to be whiskey" and became vile "rot-gut." Not content to merely destroy and monopolize the whiskey industry, he went on, Jews set out to damage American culture with their product. In the South in particular, Ford wrote (relying on Will Irwin's essays from *Collier's*), Jewish-produced "nigger gin" wrought damage on race relations, with tragic results for all. Few, however, had the vision to "point a finger at the solid racial phalanx lined up behind the whole rotten combination." Instead, Ford asserted that Americans mistakenly blamed the alcohol itself and the saloonkeepers who sold it, rather than the Jews who had produced it in the first place.

The final outrage, he declared, was the Volstead Act's sacramental wine dispensation. "The Constitution is suspended in [Jews'] favor," Ford insisted, "when the Ten-Gallon Permit is given." Ford suggested that Jews had planned for such a turn of events all along, since the rabbinical wine exemption would grant them continued access to alcohol commerce. "They did not favor Prohibition," he wrote, "but they did not fear it; they knew that it would bring certain illegitimate commercial advantages; they would be winners either way. Jewish luck!" To substantiate his claims, Ford quoted Leo Franklin, rabbi of the Reform temple in Ford's hometown of Detroit. In a recent address to the CCAR, Franklin had complained that the majority of rabbis who had requested authorization to distribute sacramental wine were "men without the slightest pretense at rabbinical training or position" who had declared themselves rabbis "for the purpose of getting into the wholesale liquor business."[53]

Ford's (and Franklin's) complaint would certainly have resonated for members of the Ku Klux Klan, which was nominally revived in 1915 after the murder of Leo Frank but did not become a truly popular movement until the early 1920s. The Klan also regarded Jews as a threat to Prohibition. In addition to agreeing with Ford's vision of a Jewish economic conspiracy, they were also of similar mind when it came to Jewish bootleggers. "My fight right now," declared *Colonel Mayfield's Weekly*, a Klan-affiliated newspaper in Dallas, "is against the Homebrew and the Hebrew."[54]

For both Ford and the Klan, Jewish involvement in American popular culture threatened American morality in general and Prohibition enforcement specifically. Ford wrote that Jews were able to broadcast their boozy "propaganda" through theater (which was "Jew-written, Jew-produced, and Jew-controlled") and popular music. "There is not a dialogue on the stage today that does not drip with whiskey," he wrote. "This idea of drink will be maintained by means of the Jewish stage, Jewish jazz and the Jewish comics until somebody comes down hard upon it as being incentive of treason to the Constitution."[55]

The Ku Klux Klan concurred: Jews, they insisted, were responsible for a national slide into moral decay. According to the Klan, American values were under attack; modern amusements, mass production, and cosmopolitanism economically undermined the middle class, subverted gender roles, and encouraged youth to embrace a pleasure-seeking ethos. Many anxious and ambivalent Americans associated these cultural shifts with Jews, who were highly visible in popular entertainment and often promoted modernity, urbanity, and cultural pluralism in their work. Accusations that Jews brought a vulgarizing influence into American life became increasingly common during the 1920s and into the 1930s. Nondenominational social clubs removed Jewish affiliates from their rosters. Job advertisements often specified that "Christians only" need apply. Harvard and New York University, among others, imposed quotas to keep the Jewish percentage of their student body at a minimum, out of concern that Jewish students were too "crude" to fit in.[56]

The Klan's anti-Semitism was thus an extreme and especially vocal variant of a broad national phenomenon. As historians have recently noted, the Klan did not lurk in the political and cultural margins during the 1920s; the organization's national membership was estimated to be four million at its height, with klaverns not only in the South but also in the Northeast, Southwest, Pacific Northwest, and upper Midwest. They fashioned themselves as defenders of white, native-born, Protestant interests in the United States, and focused their attention on immigrants, especially Catholics and Jews, whom they regarded as "unblendable" and therefore a threat to American civilization. (According to the KKK founder William J. Simmons, the American "melting pot" was more like a "garbage can.") The Klan articulated a militant version of common and widespread anti-immigrant sentiment, which, in its more mainstream form, resulted in a series of federal laws that severely restricted immigration to the United States and culminated in the Johnson-Reed Act of 1924.[57]

Even though the Klan proved to be among Prohibition's greatest enthusiasts, they never formed an open or consistent relationship with the ASL. The organizations allied in their shared passion for the dry cause and occasionally worked together on the local level—as when Klan "vigilance" investigators reported bootleggers to regional ASL officials—but their tactics, and their organizational method, were too different. "Neither partners nor antagonists," writes the historian Thomas Pegram, "the Klan and the ASL struggled to make prohibition work, eyed one another warily, and left the public to speculate as to the nature of their relationship."[58] A decisive difference between the groups was that the Klan's desire to rid the country of alcohol was not roused by progressive ideology. Theirs, like Ford's, was the nativist, nostalgic, and paranoid version of prohibitionist sentiment, a twisted iteration of the populist version of anti-alcohol politics. Klansmen proclaimed that liquor was at the root of American immorality, and that the Eighteenth Amendment, properly defended, would protect the country from its ravages. Yet immigrants and other un-American interlopers threatened to undermine the Volstead Act and American virtue with their sinful European attitudes toward drinking. Klansmen argued that Prohibition's opponents were "mainly alien," and they often targeted immigrants in their bootlegging raids. Catholics received the brunt of this rage, but Jews were subjected to it as well, as when a reader of the *Minneapolis Saturday Press* (which, although not openly affiliated with the Klan, was published in one of the midwestern cities where the Klan was strongest) insisted that "every vendor of vile hooch, every owner of a moonshine still . . . in the Twin Cities is a JEW."[59]

According to the Klan, Jews and alcohol posed a similar threat to American morality. Both were products of city life, which the Klan viewed as a stronghold of sin and moral relativism. Both Jews and alcohol, the Klan insisted further, promoted and facilitated improper social behavior; alcohol loosened inhibitions, and Jews were at the forefront of new forms of mass entertainment that facilitated contact between the genders, such as popular music (which encouraged dancing) and movies (where boys and girls could sit together in the dark, unchaperoned). Colonel Mayfield pointed to a popular song of the day as proof of Jews' willingness to use alcohol to defile young women, although he offered no evidence to back up his assumption that the songwriter was Jewish. "Say it with liquor," the song recommended, "and you're bound to win / The heart of the girlie you love." "90% of the songs of this country, and all of the filthy ones," Mayfield raged, "are written by Jews; they don't give a continental doggone how much they degrade the young gentile girls of this country."[60]

Defenders of an idealized WASP United States were not alone in lashing out against Jews' entrepreneurial and illicit relationship to alcohol during Prohibition. One of Harlem's prominent black weekly newspapers, the *New York Age*, had previously found occasional commonalities between blacks and Jews, even if only in that "one is despised almost as much as the other."[61] But neighborhood relations between the two groups had deteriorated, as the interests of the growing black population and the shrinking local Jewish population came into conflict. While Jews were moving to Brooklyn and other boroughs, they were still commercially active in the area. Blacks increasingly resented the neighborhood's Jewish landlords and merchants, accusing them of overcharging their customers for inferior goods and refusing to hire black employees. Some of these accusations were grounded in truth. But they quickly devolved into stereotypes about Jewish behavior, and about the neighborhood's white merchants in general: *all* white storeowners and landlords above 125th Street were seen as Jews and, therefore, exploitive.[62]

During the 1920s, Harlem was the capital of black life in the United States, the nucleus of an artistic, musical, literary, and intellectual movement that transformed American culture. It was also a neighborhood where drinks were especially easy to procure. As was true in Jewish immigrant neighborhoods downtown, some younger African Americans took up bootlegging as a venue for upward economic mobility, and just like their white counterparts, black middle-class drinkers enjoyed the rush and cosmopolitan cachet of dabbling in illegality. But many of Harlem's black leaders regarded the Volstead Act with great optimism, hoping that Prohibition would reduce neighborhood crime, empower black workers, and inspire a wave of communal self-improvement.[63]

To their tremendous disappointment, Harlem soon sprouted speakeasies by the dozen. In 1923, the *Age* ran a series of articles on Harlem's "Hootch Hell Holes." Neighborhood bootleggers were using furniture stores, cigar shops, delicatessens, cafés, and drugstores as fronts for their business, the *Age* reported. These "hootch-sellers" had bought the police, fouled Harlem with their liquor, and were now poisoning the locals (sometimes literally) and siphoning away the neighborhood's hard-earned capital, the paper alleged. As the series progressed, the *Age* noted that many of the stores in question had the name "Hyman" attached to them; they all turned out to be owned by Hyman Kassell, a well-known local bootlegger and numbers runner. The paper focused on Kassell's ethnicity, and raged against what they interpreted as a plague of white ethnic bootleggers in black Harlem. "Hebrew Operators Control Lenox Avenue Places," blared one headline, "While the Italian Group Controls Hootch Joints Which Have Invaded the 7th Avenue Residential District." Within a few months, local community groups were protesting against a Jewish-owned nightclub, and had complained to authorities about a "gin joint" and brothel run by "a Jew known as Archie." "There is a decided increase in sentiment," the *Age* declared, "opposing the coming to Harlem of any more 'cheap' Jews and other of the bootlegging gentry" who cater to "the weaknesses of a lower class of Negro, satisfying a vicious appetite with dangerous and life-destroying liquor." A boycott of "the interests allied with this sinister menace" might be in order, the paper suggested.[64]

The accusations leveled by the *Age* resembled nativist claims that Jews were economic parasites and moral defilers. (They also resembled white supremacist assertions that a "lower class" of black man was unable to control his thirst.) It is important to keep in mind, however, that Harlem's black leaders were responding to legitimate concerns. The bootlegging trade proliferated with shocking speed in Prohibition-era Harlem, and the owners of the neighborhood's speakeasies, nightclubs, and gin joints—like the owners of area businesses in general—were far more likely to be white than black. Crime in the neighborhood was "compounded," according to the historian Cheryl Lynn Greenberg, by "white adults who looked to Harlem for their illicit pleasures."[65] Although no definitive scholarly study has yet analyzed immigrant entrepreneurial life (legal or illegal) in Harlem before World War II, Jews were unquestionably among the whites who brought liquor to Harlem. Hyman Kassell was not alone: the leading bootlegger and numbers runner Dutch Schultz shipped uncountable gallons into the neighborhood from his base of operations in the Bronx; Connie Immerman, owner of the nightclub Connie's Inn on 131st Street, was roundly condemned by the *Age* for his bootlegging activities; and, on a less glamorous note, Izzy Einstein tracked down and confiscated "$35,000 worth of 'sacramental' Dubonnet" in a Harlem garage.[66]

American Jews participated in the illegal alcohol trade during Prohibition for many of the same reasons as did other Americans: it was potentially lucrative, even in modest quantities; the law was inadequately enforced and relatively easy to evade; and Prohibition was viewed by many Americans as a joke and an inevitable failure, which lessened the stigma of breaking the law. While many regarded Jewish bootlegging as proof that Jews were incapable of conforming to American values, one might instead regard it as evidence of Jewish acculturation, since the flouting of Prohibition law was practically a national pastime.

But there were important differences, too, including and especially the situation created by the sacramental wine dispensation. Section 6 had poked a gaping, leaky hole in the Volstead Act, one that was further dilated by American Jewry's long history of hostility toward the anti-alcohol movement. Even as some Jews availed themselves of the opportunities it created, others frantically sought to seal the breach. It was a *shande*—an embarrassment—and, potentially, a threat to American Jews' status. The New York Jewish community leader Elias Cohen expressed these concerns to Louis Marshall in 1923, complaining not only of Jewish participation in the illicit alcohol trade, but also that American Jewry was "a house divided against itself" on the matter of Prohibition. The lack of consensus, he feared, would "lend itself . . . to wilful [*sic*] misrepresentation on the part of our enemies."[67] The house, such as it was, needed to be put back in order if Jews were going to be able to defend themselves against accusations that they were insufficiently dedicated to the American way of life.

6

"The Law of the Land Is the Law"

Jews Respond to the Volstead Act

Prohibition had put Louis Marshall in an unenviable position. As leader of the American Jewish Committee (AJC), an organization founded in 1906 to defend the rights of Jews in the United States and abroad, Marshall was one of American Jewry's most visible advocates, and combating anti-Semitism weighed heavily among his responsibilities. So in 1922, when his testimony in defense of Jewish immigrants before the House Immigration Committee was interrupted by a committee member pointing out Jewish prevalence in the illegal alcohol trade, one would have expected Marshall to vigorously refute the congressman's claim.[1]

But he did not. He could not, considering how many Jewish leaders were themselves complaining about Jewish involvement in illicit alcohol commerce. It was one thing for Marshall and the AJC to facilitate the publication of "The Peril of Racial Prejudice," a petition signed by more than a hundred religious leaders, politicians, and intellectuals denouncing Henry Ford's anti-Semitic campaign as "wholly at variance with our traditions and ideals and subversive of our system of government."[2] Marshall would have been hard-pressed, however, to counter Ford's pronouncement that bootlegging was a "Jewish industry in which a certain class of rabbis have been active," when Leo Franklin and other American rabbis were similarly wringing their hands about the problem.[3]

Given the opportunity to speak out against such accusations, Marshall preferred, and advised others, to stay silent. In 1925, when Sieg Natenberg of the Chicago Jewish Educational Alliance expressed dismay about a local minister who had leveled imputations similar to Ford's, Marshall counseled that it was "not worth while to engage in any correspondence with a man who would be willing to make such a statement." Better to ignore him, Marshall suggested, since a skirmish would give the minister's claim "greater publicity" and the minister "the limelight that he desires," both of which were to be avoided at all costs.[4]

Marshall's advice was in keeping with the AJC's style of quiet advocacy, which eschewed public clashes with antagonists and favored behind-the-scenes lobbying efforts through one-on-one meetings with influential figures. But Marshall's reticence also came from his own concerns about American Jews' involvement in the alcohol trade, both currently and historically. "I have no doubt," he wrote to Natenberg, "that on examination it will be found that a very large percentage of wholesale liquor dealers in pre-Volstead days were Jews. The business of that time was at least lawful," he continued, "though I always regretted that Jews were engaged in that business to as great an extent as they apparently were."[5]

Marshall's claim to have "always regretted" the presence of Jews in the American alcohol trade is debatable, since he had asserted several decades earlier that "there is nothing immoral in the sale of liquor." While himself a self-professed teetotaler, Marshall disagreed with the very premises of Prohibition, which aligned him with the predominant American Jewish opinion on the matter. He believed that it was the right of the individual "to indulge his tastes in that regard so long as by doing he does not interfere with the public safety," and he was generally suspicious of progressive tendencies to curtail individual liberty for the sake of the common good. Any regulation of the liquor trade, he wrote, was properly a state matter, and "it should have been left to them to determine as to whether or not prohibition was desirable."[6] Nevertheless, Prohibition had been made national law, and it was now "the duty of every good citizen to insist upon the observance of the people's mandate and of the action of Congress, regardless of previous convictions as to the merits of the question."[7] Felix Frankfurter and Louis Brandeis, also Jews and prominent American jurists of the day, agreed. "The Eighteenth Amendment *is*," wrote Frankfurter, and despite his initial resistance to the adoption of the law, both he and Brandeis called on the government to fully enforce it and citizens to follow it.[8]

Yet too many Jews refused to adhere to the law, and many others remained openly contemptuous of it. How to change American Jewry's collective mind and transform their behavior so that both aligned with American law? How to convince Jews to choose the universal over the particular, and to acquiesce to an aspect of American culture so discordant with Jewish history and practice? This dilemma confounded Jewish leaders, including many who had themselves spoken stridently and confidently against temperance legislation in the past. Now they needed to do more than reorient their own political stance and rhetoric; they were charged with the task of convincing the American Jewish population to concede to and abide by a law that they had all collectively denounced as unnecessary, puritanical, and in direct contradiction to both Jewish culture and American values.

Some, like Rabbi Solomon Foster of Newark, insisted that the Talmudic edict *dina d'malchutah dina* ("the law of the land is the law"), which grants primacy to the legal decrees of the host country when they are at odds with Jewish law and custom, commanded Jews to accept the new state of affairs. "Regardless of our personal opinion in the matter," he declared, American Jews must now "observe the law as it has been drawn and aid in its universal enforcement. . . . Sound Jewish doctrine has never deviated from the principle that the law of the land is our law."[9] Others made clear that they acquiesced only grudgingly: "Since Prohibition is the law of the land it has been *my* law," Rabbi Israel Heinberg of Monroe, Louisiana, wrote privately, "while in principle I have been and shall remain *against* it."[10] Meanwhile, less-acculturated American Jews—the traditionally oriented Orthodox in particular—reminded their accomodationist Reform and Conservative brethren that they were in fact obeying the law of the land, since they were "entitled as the Constitution recognizes to the proper use of that wine for Ritual purposes."[11] Consensus would not be easy to achieve. In fact, it proved impossible.

American university students in the early twentieth century were wildly enthusiastic about sports and other competitive displays of school spirit, and the young rabbis-in-training at Hebrew Union College in Cincinnati were no different. The campus lacked fraternities and intercollegiate sports teams, but they still had school pride, if *HUC Songs and Yells*, a short pamphlet distributed to students in the years just before the First World War, is any indication.[12]

HUC Songs and Yells contains lyrics to a dozen spirited chants and singalongs, including, improbably, a song titled "We're Marching," which seems to have been taken straight from the Woman's Christian Temperance Union songbook:

> We're marching, we're marching, a brave little band.
> On the right side of temperance we'll all take our stand.
> We don't use tobacco, and here's what we think,
> That such as does use it most always does drink.
> Down with King Alcohol.[13]

But lest one think the rabbinical students had suddenly become teetotalers, the history of "We're Marching," which predates its presence in the HUC booklet, suggests that they included it in their repertoire to poke fun at the anti-alcohol movement. Originally written in the late nineteenth century by temperance advocates, "We're Marching" was co-opted by wets, appended with a series of satirical verses, and was thereafter most often sung to mock the WCTU.[14] Consider, too, the lyrics to another of the booklet's offerings: "I earn my hundred bucks a year, which goes to pay for all my beer."[15]

That about sums up American Reform Jewry's attitude toward prohibition at the time, among the leadership as well as the lay congregants. As late as 1914, the Central Conference of American Rabbis stated its opposition in forceful terms that almost exactly echoed the comments of their founder, Isaac Mayer Wise, nearly thirty years before. Prohibition, the organization announced, was "born of fanaticism [and] disregard of the actual needs of life" and its success would manifest "the ambition of ecclesiastical tyrants." It was the responsibility of Jewish leaders, the rabbis insisted, to "take a stand on the question of Prohibition," and "go on record, declaring [themselves] of temperate habits . . . but at the same time declare that [their] conception of religious ethics does not condemn the moderate use of alcoholic beverages."[16]

There were, however, a few outliers. For instance, more than a thousand residents of New York City's Eighth Assembly District, which encompassed the Lower East Side, voted for the Prohibition gubernatorial candidate in 1914. Were they Jewish drys? It would be difficult to know for sure, since non-Jews lived in the neighborhood, too. And even if these voters were in fact Jews, the candidate in question, William Sulzer, had advocated for humanitarian reform of immigrant intake practices on Ellis Island. He was running on an American Party–Prohibition Party fusion ticket, but he had earned the loyalty of the neighborhood, and Jewish voters might have cast their ballot for him *despite* his party affiliation.[17]

Still, we cannot dismiss the possibility that some Jews voted dry because they agreed with the anti-alcohol movement. We do know without doubt that toward the end of the decade, as the movement for a constitutional amendment was gaining political sway, a handful of prominent American Jews came out as its supporters. In January 1917, amid the national debates raging over alcohol commerce and war, Rabbi Stephen S. Wise urged American Jews to join forces with the anti-alcohol movement. "The prohibition question is no Jewish question," he implored them from his pulpit. "It is an American problem. Do not let us think about ourselves, but let us think of the welfare of the whole country. Let the verdict be, 'Alcohol must go.'" In another speech that month—this one at an interdenominational meeting at Carnegie Hall—Wise reiterated his views in front of a largely Christian audience. Alcohol, he announced, was "an American problem, and the attitude of the Jew must be the American attitude. . . . The Jew must not in this case be a moral laggard."[18]

Wise was a politically progressive clergyman and social justice activist. He had founded New York City's Free Synagogue as a venue for the promotion of egalitarian politics, and was one of the city's most outspoken advocates for progressive causes, including urban reform and workers' rights.[19] While a Christian clergyman with Wise's political leanings would be expected to support prohibition, an American Jew uttering these words surely took many by surprise. That Rabbi Wise's sermon was reported in the *New York Times* suggests it was a rare event; that it was given a full page in the *American Issue*, the Anti-Saloon League's monthly magazine, indicates that the ASL hoped to use Wise's words as proof that a well-respected leader of one of the country's most obdurately wet communities now understood the virtue of prohibition. Perhaps they hoped that Wise might even sway other Jews to their side.

Sadly for the ASL, Wise remained one of only a few American Jewish public figures who allied with the prohibition movement before the passage of the Eighteenth Amendment. These Jews remained anomalous in their communities and did not join together as a faction of Jewish prohibition advocates. In many ways, they had little else in common besides their anti-alcohol politics. Their motivations and methods varied, as did their broader range of political commitments. But they did share one notable characteristic: Of all sectors of American Jewry, German Jews—or, more accurately, Jews of central European birth or descent and of a German cultural milieu—were more likely to support prohibitionist legislation and try to bring American Jewry into alignment with the "new normal" of national sentiment than were Jews of other ethnic backgrounds.

Stephen Wise certainly fits within this category. Born in Budapest and brought to the United States as a toddler, Wise followed his father (and grandfather) into the rabbinate. His intellectual lineage stemmed from the German Reform school of Judaism, which advocated the modernization of Jewish belief and practice, although he came to regard the institutions of American Reform Judaism as too radically assimilationist. His ideas about American Jewish identity combined classical Reform's universalism and traditional Judaism's commitment to the particular. He maintained the belief that Jews should cultivate historical and spiritual difference, and he was an early Reform advocate of Zionism. But he also saw it as part of his rabbinic mission to participate in nonsectarian movements to reform and improve civic life, and consistently did so as a social liberal and progressive: he was

Prohibition
Concerns *the* Jew

So Says RABBI WISE, of NEW YORK

ALCOHOL must go, according to Rabbi Stephen S. Wise, of New York City. At a meeting of churches representing almost every important religious denomination in the city, at Carnegie Hall, the learned rabbi discussed the drink evil from the standpoint of the Jew.

This standpoint, he declared, was not and could not be peculiar to the Jews.

"It is an American problem, and the attitude of the Jew must be the American attitude," said Rabbi Wise. "Alcohol must go. It is a blessing only for the idle rich—for the extinction of their kind and as a means to make their perpetuation impossible. Rum is a race poison. It poisons generations; it poisons the child before it is born. Industrial efficiency, domestic happiness, national security—all are incompatible with that demon, Alcohol.

"The Jew has been temperate, but he has been cold to prohibition. The tender and precious memories which wine plays in the religious life in his home and synagogue account for this passive attitude. But no fundamental rights of life and liberty are endangered by prohibition, and the Jewish attitude must become one of active opposition to alcohol. Always a moral pioneer, the Jew must not in this case be a moral laggard. Not to prohibit the use of liquor is to sanction it."

VOTE DRY

Series C, No. 4. Postpaid—100, 30c; 500, $1; 1M, $1.85. Attractive quantity rates.

AMERICAN ISSUE PUBLISHING COMPANY.

Department of Literature Westerville, Ohio

14. The Anti-Saloon League's announcement of Rabbi Stephen Wise's prohibitionist sermon, 1917. Stephen Wise was one of a few American Jews who came to support Prohibition during the Progressive era. His stature as a Jewish leader and progressive reformer lent his urgings clout, and the Anti-Saloon League hoped that he would bring other Jews into the movement. (Courtesy of the Brown University Library)

a founding member of both the NAACP and the ACLU. Like many other progressives, Wise voiced pro-Anglo and anti-German sentiment as the war in Europe began. When the United States joined the fight, he praised American military action in ecstatic, Wilsonian terms: "It is not too late to save the world," he declaimed in a wartime speech, "to rebuild an order of life that shall be just and righteous altogether."[20]

Wise's prohibitionism emerged out of his pro-war progressivism; he regarded the war against Germany as a positive endeavor, and alcohol as a threat to the Allies' success. After the Amendment was ratified, Wise continued to speak out in favor of prohibition law. "There will be no wise or sane or just solution of any of our social problems," he wrote in 1921, "until liquor goes out of all lands." He also tried to explain why American Jews had historically found prohibitionist arguments uncompelling. "Drunkenness has never been, so far as I know, a vice among Jews," he wrote. "Therefore it wasn't an easy thing to stir Jews up about the whole problem." But now, he insisted, Jews were willing to reject particularism for the sake of the common good: "I don't believe that any decent Jew in America wants liquor brought back to our land."[21]

Wise's friend and fellow progressive Lillian Wald would not have offered such an overgeneralization about Jewish support of prohibition. Nor was she as exultant as Wise about American military efforts in Europe. But the founder of the Henry Street Settlement on the Lower East Side knew that the liquor trade hurt her neighbors more than it helped them. Born to German Jewish immigrants just after the Civil War, Wald had moved from Cincinnati to New York as a young woman to help improve living conditions and provide services for impoverished immigrants. "She rejoiced when the Prohibition Amendment was passed in 1919," one of her biographers has claimed; "she had seen too much to mourn the passing of the old-time saloonkeeper," offers another.[22] By decade's end, her position was less clear. She bemoaned the nation's lackadaisical attitude toward the law, and in 1927 wrote a short forward to *Does Prohibition Work?*, a report from urban settlement houses that proffered an optimistic vision of the law. The following year, however, she supported the presidential bid of the Democratic candidate Al Smith, who openly opposed Prohibition and wanted to see the law fundamentally reformed, and perhaps even repealed. Wald's attitude toward Prohibition can best be characterized as inconsistent.[23]

Thousands of miles to the west, two American Jewish governors put their far more unequivocal prohibitionist sentiments to political use. In 1916, Moses Alexander, originally of Bavaria and the first Jew elected as governor of an American state, signed a statewide prohibition law in Idaho.[24] His experience in the American West paralleled in many ways that of Simon Bamberger, the first non-Mormon governor of Utah. Bamberger was born in Hesse-Darmstadt, immigrated to the United States on the eve of the Civil War, and settled in Salt Lake City in the 1870s. By 1900 he had made his fortune in hotels, mines, and railroads; as had Alexander in Boise, he had become a member of the economic and social elite in a city and a state where Jews constituted an almost imperceptible minority.[25] Bamberger was elected to Utah's state senate in 1903, where he developed a reputation as an energetic progressive reformer. Even then, he declared his support for prohibition and spoke of his own teetotalling habits. This endeared him to his Mormon electorate, whose religion forbade consumption of alcoholic beverages.[26]

Despite his previous affiliation with the Democratic Party (which was a disadvantage in a largely Republican state) and the fact that he was Jewish (he was the subject of a brief anti-Semitic smear campaign), Bamberger won the gubernatorial election on the Republican ticket in 1916. His campaign promise to enact strict anti-alcohol laws had attracted many voters, and in February 1917 Bamberger signed a statewide prohibition statute into law.[27] Two years later, on January 16, 1919—the very day that the amendment achieved ratification by three-quarters of the states—Bamberger oversaw his state's official endorsement of the Eighteenth Amendment. It might therefore be said that Bamberger's leadership directly resulted in the passage of Prohibition law.

Wise, Wald, Alexander, and Bamberger's prohibitionist leanings were expressions of their progressive worldviews. All four regarded the liquor traffic as a corrupting influence on politics, and all despised the saloon, in particular, for its demoralization and impoverishment of the working class. In addition, all of them were acculturated Jews who had come to share the anti-alcohol sentiments of the larger culture in which they lived. Becoming fully "American" meant not just accepting the law once it was passed, but championing the movement that had captured the imagination and sympathy of so many of their countrymen.

They might also have been reacting defensively to the xenophobia of the day, although none of them said as much. Alcohol symbolized foreign power and alien behavior, and prohibitionists insisted that its abolition would protect American political and economic interests and force immigrants to conform to American moral standards. Some prohibitionists went further, claiming that the presence of immigrants in the United States *was* the problem. While we should not assume that Jewish prohibitionists were motivated solely by insecurity, they undoubtedly noticed that both German Americans and Jewish Americans were often viewed as prohibition's enemies, or at least as forces of obstruction. Even if these four individuals, themselves of central European Jewish descent, genuinely found prohibitionist arguments convincing, they may have hoped that their efforts would shield Jews from the ugly public acrimony being directed toward immigrants whose anti-prohibitionist politics and engagement in the alcohol trade had become a political and cultural burden.[28]

The desire to protect Jews from accusations of disloyalty and unpatriotic leanings moved the Louisville distiller Isaac Wolfe Bernheim to action as well. Bernheim never supported Prohibition, but he was a German immigrant amid anti-German hysteria and a Jew in an increasingly anti-Semitic culture, and thus had multiple political and psychological motivations for proving that American Jews did not waver in their love of country.

In addition to his public displays of patriotism in Louisville—including his donation of statues of Thomas Jefferson and Henry Clay to the city—he also became an outspoken anti-Zionist, accusing Jewish supporters of the Palestinian *Yishuv* of disloyalty. As treasurer of the American Jewish Committee, Bernheim availed himself of the bully pulpit several times between 1918 and 1921 to warn Reform Jews against the "poisoned seeds of Nationalistic Zionism." "These mischievous campaigns for an alien flag and a political loyalty outside our own land," he wrote, "ultimately must result in the impeaching of our standing as citizens." The United States, he insisted, was "our Zion," and American Jews were duty bound to regard it as their one and only homeland.[29] Bernheim's statements articulated an especially vehement version of Reform Judaism's long-standing anti-Zionism. The AJC, UAHC, and CCAR had all made great efforts to distance themselves from political Zionism since the nineteenth century. But the Zionist movement was a subject of rancorous debate within Reform organizations and congregations during the 1920s. Bernheim was stepping into an ideological minefield, and he knew it.

If Bernheim had stopped there, he would have remained within the parameters of the debate. Instead, in his eagerness to prove that "we are Americans by nationality, and that our longings are not for an Oriental Palestinian homeland," he called for the formation of a new organization: the "Reform Church of American Israelites." Bernheim appropriated the teachings of his Louisville rabbi, Adolph Moses, who preached a radically assimilationist interpretation of American Judaism. His new group would stop calling themselves "Jews," Bernheim declared, since the word had been "corrupted into a term of reproach" by anti-Semites. He advocated replacing words of "foreign origin" like "synagogue" and "temple"; American Israelites would worship in churches of their own. Employing a current and extremely loaded turn of phrase, he insisted that the membership of the Reform Church of Israelites "must consist of 100% Americans."[30]

Rabbis of all denominations lined up to castigate Bernheim and criticize his manifesto. The Reform rabbi Edgar Magnin of Los Angeles took a relatively respectful tone, suggesting that Bernheim's reforms might weaken American Judaism rather than strengthen it. Less deferential was Nehemiah Mosessohn, an Orthodox rabbi and the editor of the *Jewish Tribune*, who called Bernheim "demented" and a "contemptible fabricator," as well as a purveyor of "rank ignorance and Jew-hatred." Bernheim's ideas received their most brutal thumping from Stephen Wise. The aim of Bernheim's plan, Wise wrote, "is not so much to emphasize the Americanism of American Jews" as to "sever" the historical and spiritual bond between American Jewry and Jews elsewhere. Jews like Bernheim, Wise concluded, should not be empowered to "weaken the loyalty of those of us who view our Jewishness not as a shame and tragedy but as our exultation and exaltation."[31]

Bernheim's critics regarded his efforts as little more than pathetic acts of self-defense. The "Reformed Church of American Israelites" was Isaac Wolfe Bernheim's way of channeling his frustration with the anti-Semitism he encountered, insisted Rabbi Wise; such Jews should not be in a position "to empoison Jewish life with their own fears and timidities" by insisting that Jews could expect to be accepted in the United States only if they become more like Christians. Rabbi Magnin was of the same mind as Wise: "Calling myself an Israelite," he wrote, "will not compel Mr. Ford to discontinue his unreasonable and savage attacks," nor would it gain Jews entrance "into an exclusive Gentile golf club." The *Baltimore Jewish Times* caustically invoked Henry Ford, too: Bernheim's project "reminds us somewhat of Mr. Ford's Peace Ship enterprise," they sneered, referring to the automaker's embarrassing failed attempt to end the war in Europe, and, perhaps, Ford's subsequent revelation that Jews were responsible not only for the war, but also for all the evil in the world.[32]

Stephen Wise, alongside Bernheim's other detractors, interpreted the proposal for the "Reformed Church" as sublimated self-hatred expressed as jingoism. But Wise seemed not to realize that he, too, was capable of sounding like a nativist and offering a disquietingly circumscribed vision of civic identity. When the Hungarian-born New Yorker accused urban East Coast Prohibition critics of living in "metropolitan suburbs of Europe," which "are not America," it betrayed an awkwardness that may have come of trying too hard to prove that he was truly American.[33]

Throughout the Prohibition era, Jews felt the pressure to prove themselves, at the very least, loyal to the law. The first test for Rabbi Samuel Price of Springfield, Massachusetts, came in March 1920, the first Passover of the Prohibition era. Despite the complexity of Volstead's sacramental wine rules, Price thought he had everything under control. He had prepared for the holiday by acquiring three hundred gallons of wine from an official dealer in Hartford, about thirty miles away. He cheerily noted in his diary that he had made the purchase and planned to allocate the wine among his congregants. But Rabbi Price was thrown for a loop a few days later, when Prohibition authorities raided the home of a local Jewish tailor and confiscated four hundred gallons of homemade Pesach wine. Prohibition law allowed for home production and consumption of two hundred gallons of fermented "cider and fruit juices" per household per year. The Springfield tailor, however, had made twice the legal limit and intended to sell it.[34]

Price responded to the tailor's arrest with profound discomfort and hoped to avoid the whole mess. "The newspapers made a bad noise about it, very unbecoming," he wrote. "I would not interfere, as I do not desire to have my name connected with it." Usually, American rabbis understood that serving as Judaism's interpreters to police, newspapers, and other religious groups was part of their job, and they would come to the aid of local Jews, even those outside their congregation, when their religious or social customs conflicted with American laws and practices. A Russian immigrant, Price had lived in the northeastern United States for several decades and been the rabbi of Springfield's Conservative synagogue since 1913, and would certainly have been in a position to act as an intermediary. But he was so unnerved by the tailor's alleged crime that he avoided getting involved in the matter at all. The following year he delegated the responsibilities of acquiring and distributing Passover wine to someone else.[35]

He was not alone in his anxiety. Prohibition officials and Jewish leaders had intended that section 6 of the Volstead Act would allow Jews free exercise of religion and align American law with Jewish custom. But by that first Passover, it was all already going terribly wrong. Instead of enhancing Jewish life, it facilitated illegal activities both by Jews and in the name of Jews all over the country. Correct in their fear that anti-Semites would see sacramental wine crimes as evidence that Jews exploited the concept of religious freedom for their own economic gain, they began to worry that section 6 provided too many opportunities for unscrupulous behavior. Just as worrying was the possibility that the privilege itself created the perception that

Jews held themselves to different standards of legal and moral conduct than did other Americans—a development that acculturated Jewish leaders had worked hard to avoid since the nineteenth century. "We are entitled to equal rights," wrote Louis Marshall, but "we are not entitled to and should not seek privileges." For Marshall, this was especially important in matters pertaining to Prohibition, about which "the American people are greatly aroused."[36]

Organizations representing acculturated Jews offered a solution to the sacramental wine bootlegging problem by, in effect, negating fifty years of Jewish anti-prohibition argument: do away with section 6's dispensation, they proposed, and we will use grape juice instead. The CCAR announced to its members that "unfermented wine (grape juice) may be used by Jews for all ritual purposes," and pressed on the Reform rabbinate "the desirability of persuading their members to use unfermented rather than fermented wine." Conservative Jewish organizations followed suit after Rabbi Moses Hyamson, a scholar at the Jewish Theological Seminary of America, informed the New York Board of Jewish Ministers that wine need not be intoxicating for use in Jewish ritual. This was not meant to be an absolute dictate, and the CCAR knew they did not have any power over other denominational institutions. Further, they insisted, they did not "wish to impugn the motives of the large number of our Orthodox brethren, who conscientiously believe that fermented wine is indispensable for the fulfillment of their religious obligations." These traditional rabbis had "a perfect right to avail themselves of the exemption which the law of the land grants them," they declared.[37]

Hoping to bring all of American Jewry on board and create a cross-denominational consensus, Marshall wrote to Moses Z. Margolies, the president of the Union of Orthodox Rabbis, and asked him to encourage his rabbinate to "abstain from placing themselves in the position of asking for exceptional treatment in respect to the use of wine." If Orthodox Jews were unwilling to relinquish section 6's special dispensation, he suggested, perhaps the union would provide a theological responsum to substantiate their claim that Jews were required by rabbinic law to use intoxicating wine in their rituals. Margolies never responded to the overture; later, Marshall was shocked to learn that Margolies had met with officials from Internal Revenue in early 1920, and offered the Orthodox union's services as the exclusive authority for the issuance of sacramental wine permits. Clearly, Margolies was not only uninterested in foregoing rabbinic access to wine, but in fact eager to establish total Orthodox control over its availability.[38]

Tensions between Orthodox and Reform Jewish organizations worsened over the next several years, as sacramental wine offenses increased in number and offenders grew more brazen. One incident gained particular notoriety during preparations for the Passover holiday in 1921, when the Menorah Wine Company in downtown Manhattan, an official sacramental wine distributor, was raided—by Izzy Einstein, no less—and found to be selling wine to customers without permits. So far, a run-of-the-mill scandal; but to Einstein's vexation, and, no doubt, to the chagrin of Jewish leaders following the story, the chief of Prohibition enforcement in Washington ordered local agents to return the wine to Menorah, and the company was mysteriously granted permission to sell their goods for the holiday.[39] Everyone knew that Prohibition's enforcement agencies were understaffed and overwhelmed, and, in many too cases, eminently bribable; but were they so corrupt that they would actually help a bootlegger to distribute his wares?

Journalists investigating the case discovered that Menorah's founder was a Jewish olive oil importer who saw in section 6 a business opportunity. He had purchased 750,000 gallons of high-proof Spanish wine, enlisted the twenty-year-old son of a Washington, D.C., Orthodox rabbi to have the wine falsely certified as kosher, and found a New York Orthodox rabbi who would issue Menorah the necessary permits to sell sacramental wine. The Menorah scandal seemed like a simple case of sacramental wine fraud, albeit perpetrated by someone with especially powerful friends.[40]

But it was not so simple. The scandal illuminated a turf war between two Orthodox rabbinic associations that were in competition with each other for market share. On one side was Moses Margolies of the Union of Orthodox Rabbis, who had attempted to establish an Orthodox monopoly for sacramental wine commerce. It turned out that he had not only sought to exclude Reform and Conservative Jews from the process; his goal was to keep Orthodox rabbis who were not affiliated with his organization from participating in the lucrative business of kosher wine supervision. On the other side stood the Assembly of Hebrew Orthodox Rabbis of America, which was formed by a collective of New York Talmud scholars and communal leaders opposed to Margolies's exclusionary tactics. Considering that Margolies was paid the equivalent of 25 percent of the price of each bottle of wine he certified as kosher, it is clear why both groups wanted as much of the business of sacramental wine supervision as they could get.[41]

The incident reflected poorly on New York's Orthodox rabbinate and generated a great deal of negative press that reached beyond the Menorah case. The CCAR bemoaned the damning newspaper headlines the sacramental wine scandals had generated, such as "Jewish Rabbis Reap Fabulous Sums by Flouting Dry Law." Mortified by rabbinic malfeasance and afraid that all

American Jews would be regarded as criminal because of the acts of a corrupted few, acculturated Jewish organizations once again tried to minimize the damage by offering a counter-narrative that proved their eagerness to follow American law. Louis Ginzberg, a leading Conservative scholar of Talmud and Jewish law at the Jewish Theological Seminary of America, undertook a lengthy study of rabbinic debates surrounding *yayin* and *tirosh*. He published his study in early 1922, having concluded that "while the use of fermented wine is not forbidden there is a distinct preference in favor of unfermented wine" for ritual purposes.[42]

The CCAR had already passed a resolution directing its members to "refuse to sign any and all requests for the use of fermented wine for sacramental purposes." Now, armed with both Hyamson's and Ginzberg's pronouncements, Louis Marshall, as president of the AJC, and the CCAR in its official capacity as the collective voice of the Reform rabbinate, wrote to the commissioner of Internal Revenue beseeching him to revoke section 6 outright. The majority of American Jews, the CCAR's executive board declared, were "law-abiding" and "honorable," and "would rather surrender a privilege or even a right that may tend to desecrate the name of their God, than to insist upon it and occasion dishonor."[43]

A few—very few—Jews from traditionally oriented communities came to their side. One of them, Leonard Landes, produced that rarest of texts: a Yiddish anti-alcohol tract. Landes was a physician (though the head of the Boston Dispensary referred to him as a "quack") and author of several sex and marriage manuals. Although his personal religious affiliations are unknown, he meant for *Di Drey Leydenshaften* (The three passions) to be read by Yiddish speakers, many of whom were traditionally oriented Jewish immigrants. Landes explained the chemical process of fermentation through a bizarre anthropomorphic folk tale about the murder of families of molecular yeast "creatures." Alcohol, for Landes, was "Der Getrank fun di Toyt" (the drink of death), and not just because of what it did to drinkers. But drinkers suffered, too; "even the innocent beer," he warned, "which many drinkers don't think of as strong drink, contains enough alcohol to make one a slave." Landes was skeptical that Prohibition law would prove effective, but he approved of the government's decision to take the drastic action necessary to "fight the plague of drunkenness."[44]

Rabbi Isidore Koplowitz came to a similar conclusion, though the Talmud, rather than folk tales, served as his chosen source. Koplowitz had served an Orthodox congregation in Kansas City before he moved to Detroit, where he self-published *Midrash Yayin Veshechor: Talmudic and Midrashic Exeget-*

ics on Wine and Strong Drink in 1923. Through a selective compilation of excerpts from the Talmud, Koplowitz argued not only that Jewish law did not require fermented wine for ritual purposes, but that the rabbis of Jewish history abhorred drunkenness. All claims to the contrary were, in his opinion, "blasphemous." Koplowitz thus used Jewish law to corroborate Marshall's position, calling on his readers to "forego the privilege of obtaining fermented wine for religious purposes. . . . Let us cause our Government to cancel and recall this special privilege speedily."[45]

And then there was Izzy Einstein, the Jewish immigrant who became one of the most famous employees of the Bureau of Prohibition. He was, from the beginning of his illustrious if unconventional career with the bureau, an unlikely Prohibition agent. He had been working as a mail sorter—much to the dismay of his Orthodox father, who hoped that he would enter the rabbinate—when he applied to the Prohibition Unit's Manhattan office in 1920. The office chief initially dismissed him as an unconvincing law enforcer; as Einstein himself admitted, he "didn't look like a detective." Prohibition agents were expected to be athletic of build and stony of countenance. Izzy was decidedly neither. *Time* magazine described him as a "fat little Austrian Jew," and indeed he was, at five feet five and well over two hundred pounds. But Izzy successfully made the case that the bureau could use his tubby stature, waddling gait, and stereotypically ethnic *punim* ("face" in Yiddish) to their advantage: he "would never be spotted as a sleuth," he promised, and therefore "could get results that the regular plainclothes man couldn't."[46] He might not be able to outrun bootleggers and saloonkeepers, but he could outwit them by looking like one of their customers.

Americans loved hearing about Izzy's exploits, and even bootleggers regarded him with bemused affection; one Georgia moonshiner named his dog after him.[47] He and his partner, Moe Smith, gained national fame because of their productivity (4,392 arrests in five years, with a 95 percent conviction rate—an agency record) and Izzy's tireless self-promotion (for which he was regularly reprimanded, and eventually fired, by bureau officials). But newspapers kept reporting on "Izzy and Moe" because of their investigatory methods, which were idiosyncratic and often comic. They regularly busted speakeasies and exposed illegal liquor distribution networks by disguising themselves in urban camouflage: they dressed up as musicians, society dandies, pickle peddlers, college athletes, and a bourgeois couple (Moe donned the dress and cloche hat) out for a night on the town. Izzy used his knowledge of Yiddish (his mother tongue), German, Polish, Hungarian, Bohemian, and Italian to infiltrate immigrant communities in cities all over

15. The former Prohibition agents Izzy Einstein (*left*) and Moe Smith (*right*) enjoying *abisl mashke* in 1935, after Repeal. (Library of Congress).

the country, which most native-born bureau agents could not do. On at least one occasion, he passed himself off as African American by blackening his face, as if he were performing in a minstrel show, and driving a coal wagon through the streets of Harlem, "stopping at sixteen saloons to peddle coal."[48]

Agent Einstein cut a peculiar figure in the nation's Prohibition landscape. His admirers delighted in the oddness of a flamboyantly ethnic Jew, a member of a community that had long engaged in alcohol production (and continued to do so during Prohibition), prosecuting the law, and his fellow Jews when they broke the law, with affable and irrepressible gusto. Jewish identity proved crucial not only to his celebrity, but also to his modus operandi. On one occasion, he was served liquor at a midtown club only after convincing the bartender that he was a rabbi; on another, he convinced a saloonkeeper who recognized him that he was not Izzy Einstein by pretending to eat a ham sandwich, something the real Izzy, who kept kosher, would never do.[49] Einstein clearly reveled in the role of Jewish trickster, and he embraced his resemblance to a Jewish stereotype as a useful tool of his trade. As he told a reporter in Mobile, Alabama, he fooled saloonkeepers so well because he was regularly "taken for granted as a traveling salesman. I just happen to be that type." For readers who did not understand what "that type" was, the reporter elaborated: Einstein's "Hebraic personality and his foreign accent," he wrote, "are invaluable assets in his work."[50]

Unlike Koplowitz, Landes, and Einstein, however, the vast majority of Orthodox and Yiddish-speaking Jews remained hostile to Prohibition and its enforcement. As representative of the New York Kehillah (the city's cross-denominational Jewish communal organization), Elias Cohen, himself a Conservative Jew, rebuked Marshall on behalf of traditionalists. "It is not for those who do not believe in the use of Ritual Fermented wine," he protested, "to act as a unit without consulting the rest of us who do."[51] Though at least one publication, *Der Tog* in New York City, suggested some sympathy with Marshall's claim that Jews should demonstrate their acceptance of American law by refraining from drinking sacramental wine, Yiddish-language newspapers, radio entertainers, and even Talmud scholars satirized the Puritanism of the law itself and the ineptness with which it was enforced.[52] And Orthodox Jewish organizations themselves barely responded to Reform Jewry's entreaties.

But once other religious groups—the Catholic Church in particular—angrily entered the fray, the Orthodox did not need to respond. Catholic leaders expressed alarm, both publicly and to the Bureau of Prohibition directly, at the possibility that their access to sacramental wine might be curtailed. They claimed that the use of unfermented wine was "against the principles" of their religion, and that they would never acquiesce to such radical revision of the Volstead Act. Further, they insisted, the Catholic Church had committed no crime and should not be punished; the wine abuses had developed because Jews, not Christians, had taken advantage of loopholes in the law. Of course, this was not quite true, since Catholics were among those Christians who posed as Jews in order to get their hands on wine and participated in a gamut of imaginative sacramental bootlegging schemes. What could truthfully be said was that the home use stipulation in section 6, which had been written with Jewish ritual in mind, had proved easy to manipulate.[53]

Prohibition authorities were unwilling to revise the law, as they might be accused of limiting religious freedom. They assured the National Catholic Welfare Council that the bureau was "in no wise concerned with the enactment of laws which would tend to do away with the use of wine for sacramental purposes," and called any statements to the contrary "preposterous."

Marshall and the CCAR, sensing that the request for repeal of the exemption had been a step too far, decided to abandon this tactic. They did not want to create tension between themselves and those Christian churches that also used wine in their rituals; but even more worrying was the possibility that the revocation of sacramental wine privileges "might come back to plague us later," since "to broach the question of religious liberty as guaranteed under the Constitution in a manner that might even only remotely affect its strength would be unwise." A constraint on religious use of wine might at some future point be used as a precedent to weaken guarantees of freedom of religious practice.[54]

Intending to placate both Jews and Catholics as best they could, and aiming to make the law more effectual as well, in the fall of 1922 the bureau announced new restrictions that they hoped would tighten the controls around rabbinic distribution of sacramental wine. Rabbis would no longer be permitted to store wine outside their home or synagogue, and would have to keep more detailed records than previously required. "FAKE RABBIS ELIMINATED," trumpeted the *New York Times* in a moment of ebullient overenthusiasm, seeing as both the Prohibition Unit and mainstream Jewish organizations were still desperately trying to find a solution to the problem three years later.[55] The latter's efforts to convince Orthodox Jews to replace wine with grape juice had come to naught; and while the American Episcopal Church briefly contemplated the omission of wine in communion ritual (the communicant could "receive the cup into his hands" as a symbolic act without drinking from it), the Catholic Church continued to regard such suggestions with utter contempt. "They can send us to jail until we rot," roared one Denver priest, "but the mass will be celebrated with fermented wine, and celebrated regularly" in his diocese.[56] Meanwhile, millions of gallons of sacramental wine were distributed throughout the nation every year, much of it for recreational consumption.

Starting in 1925—the peak year of sacramental wine withdrawals—Prohibition authorities began to modify the rules of the law enough to have significant effect. First, they reduced the amount of wine available to Jewish families from ten to five gallons annually. They revoked the two-hundred-gallon homemade wine permit, even for rabbis with recognized accreditation. Having decided that official domestic manufacturers produced a sufficient amount of sacramental wine for American Jewish needs, they halted importation of kosher wine from Palestine, ignoring those who insisted that Palestine wine was "more sacred" than American-made kosher wine.[57] Then, early in the fall of 1926, they closed more than two hundred sacramental wine stores in New York City. The bureau went so far as to revoke all rabbinic wine permits, insisting that each rabbi appear at the local Prohibition office in order to have his request approved. Orthodox rabbinic organizations railed against the new rules and even hired counsel. Their lawyer pointed out that many Orthodox rabbis were recent immigrants and could not "speak enough English to find their way to the prohibition offices." He warned that the new stipulation might have an unintended consequence: if Orthodox rabbis were stymied in their efforts to access wine for the upcoming High Holidays, their congregants might seek out bootleg wine instead.[58]

The bureau pressed on, increasing its investigations of rabbinic wine distribution. In 1927, more new rules went into effect, demanding that all clergy requesting sacramental wine permits provide an alphabetized list of the names and addresses of their congregants, information about where the wine would be stored, and an account of all previous withdrawals. By the end of the year, rabbis were required to "file with the [Prohibition] administrator a [notarized] report . . . showing the date and quantity of each delivery of wine made by him, with the name and address of the person to whom each such delivery was made, and a statement of the quantity of wine remaining in his possession on the date of such report." These new regulations seemed to have their intended effect: already by the end of 1926, sacramental wine withdrawals were less than a fourth of what they had been the previous year, and that amount continued to decrease for the rest of the Prohibition era.[59]

But Jewish leaders still felt themselves to be under tremendous pressure. Prohibition had revealed deep fissures within American Jewish culture, a development that filled Louis Marshall with dread. Jewish infighting about the law did not merely "bode ill for peace and harmony" between Jewish communities, he wrote. It also produced "an unpleasant spectacle for the general public, which naturally must be avoided."[60] Concern that the non-Jews who constituted the "general public" might witness intra-group disagreement and judge American Jewry negatively was one of the reasons that Marshall and other acculturated Jewish leaders wanted to keep Orthodox Jews from using wine in their rituals. In the process, however, they enacted a civic version of nineteenth-century temperance Christians' pietism, demanding that all Jews conform to their interpretation of proper compliance with the law. Traditionalist Jews responded by continuing to avail themselves of their legal right to access wine and refusing to join their Reform and Conservative colleagues in a "boycott" of section 6. The Jewish people, they sniffed, had maintained ancient practices in the face of deadlier enemies than the Bureau of Prohibition. "We never ran away from the stake, from the rack, or from the sword," wrote one Orthodox Jew, "and now it proposed [that we should] run away from the bootlegger!"[61]

The aforementioned Jewish Baltimorean, in his letter to his city's *Jewish Times*, bespoke acculturative Jews' scorn for Orthodox Jews' willingness to sully the larger Jewish community's reputation. "I lay the blame with the Orthodox Jews," he wrote in response to rumors that a local Orthodox rabbi had claimed to hold "no objection to any member of his congregation bootlegging." A rabbi was supposed to be a teacher and a moral authority; if one took such a loose attitude toward Prohibition, the letter writer contended, he should be "unfrocked, tarred, and feathered." Pointing a sanctimonious finger at his city's less-assimilated Jewish community, he reminded them that *dina d'malchutah dina*: "The fact that the Eighteenth Amendment is unpopular . . . is not any excuse for a Jew to violate the law."[62]

But Prohibition exposed and amplified other disagreements within American Jewry, including an especially divisive issue of the day: Zionism. The American Zionist movement had grown since 1917, when the Balfour Declaration offered Palestine as "a national home for the Jewish people." It expanded further after the passage of immigration quota laws slashed the number of Jews who could be admitted to the United States. Zionism gained American adherents throughout the rest of the decade, even among segments of the Jewish population historically averse to Zionist claims of Jewish national difference. The CCAR, which had been formed by advocates for the universalist mission of classical Reform Judaism, had begun to express some sympathies for the movement. They passed a resolution supporting the *Yishuv* in 1923, quietly acknowledging that American Jews increasingly looked on the idea of Jewish settlement in Palestine with hope and pride.[63]

Though their position toward Zionism had softened—shifting from anti-Zionism to openness to the idea of a Jewish cultural and religious center in Palestine[64]—they remained resolute on the subject of Prohibition and sacramental wine. Perhaps the New York entrepreneur Fred Goldberg was unaware of the CCAR's steadfastness on the matter when he wrote to Hyman Enelow, the organization's president, in 1928. The ban on importation of Palestine wine had been rescinded, and Goldberg informed Enelow that he and several rabbis had met with Prohibition officials the week before. His motivations were twofold, he announced: to "bring order out of chaos and to eliminate so-called Rabbinical Bootlegging" and "to further the sale of Palestine wines," since an increase in their importation to the United States would "mean a real help" to the *Yishuv* economy and the Zionist cause. To that end, he had proposed to the Prohibition Unit that only wines made and bottled in Palestine be considered kosher and legitimate for sacramental use. Goldberg reported that federal Prohibition administrators had expressed willingness to consider the proposition, and Chaim Weizmann, president of the World Zionist Organization, approved of the arrangement.[65]

Unfortunately, Fred Goldberg remains something of a mystery. Beyond the address he gave for himself in his letter, nothing is known: the details of his life and his project; his occupation and his organizational affiliations. It is also unclear whether Enelow had any previous dealings with Goldberg—although if this was their first interaction, Enelow's reply suggests that Goldberg had not made a very good initial impression. "I do not see what Dr. Chaim Weizmann has got to do with this question," came Enelow's contemptuous response. "As far as I know, he is neither an authority on Orthodox Judaism nor on the requirements of American law." Further, he snapped, the Bureau of Prohibition could not claim any authority over the kosherness of wine from Palestine or anywhere else. When Enelow received another letter—this one from the New York administrator from the Department of the Treasury informing him that in response to Goldberg's queries, an official meeting had been arranged between the Prohibition Unit and representatives of "a number of the Rabbinical organizations in the Metropolitan District . . . to discuss the distribution of Sacramental Wine"—Enelow wrote a short, angry missive to Goldberg and forwarded it to the bureau. "You have absolutely no right to use the name of the CCAR in connection with your prohibition activities and business enterprise," Enelow told Goldberg, "and I earnestly hope that you will remove it from your list."[66]

For Enelow and the CCAR, Goldberg's efforts to restructure section 6 so that it functioned to the advantage of the Zionist settlement in Palestine rang every possible alarm. Even though the rabbinic organization was not as hostile toward Zionism as it had been before the First World War, Reform Jewry was still split on the matter, and many of their leaders regarded Jewish nationalism apprehensively. What would the "general public" think, Enelow must have wondered, if, in the process of consuming alcohol that was off-limits to the rest of the American population, Jews financially aided a project that regarded Jews' true home to be on the Mediterranean Sea? Goldberg's proposition presumed Jewish difference in too many ways for Enelow's comfort.

Eventually, just as Zionism had done, the issue of Prohibition undermined "peace and harmony" within the CCAR itself. The organization's rabbis even disagreed about the wisdom of American Jews expressing their disapproval of the law; while a few were openly and publicly contemptuous of it, most feared that Jewish criticisms of Prohibition would be received as self-serving or unpatriotic. Rabbi Enelow voiced the organization's consensus and public position in a sermon to his congregation at Temple Emanu-El in New York. "From a Jewish point of view," he stated, "you may work for a modification of the Prohibition law, if you think you must. But . . . Judaism bids us obey the law, and so long as the Prohibition laws are in effect, it is for us to obey them, if we would be regarded as good Jews."[67] Opposition to the law, he reminded his audience, was not a reason to break it.

But what if a member of the CCAR were to take Enelow up on his revision of *dina d'malchutah dina* by seeking to change the law of the land? In 1926, CCAR secretary Rabbi Morris Lazaron did exactly that by publicly supporting the Association against the Prohibition Amendment (AAPA). Founded in the months before ratification, the AAPA spent the first half-decade of its existence failing to have much impact on American politics. In 1925, the organization began to attract powerful allies, former legislators and wealthy industrialists among them. Through the rest of the decade and until the repeal of Prohibition in 1933, the AAPA gained hundreds of thousands of members who agreed with the organization's position that Prohibition was both ill conceived as legislation and insufficiently enforced by the government. Federal control over liquor production and consumption, they insisted, gave power to Washington that rightly belonged at the local level.[68]

By early 1926, Lazaron had come to doubt the wisdom of Prohibition and decided that he needed to take action. He began with an investigation into Jewish public opinion. Without consulting his colleagues on the CCAR's executive board, Lazaron sent a questionnaire to all 303 of the organization's members. He asked his fellow rabbis for a description of local sentiment regarding Prohibition: did their communities approve of the law as it stood, or did they seem to favor its modification or even repeal? He also asked if their communities were of split opinion, and if so, which groups seemed to favor the law and which ones wanted change. Finally, he inquired into their personal opinions: "Do you believe that the enactment of the prohibition laws has brought more harm than good? What do you think should be done?"[69]

The 122 responses he received showed that Reform rabbis were in as little agreement as the rest of the country's population. The vast majority indicated that community opinion was either resolutely against the law or fairly divided. (Though several respondents pointed out that Lazaron's intended meaning of "community"—whether he meant the word to refer only to Jews or to the general local population—was unclear.) Nearly every rabbi, from every region, asserted that only two groups seemed to favor Prohibition. The first was evangelical Christians—or, as a rabbi from Trenton, New Jersey, described them, "pious long-faced religious fanatics who are looking for a kick out of life in some future world." The second group was bootleggers, for whom Prohibition had turned out to be a windfall.

When asked which groups favored a change in the law, however, responses varied. Some pointed to laborers, and others to Catholics and the foreign-born. Several mentioned the "liberal element," "lovers of liberty," "professional men," secular citizens, or, as a New York City rabbi asserted, "the drinkers and the thinkers." Nearly half the rabbis stated that in their area, *everybody*, or "the majority of the people," thought the law was deeply flawed and in need of significant repair. Twelve rabbis stated, specifically, that the Jews of their city were entirely and uniformly opposed to Prohibition. "In the Jewish community" of Wilmington, Delaware, according to the local Reform rabbi, "the overwhelming majority of individuals neither observe nor sympathize with the present Prohibition law."

The failure of middle-class and otherwise law-abiding people, Jewish and gentile, to comply with the law frustrated several of Lazaron's respondents. "In the circles in which I move," wrote the rabbi of Portland, Oregon's establishment temple, "Prohibition is flaunted." Many others decried the "hypocrisy" and the loosening of morals that the law had inspired, and suggested that the illegalization of alcohol had the opposite of its intended effect. In Milwaukee, the local rabbi wrote, the Volstead Act had "encouraged youth, adolescents, and former temperance people into curiosity of tasting, then acquiring [a] drink habit on the sly." A Cleveland rabbi despaired about Prohibition's effect on American youth in particular: "I am convinced that homebrew of whisky has made a criminal of many a good young man and ruined the virtue of many good girls."

Asked for their own personal feelings about the law, most favored modification so that it permitted the production and consumption of low-proof alcohol. "If light wines and beer were allowed," a rabbi from Tacoma, Washington, suggested, "there would not be such immoderate and indiscriminate drinking, crime would decrease, and the general moral tone of the American public would be higher." Many respondents, including those who favored repeal, expressed that they would "dislike to see the return of the saloon" under any circumstances. Those who favored the status quo, unsurprisingly, were far in the minority. By Lazaron's count, only eleven rabbis thought that Prohibition should remain as it was and be more strictly enforced, rather than repealed or modified.

This minority turned out to be as much a source of worry to several members of the executive board as was the furious letter from a Baltimore rabbi who called on CCAR to "courageously give utterance to a reversal of position" by not only publicly insisting on Jews' right to access sacramental wine, but also acknowledging that Prohibition had "effected a demoralization of American life and a break-down in American morals." But the very act of having a public opinion on the matter, according to Henry Englander, a member of the faculty at Hebrew Union College in Cincinnati, could work to the detriment of the Jewish community. "Religious bodies ought not to take the initiative in having the law repealed," he wrote; rather, "it ought to be purely a political or social movement. I am opposed to Jewish bodies as Jewish going on record as opposed to prohibition."

CCAR president Louis Wolsey found Lazaron's questionnaire and the responses it prompted to be even more unnerving. "It is a bit indelicate and imprudent," he wrote to Lazaron, "for a rabbi to express himself publicly on this question." Those who favored Prohibition could potentially cause trouble by creating dissention "within our ranks," since the majority of Reform rabbis opposed the law. But what Wolsey feared most was the possibility that Jewish anti-prohibitionist sentiment might provoke the anger of Christian "drys," who were "intolerant [and] liable to say that Jews and saloonkeepers are trying to destroy the country." The issue was too much of a "cactus," and if Jews tried to take it in hand they would come away injured. Silence, he counseled, was the only wise option: "the whole prohibition question is a Protestant-Anglo-Saxon matter," he concluded, that "Jews ought to keep out of."[70]

What were Wolsey and Englander afraid of? Their warnings to Lazaron suggest concern that developments since the passage of the Eighteenth Amendment had heightened American Jewish vulnerability. The sacramental wine scandals and Henry Ford's vicious accusations earlier in the decade had led Americans to believe that Jews disregarded Prohibition law; for a Jewish leader, an executive of a national Jewish organization, to speak out for the law's repeal might confirm those suspicions. Perhaps, too, they wished to discourage Jews from voicing their positions on the law from a specifically Jewish platform, whatever those positions might be, because of the chaos it would invite. Two Jews, three opinions, as the saying goes; but creating a space for Jews to disagree about the Jewish position on Prohibition law would invariably lead to confusion, misinterpretation, and fragmentation. From either standpoint, the best way for Jewish leaders to protect themselves and their communities was to avoid speaking on the subject at all.

Lazaron acquiesced, mostly, to the insistences of his more cautious colleagues and elders. He did write a passionate letter to AAPA founder William H. Stayton expressing his approval of their efforts. Prohibition was "a national scandal," he wrote; "the present law cannot and in the nature of things never will be enforced," because Congress was unwilling to appropriate sufficient economic resources and "it overrides the sentiments of too large a proportion of our population." But he also declined Stayton's invitation to speak at a congressional hearing on behalf of the AAPA.[71]

There is a third possible interpretation of Wolsey and Englander's request that Lazaron remain uninvolved in debates about the future of Prohibition law. When Wolsey wrote that Prohibition was a "Protestant-Anglo-Saxon matter," he might have been alluding to the fact that the movement to repeal Prohibition was already well underway, without any Jewish participation; let the Christians fight it out, in other words. That is precisely what happened, and it would not be long before the AAPA had its way.

By the time Franklin Delano Roosevelt defeated Herbert Hoover in the 1932 presidential race, the American public's patience for Prohibition was clearly not what it had once been. In addition to the AAPA and the Women's Organization for National Prohibition Reform, whose memberships were primarily white and upper middle class, working-class Americans, and especially ethnic workers, also began to make their discontent with Prohibition a political issue. They were angered by the law's seemingly selective, classist enforcement, according to the historian Lizabeth Cohen. "A rich family could have a cellar full of liquor," she writes, "but if a poor family had one bottle of home-brew, there would be trouble." Further incensing ethnic workers was their suspicion that their own employers enjoyed the privilege of a private stock of liquor, even as they denied workingmen the right to a beer. Prohibition in the name of industrial productivity, it seemed, extended only to the workers, not to society as a whole.[72]

Prohibition's contradictions were further illuminated by the 1931 release of the Wickersham Commission report. Appointed by President Hoover in 1929, the commission examined the state of the nation's commitment to Prohibition, in terms of both public observance and law enforcement. Their findings: Prohibition had been badly and inconsistently implemented from the start; sufficient resources had never been committed to the task of administration and enforcement; and public opinion, which had once supported the law (or at least been willing to go along with it), had "changed into non-observance or open hostility."

Much of the report reiterated the claims of the AAPA. But even though a majority of the committee considered Prohibition's current state unsustainable and advocated the law's radical modification, and two (including the commission's only Jewish member, Monte M. Lemann of New Orleans) called for immediate repeal, the report itself stopped well short of recommending anything other than the redoubling of enforcement efforts. Hoover presented the report to the public as if it unequivocally supported the law as it stood. The findings of the report, the timidity of its conclusions, and the dishonesty of Hoover's synopsis increased the nation's general skepticism about Prohibition.[73]

In addition, changes in American culture, and especially in national attitudes toward immigrants and ethnic communities, undermined support for Prohibition. Prohibition's nativist argument had lost traction since the 1928 presidential election, when the Republican Hoover trounced the Democratic candidate Al Smith. Smith was a Catholic product of urban ethnic politics and a long-standing "wet," and he had prodigious support from ethnic voters. When the Anti-Saloon League joined Herbert Hoover's campaign, ASL spokesman Bishop James Cannon, Jr., used these alliances to his best advantage. "Governor Smith wants the Italians, the Sicilians, the Poles and the Russian Jews" to continue to immigrate to the United States, Cannon told a Maryland campaign crowd. "He wants the kind of dirty people you find today on the sidewalks of New York. . . . That kind has given us a stomach ache. We have been unable to assimilate such people in our national life."[74] But a growing number of Americans, even those sympathetic to the Prohibition cause, regarded Cannon's nativism as distasteful and repellant.[75] In the end, accusations of financial misdoings, including stock market speculation and wartime profiteering, led to Bishop Cannon's downfall in the eyes of the American public. His malfeasances reflected poorly on his organization; by the time he was accused of adultery in 1930, his career was ruined, and the ASL's close association with Cannon had severely tarnished the organization's reputation.[76]

Public opinion also changed, in response to ethnic communities' accelerating assimilation into national life. Immigrants from southern and eastern Europe, previously a source of profound cultural anxiety, were "fitting in" and becoming more integrated into American culture. With no new influxes of exotic and impoverished "unblendables" since the passage of immigration restriction legislation earlier in the decade—not to mention the fact that no one ethnic, religious, racial, or economic group had a monopoly on illegal alcohol purveyance or consumption—claims that immigrants' drinking habits or relation to alcohol posed a threat to American society had become less convincing than they once had been. In general, immigrants were settling into their new American home with minimal trouble.

By the end of the decade, prohibitionists were themselves regularly held responsible for the lawlessness of the period. Congressman Adolph Sabath of Illinois joined the AAPA in denouncing the prohibitionists of the ASL "and their allied forces and co-workers, the Ku Klux Klan fanatics," accusing them of having engendered the crime and violence that had plagued the nation, and his Chicago district in particular, since 1920. Himself a Jewish immigrant from Bohemia, Sabath was first elected to the House of Representatives in 1895 and went on to serve his district for twenty-three consecutive terms. Like the majority of urban leaders with primarily ethnic constituencies, Sabath actively opposed Prohibition, and nearly every year between 1925 and 1933, he introduced bills to amend the Eighteenth Amendment and the Volstead Act so that they allowed for commerce in beer and wine. In 1929, he responded to prohibitionist claims that Jews and other immigrants were responsible for the era's surge in crime by turning that blame back on them. "The bootlegging and gang killings . . . are not the by-product but the direct product of the Volstead Act," he said in a speech to the House, "and the supporters of this crime breeding legislation must claim this new cult of American criminals entirely as their own."[77]

But Prohibition's strength was most decisively sapped by the Great Depression. By 1932, even the most ideologically devoted prohibitionist would have to admit that worse things could happen to an American citizen than that he or she had an occasional drink. Twelve million Americans were unemployed, and millions more were desperately in need of assistance. American manufacturing had decreased by more than three quarters, and agricultural production had halved, since 1929. Thousands of banks had failed, causing millions of dollars of Americans' life savings to evaporate. The country, in short, was in the throes of a devastating financial crisis. Roosevelt campaigned on the claim that repealing Prohibition would ease the nation's pain. Before 1920, about 14 percent of federal, state, and local tax revenues came from alcohol commerce. By restoring this source of revenue, Roosevelt insisted, and ending the exorbitant costs of Volstead's enforcement, the government could begin to provide greater relief. Repeal would also put people to work, in breweries and distilleries and bottling plants, and would increase consumer spending as well. These economic considerations, along with the increasingly common insistence that Prohibition had created more evils than it had eradicated, gave the repeal movement the force and the widespread appeal that it needed to succeed.[78]

Before President Roosevelt was two weeks in office, he pushed Congress to pass legislation that allowed the states to legalize and regulate the sale of beer and wine, and proposed a federal tax on both products. Congress formally put forward and approved a total repeal amendment in early 1933, and sent it to state legislatures for approval. Thirty-seven states held popular elections to determine their position, and of the twenty-one million Americans who voted on the matter, nearly 73 percent favored the repeal of the law. Polls showed that even though there was still an urban/rural split in Prohibition sentiment, rural areas were now voting wet, too, and in surprisingly substantial numbers.[79]

The Twenty-First Amendment—which declared that "the eighteenth article of amendment to the Constitution of the United States is hereby repealed"—was ratified in December 1933. Alcohol was once again legal, and the nation responded not with debauch and abandon (as many had expected and feared), but with a sigh of relief. Politicians and newspapers around the country expressed hope that state legislatures, where the power to regulate alcohol commerce now resided, would soon put reasonable and effective laws in place. They also wished for a new sense of shared national purpose to replace the ideological shrillness and divisive rhetoric of the previous decades. Even the USBA warned consumers against "untoward celebration," encouraging beer drinkers to enjoy their reinstated freedom moderately— and, assumedly, without untoward gloating.[80]

For American Jewish leaders who had regarded Prohibition law as a dilemma for their own communities, Repeal offered special relief. Now that the law was gone, Jewish practices of alcohol consumption and American laws agreed once again, and Jews' historical engagement in alcohol commerce, they hoped, would no longer evoke suspicion. Some Jewish leaders hoped to facilitate reconciliation between the formerly warring sides of the debate. They endeavored to make amends, and even to make some allies out of former adversaries. This was the goal of Rabbi Ferdinand Isserman of St. Louis, who gave a radio sermon a month before the Twenty-First Amendment's ratification. He directed his speech toward a nondenominational audience, encouraging his listeners, a group that might well have included Protestant prohibitionists as well as his own Jewish congregants, to consider that "not all drys were bigots, nor fanatics." Isserman defended Prohibition's advocates, and reminded those who disagreed with them that "the overwhelming majority" of anti-alcohol advocates had been "animated by the highest motives and seeking to conquer a problem of serious proportion." It was time, Isserman insisted, for the two sides to put away old differences and find common cause as they created new legislation, which, he suggested, should include laws that abolished the saloon once and for all and prevented "the reign of king rum in the political arena."[81] On some things, Isserman intimated (and hoped), all Americans could agree.

With Prohibition's inglorious demise came the resurrection of the alcohol trade. The industry did not take long to bounce back. In the middle of 1936, the Department of the Treasury announced that 348 million gallons of distilled liquor were currently stored in bonded warehouses, up from only 91 million gallons two years before. "A further increase in production is expected," Treasury officials reported, "as some forty distilleries not yet in operation complete arrangements to begin manufacturing." That same year, 739 breweries produced more than 50 million barrels of beer—a decrease by a dozen in the number of breweries in 1934, but an increase in production by 14 million barrels.[82]

Jews were among those who entered the revived industry. Brooklyn's Liebmann family had survived the previous thirteen years by manufacturing nonalcoholic near beer and lemonade. They relaunched their Rheingold brand of beer, and in the decade that followed initiated a monumentally successful advertising campaign—the "Miss Rheingold" Contest—that made the brand one of the leading sellers in the lucrative New York City market. (The company stumbled badly in the 1950s, when they purchased breweries in California in an expensive and failed attempt to market their beer on the West Coast.)[83]

Several of the Jewish alcohol entrepreneurs who reentered the industry in the years following Repeal had been engaged in alcohol commerce while it was still illegal. Kosher vintners who had remained in business during the Prohibition era could now sell their product in unlimited quantity, though they struggled to compete against the Palestine wine trade, which aggressively courted American Jewish consumers. One of these stateside manufacturers, Brooklyn's Monarch Wine Company, inked a deal in 1936 allowing them to use the Manischewitz brand name for their product. By the 1950s, Manischewitz Concord Grape dominated the national kosher wine market—thanks in no small part to non-Jews who preferred sweet wine. The Canadian distiller Samuel Bronfman also hit the ground running after Prohibition's end. Bronfman's agents had shipped countless millions of gallons of contraband liquor to American bootleggers during Prohibition. In 1936, Bronfman moved his corporate headquarters to New York City, and paid the

American government $1.5 million to settle claims against his company for violations of the Volstead Act—a settlement far smaller than what he actually owed, according to his critics.[84]

One of Bronfman's competitors, Lewis Rosensteil of Schenley Distillers Corporation, came from a Jewish family that had been in the distilling and rectifying business since before Prohibition. Schenley operated as a government-sanctioned medicinal alcohol distributor in the thirteen years that followed. Observers suspected that the business was a bootlegging front, however, pointing out Rosensteil's purchase of one distillery and whiskey warehouse after another, which enabled him to stockpile far more liquor than a medicinal distributor could possibly need. Rosensteil eventually accumulated thirty distilleries and all of these distilleries' warehoused liquor—including, in 1937, the Bernheim Brothers' flagship Louisville distillery. By the time of Repeal, Rosensteil had amassed a tremendous supply, and as early as 1934, when most distilleries were just beginning to barrel and warehouse their new whiskey, Schenley's sales were already reported at $40 million. Other Jews in the revived liquor trade had made minimal effort to hide their bootlegging endeavors during Prohibition: Newark's bootleg kings, Longy Zwillman and Joe Reinfeld, also stayed in the liquor distribution business after 1933, though they sold their corporation, Browne Vintners, to the Bronfmans in 1940.[85]

These businessmen surely understood that even if their entrepreneurial activity during Prohibition had made them wealthy, it had done their reputations substantial harm. As one historian of Prohibition's most prolific bootleggers has written, for many of these bootleggers, "the liquor business was not an interlude of the 1920s but a means by which they gained the resources to control the legal liquor business and thereby achieve success and respectability."[86] Bronfman and Rosensteil sought to further their respectability through philanthropy, and both men were effusively generous in their charity to Jewish organizations in the decades after Repeal. The Bronfmans contributed millions of dollars to universities, medical institutions, and scholarship on Jewish subjects in Canada, the United States, and Israel. Rosensteil donated $20 million to Brandeis University in the 1960s, recalling the Bernheims' and Freibergs' donations to Hebrew Union College in the early twentieth century. Bronfman's and Rosensteil's gifts to Jewish institutions lent tremendous and unparalleled support to Jewish communal efforts, and it should not discredit their generosity to suggest that they also hoped that their munificence would help to blot their Prohibition-era businesses from the public mind.[87]

Jews' economic relationship with the newly legal American alcohol trade attracted the attentions of *Fortune* magazine, which published several articles that alluded to Jewish involvement in many of the industry's biggest companies. In 1933, as the Twenty-First Amendment was making its way through the states, the magazine referred to "four gentlemen of the faith" who owned or were highly placed in the nation's largest distilling conglomerates, and intimated that their industry leadership represented a preponderance of Jews in the field. These men "once ran the whiskey business" in the United States, *Fortune* claimed, and "are far from unimportant today." The following year, the magazine commented, in language that seems especially repugnant from the other side of the Holocaust, that "for better or for worse, the industry today has hardly the ruling caste that a Hitler would be happy about." Even *Fortune*'s 1936 attempt to counter contemporary accusations that Jews dominated and controlled the American economy noted that "about half the important distilling concerns are Jewish."[88]

Indeed, Jews did reenter the American alcohol business at all levels. But aside from *Fortune*'s articles, their presence in the post-Repeal American alcohol trade elicited minimal response. This was not the result of diminished anti-Semitism, since anti-Jewish sentiment actually intensified during the 1930s and through the end of the Second World War, due to the anxieties wrought by economic crisis at home and political and military trouble abroad. Conspiracy theories abounded, as Jews were accused of dominating the national and global economies and of devising President Roosevelt's New Deal (or, as some called it, the "Jew Deal") for their own benefit.

But Jewish alcohol entrepreneurs were no longer subjects of scrutiny, in part because the presence of Jews in the trade had diminished significantly, especially in the spaces where their presence had roused concern. Post-Repeal modifications in the American alcohol industry itself played a role in this development. Legislators at both the state and federal level were eager to reorient public alcohol commerce and consumption so that it had no resemblance to the pre-Prohibition industry, and many of the regulations they instituted had the intended effect. Some state legislatures established rigorous licensing systems that limited the number of alcohol retailers in any given location and imposed strict regulations and high tax levies on their businesses. A few states created liquor monopolies, where consumers purchased their alcohol directly from state-run liquor stores. The "tied-house" system was declared illegal, and several localities actually forbade alcohol retailers from calling their establishments "saloons." Public drinking now occurred in taverns, bars, cocktail lounges, and grills, and fewer of them dotted the urban landscape.[89]

Changes in Jewish socioeconomic practices further diminished American attention to Jews' relation to alcohol. Jewish occupational trends shifted in the years after the Second World War, as American Jews gravitated toward white-collar occupations such as medicine, law, and education. The proportion of Jews in craft and service jobs decreased, not only relative to previous generations but also compared to non-Jews. Self-employment, one of the features of saloon or liquor store proprietorship that practitioners found most appealing, also declined among Jews during the postwar period.[90] American Jewry's mass entry into the professional middle class resulted in their gradual abandonment of the commercial tendencies that had led American Jews into the production and purveyance of alcohol in the first place. Further, the children of Jews in small businesses were less likely to follow their fathers into that line of work; but for those who did take over the family businesses, if the alcohol trade had been the family business before Prohibition, they had almost certainly abandoned it during the 1920s and found a new product to sell.

Jews were not the only alcohol entrepreneurs for whom this was the case. Thousands of brewers, distillers, wholesalers, and retailers, of all ethnic backgrounds, had left the business when their product became illegal. Only a few maintained or developed their stock; most sold everything, including manufacturing and storage facilities. When Repeal came, the small number of firms that kept their businesses intact—on the off chance that just this day would eventually arrive—had a significant advantage over their competitors. As Daniel Okrent wrote of the American brewing industry, these farsighted alcohol entrepreneurs had a "head start . . . [that] triggered a consolidation of the market that would never end."[91] As we have seen, a few Jews benefited from a similar consolidation process in the liquor trade. For most American Jews, however, an industry that might have enticed their parents' generation was no longer as easy to enter.

Because of American Jews' diminished numbers in the alcohol business, the malevolent Jewish alcohol entrepreneur disappeared from the cast of American Jewish stereotypes. But a reduction in their number was not the only factor. Prohibitionist anti-Semitism had always been a manifestation of other anxieties, and even a small number of Jewish entrepreneurs in a worrisome industry could provoke an anti-Semitic response at a time when alcohol commerce aroused anger and alarm. The principal reason why Americans no longer thought of Jewish alcohol entrepreneurs as a threat was because they no longer considered the alcohol industry to be a menacing presence. Alcohol continued to provoke anxiety in some quarters, but the prevailing discourse on the subject reverted to pre–Civil War tactics: educating individual consumers about the dangers of alcohol, rather than seeking to condemn and suppress its production or distribution. Jews' relation to alcohol dropped out of national debates about alcohol, in other words, because those who sought to vilify the trade had lost in a most resounding way.

Conclusion

"My father owned a saloon off Grove Street in East Orange," the scholar of classical literature confided to his friend. "He was one of those Jewish saloon keepers" whose establishments could be found "all over New Jersey" in the middle years of the twentieth century. The saloon was of the rougher sort—the scholar suspected ties to the Newark mobster and former bootlegger Joe Reinfeld—and the saloonkeeper, who had only a seventh-grade education, wanted better for his son. "Everything in life," the scholar recalled, "including the saloon—*beginning* with the saloon—was always pushing me to be a serious student." After he fulfilled his working-class parents' aspirations by becoming "an ultra-respectable college professor" and then a dean of faculty, he nursed a quiet resentment against those who invoked his "barroom brawler" roots—like his college president, who "liked to tell people that my success as a dean flowed from learning my manners in a saloon."[1]

Coleman Silk, the classicist and taverner's son, proffers an autobiography that maps with precision onto the story of American Jews' move away from the retail sector of the alcohol trade in the years following the Second World War. Silk had left his father's barroom behind, ascending into a realm of American occupational life, the academic study of literature, from which Jews had previously been excluded.[2] Silk's choice of a career in academia over life behind a bar corresponded to American Jews' rising social and economic status after the war. Though Silk's story parallels the broad narrative of American Jews' postwar connection to—and move away from—alcohol commerce, it is, in truth, just a story. As readers of Philip Roth's 2000 novel *The Human Stain* know, Silk is a fictional character. What's more, Silk's father is a fiction within a fiction. The "Jewish saloon keeper's son" was actually a light-skinned black man. In an impulsive act of resistance against both racism and the provinciality of ethno-racial identity itself, Silk decided to pass as white and Jewish when he enlisted in the army. He had lived as a Jew ever since, marrying a Jewish woman and devising a backstory that fit within the postwar American Jewish narrative.

While Silk and his father emerged from Philip Roth's imagination, another postwar writer depicted a similar generational progression that had come from his own family experience. The playwright Herb Gardner was born the year after Repeal to a Russian Jewish immigrant father who ran a bar in downtown New York. He did not follow his father into the business; instead, he wrote a play called *Conversations with My Father*, which was produced in 1992. Eddie, the main character of the play, is a Russian Jewish immigrant who runs a bar in lower Manhattan. Eddie spent the years since he immigrated to the United States struggling to Americanize and distancing himself from his Jewish heritage. He changed his last name from Goldberg to Ross, festooned his bar with patriotic decorations, and expressed seething contempt for his neighbors and family (including his son) who wanted to maintain some connection with Jewish history. As the drama concludes, it becomes clear that these efforts have done him grave damage; like a replanted tree that fails to take root in its new soil, something in Eddie has died in the United States. The American Jewish saloonkeeper represents for Gardner the Jew as perpetual outsider, a figure who cannot become an acculturated American and remain fully himself.[3]

Gardner and Roth both depict Jewish alcohol entrepreneurs for whom assimilation and upward mobility remain elusive. Only their sons, who took up other occupations and came to adulthood in an era of waning anti-Semitism, are able to achieve what they themselves cannot. The fathers' experiences mirrored those of the generations that preceded theirs, whose engagement in the alcohol trade had complicated Jewish efforts to be accepted into American society. They embody the tensions between Jews' old communal identities, which included a long-standing relationship to alcohol commerce, and their desire to fit into American culture at a time when the alcohol trade was regarded with suspicion.

This image of the Jewish saloonkeeper as a man on the margins is in keeping with American discourses surrounding Jewish alcohol purveyance in the first three decades of the twentieth century. In the years leading up to and during national Prohibition, Jews who made a living selling liquor, or who defended alcohol's legal availability, unwittingly acted as flash points for American anxieties about immigration and capitalism. In a society undergoing rapid demographic and economic transformation, both alcohol and Jews represented elements that many WASPs wanted to hold at bay. Condemnations of Jewish alcohol entrepreneurs were initially limited to Jewish immigrants who served working-class or impoverished customers. As we have seen, critics tendered a harsh critique of Jewish saloonkeepers, and of

American Jewish economic activity, by intimating that Jews' presence in the saloon trade proved their failure to assimilate and essential incompatibility with American values. As denunciations grew in volume and frequency, they came to encompass middle-class and native-born Jewish alcohol manufacturers and wholesalers as well, and were eventually intertwined with anti-Semitic allegations that Jews sought to control or dominate sectors of the national (or global) economy.

A handful of observers continued to warn against Jewish alcohol entrepreneurs in the years following Repeal, especially in the face of the industry's rapid consolidation. If *Fortune*'s editors had seemed mildly irked by the presence of Jewish distillers in the reinstated liquor industry in the 1930s, the independent scholar Ernest Gordon was downright infuriated. One of the few Americans still decrying Repeal and warning against liquor power a decade after Prohibition had ended, Gordon adhered to an especially paranoid version of the populist school of prohibitionism. He insisted that Wall Street tycoons and liquor industrialists had manipulated American society into repealing Prohibition and conspired to reintroduce "narcotic" beer into American culture in order to "etherize radical movements." Among those at the heart of the "sinister power" of the liquor trust, he wrote in 1943, were Jews. "Formerly the German brewer took the lead" in corrupting government and society for its own profit, Gordon wrote, but "now the Jewish whisky-truster runs neck to neck with him." These Jewish liquor dealers and their Jewish lawyers operated in collusion with the Catholic Church, he continued, which had invested most of its American financial portfolio in Jewish-run whiskey businesses.[4]

Gordon also took American Jewish communal leaders to task for what he saw as their failure to publicly rebuke Jewish bootleggers during Prohibition. He expressed particular anger at Stephen S. Wise, even though Wise had been one of the few Jews to publicly support prohibition before the Eighteenth Amendment was ratified. For Gordon, that was not enough. "When Rabbi Wise tells us that 'the only hope of the world is that Israel and Christendom stand together,'" he wrote, "we ask, 'why then did you not stand with us? Why did you not rise up and rebuke those [Jews] who were destroying the Eighteenth Amendment?'" Jewish leaders' unwillingness to denounce Jewish bootleggers during Prohibition, and their reluctance to condemn Jewish alcohol industrialists currently, according to Gordon, rendered American Jews' loyalty to the United States suspect. "Jewish leaders should disassociate themselves and their community" from Jewish liquor manufacturers, he insisted, for such men were no better than "sellers of potato schnapps [from] the villages of Eastern Europe . . . with little understanding for American ideals of law and decency and freedom." American Jews' failure to amputate the whiskey industrialists from the communal body, he suggested, could mean only that they were all still aliens, too.[5] Fifteen years after Gordon's book appeared, the *American Mercury*—the journal of opinion founded by H. L. Mencken and edited by him for much of the interwar period, and which embraced a fanatical anti-Communist and anti-Semitic editorial stance after the Second World War—contended that the Rothschilds, the Bronfmans, and a cabal of American Jews (a collective of industrialists, lawyers, former bootleggers, and religious leaders) had conspired to take control of the global liquor trade and influence the American government so that the industry would be structured for their sole benefit.[6]

Neither Gordon's book nor the *Mercury*'s argument, however, garnered an audience; they occupied the remote fringes of American conversations about both alcohol commerce and Jewish entrepreneurial behavior. Indeed, it would be fair to say that in the mainstream of American culture, those conversations ceased altogether, in part because Jews' actual presence in American alcohol commerce was in decline. Further, those who remained in the trade were no longer regarded suspiciously, because alcohol itself had ceased to inspire the anxiety it had in the past. Prohibition failed to a degree that its nineteenth- and early twentieth-century advocates could not have imagined. Alcohol's menace had been almost entirely neutralized, its presence domesticated by home consumption (facilitated by new packaging technologies and household refrigeration), a general acceptance of women's social drinking, and acknowledgment by most medical professionals that moderate alcohol consumption would not lead inevitably to alcoholism, ruin, and death.[7] The increased presence of far more dangerous narcotics in American life surely played a role as well, making alcohol seem innocuous by comparison.

By the time Roth and Gardner brought their Jewish saloonkeeper characters into being, concerns about American Jews' relation to alcohol had been effectively erased from national discussions of Jewish identity. Comfortably ensconced in the mainstream of American culture, able to participate in most any sector of economic, political, and social life they chose, unequivocally included as a constituent element in the national body, Jews were far less likely to fear that their engagement in commercial occupations would cause their fellow citizens to distrust their commitment to American values. By the end of the twentieth century, Jews' historical participation in the American alcohol industry had become a nonissue.

With the evaporation of the anxieties surrounding Jewish alcohol commerce came a reemergence of alcohol-related historical figures in fiction and popular culture. Indeed, as we have seen, the last years of the twentieth century saw a surge in American Jews' fascination with the Jewish bootlegging gangster cohort of the Prohibition era; men who were once regarded as threats to national security, not to mention Jews' security, have since been reimagined in popular culture as figures of kitschy ethnic pride. Such affection is certainly not immaterial for the makers and marketers of "He'Brew," an independent craft brewing company that advertises its product as "The Chosen Beer" and employs a range of Jewish religious and cultural icons, from Hasidim to Lenny Bruce, in its cheeky packaging.[8] While Louis Marshall had "always regretted that Jews were engaged" in the alcohol trade, it is certainly not a subject that inspires regret in these modern American Jews.

Roth's and Gardner's allusions to Jews' connection to alcohol commerce, on the other hand, were far bleaker—and they were not alone. Bernard Malamud also offered unhappy characterizations of Jewish alcohol entrepreneurs. Nat Lime, the protagonist of Malamud's short story "Black Is My Favorite Color" (1963), owns a struggling liquor store in Harlem and is resented, even despised, by the neighborhood's black residents, whom he desperately wants to befriend. And as did Roth's *Human Stain*, Malamud's *The Tenants* (1971) features a metafictional Jewish alcohol dealer: Willie, an aspiring black writer and the story's antagonist, produces a short work called "The First Pogrom in the U. S. of A.," wherein Harlem's Jewish pawnbrokers, shoe dealers, and the proprietor of "Goldberg's Liquor Emporium" are lined up against a wall and shot.[9] For Malamud's characters, too, alcohol-related occupations obstruct their full acculturation and act as a barrier to their feeling truly "at home" in their American settings. Alcohol commerce renders them alienated men, estranged to the communities where they sold their wares, seemingly belonging to no place.

It is of no small importance that race figures centrally in Malamud's narratives. This focus alludes to the actual presence of Jewish alcohol entrepreneurs in black neighborhoods after the Second World War. This was the era of "white flight," the tail end of African Americans' migratory surge from the South to the industrial regions of the North. As blacks moved in, the newly "white" ethnic populations that had populated these quarters since the turn of the century joined the postwar American exodus to racially exclusive and exclusionary suburbs. But many Jewish shop owners and petty entrepreneurs remained in place, selling furniture, clothing, groceries, and liquor to "redlined" neighborhoods populated by increasingly ghettoized African Americans. Jewish entrepreneurs were often disliked, and sometimes even despised, by their African American customers, who accused them of exploiting their neighborhoods and strategically undermining black competitors.[10]

This tension between blacks and Jews, whose wildly divergent experiences as ethno-racially marginalized groups shaped their long and complicated historical relationship, has fascinated and distressed American Jews since the 1960s. At the same time, Jews in the process of achieving rapid upward mobility, and whose opportunities for acculturation seemed boundless, found the alienated condition of the fictional Jewish alcohol entrepreneur to be both unsettling and deeply compelling. Well after anti-alcohol ideologies had been rendered irrelevant in the United States, the Jewish saloonkeeper and liquor store owner of postwar American fiction recalled an era when American Jews' commercial activities reinforced their status as "strangers." When Jews were experiencing acceptance into the American mainstream—a state of affairs that threatened to weaken communal ties—the appearance of this marginalized figure in American Jewish fiction and popular culture suggests that alcohol commerce represented American Jews' ambivalence toward acculturation during the postwar era. Though "nostalgia" might be too strong a word, these characters acted as a metaphor for the Jewish outsider at precisely the moment when Jews' relegation to the peripheries of American society seemed to be a thing of the past. Even when grimly depicted, these characters manifested American Jews' ongoing attraction and commitment to the idea of communal distinctiveness. The continuing appeal of certain aspects of Jewish identity as markers of difference partly explains American Jews' current interest in the history of Jewish bootleggers and mobsters; repugnant though their behavior may have been, they self-identified as Jews, without hesitation or equivocation.

The history of American Jews' relation to alcohol commerce makes one fact incontrovertibly clear: Jewish entrepreneurial history matters. Jews' relationships to commercial capitalism, to particular commodities, to one another within commodity chains (even illicit ones), and to their customers and competitors profoundly shaped their experiences, both as members of a community endeavoring to define Jewish identity in their new setting, and as immigrants and outsiders striving to become more secure in their American identities. Their shared connections could tie them together in ways that nourished and comforted them. When their merchandise was reviled, as was the case with alcohol during the late nineteenth and early twentieth centuries, it not only undermined their status as Americans, but also threatened to untether their attachments to one another.

Examining this aspect American Jewish economic life shines light on broader historical developments as well. Jews' engagement in the American alcohol trade helps explain the industry's growth; and their involvement in "wet" politics offers a new angle from which to survey the political and cultural landscape of the day. Significantly, it clarifies the evolution of American attitudes during a period when both alcohol and Jews acted as lightning rods for American concerns about race and immigration, urbanization, and commercial capitalism. Jews' relation to alcohol conflicted with anti-alcohol activists' principles, which eventually became the principles of the American political mainstream. For temperance advocates and prohibitionists, to be truly American was to reject alcohol purveyance.

American Jews responded to the anti-alcohol movement variously and inconsistently, and never collectively repudiated their connection to the trade. As a result, Jews struggled to prove that they were in fact loyal Americans, even as they disagreed among themselves about whether alcohol commerce or consumption should remain a component of American Jewish identity. It was a precarious position to be in, a problem solved less by any decisions or actions on the part of Jews than by the collapse of the political movement that had vilified alcohol in the first place. But during the years between the end of the Civil War and the repeal of Prohibition, their relation to alcohol commerce typified, and even magnified, the challenges Jews faced in the process of becoming American.

Notes

NOTES TO THE INTRODUCTION

1. Izzy Einstein, *Prohibition Agent No. 1* (New York: Frederick A. Stokes Company, 1932), 232–33.

2. Herbert Asbury, *The Great Illusion: An Informal History of Prohibition* (Garden City, N.Y.: Doubleday & Company, 1950), 211–13.

3. The "anti-alcohol movement," as I use the term, refers to American efforts to limit alcohol production and consumption in the broadest sense. Ideological and strategic differences between the "temperance" and "prohibition" movements will be elaborated on in later chapters. Briefly put, the temperance movement addressed the problem of consumption most directly, and its primary strategy was to exert pressure on individual drinkers. The prohibition movement, on the other hand, focused on systemic rather than individual reform, and sought to hinder the production and sale of alcohol through political and legal channels. These two movements overlapped significantly, however. "Prohibition" with a capital *P* will only be used in reference to the law put in place after the ratification of the Eighteenth Amendment.

4. "Sermon on Jewish People," n.d., E. B. M. Browne Collection, MS 639, box 1, folder 18, American Jewish Archives, Cincinnati (hereafter referred to as AJA).

5. *Jewish Criterion* (Pittsburgh), May 31, 1918, 94.

6. "How Jews Gained American Liquor Control," *Dearborn (Mich.) Independent*, December 17, 1921, reprinted in Henry Ford, *Aspects of Jewish Power in the United States*, vol. 4 of *The International Jew: The World's Foremost Problem* (Dearborn, Mich.: Dearborn Publishing Co., 1922), 7–18.

7. Nathan Glazer, "The Study of Man: Why Jews Stay Sober," *Commentary*, February 1952, 183.

8. Thomas Pegram, *Battling Demon Rum: The Struggle for a Dry America* (Chicago: Ivan R. Dee, 1998), 91.

9. David E. Kyvig's review essay of Richard Hamm's *Shaping the Eighteenth Amendment* presents a brief, cogent, and useful summary of the historiography on the subject. See "The Character of the Cork Determines the Flow from the Flask," *Reviews in American History* 24, no. 1 (March 1996): 114–19.

10. Norman Clark, *Deliver Us from Evil: An Interpretation of American Prohibition* (New York: Norton, 1976); James H. Timberlake, *Prohibition and the Progressive Movement, 1900–1920* (Cambridge, Mass.: Harvard University Press, 1966). For a "politics from below" interpretation, see Jed Dannenbaum, *Drink and Disorder: Temperance Reform in Cincinnati from the Washingtonian Revival to the WCTU* (Chicago: University of Chicago

Press, 1984); Barbara Leslie Epstein, *The Politics of Domesticity: Women, Evangelism, and Temperance in Nineteenth-Century America* (Middletown, Conn.: Wesleyan University Press, 1981). Bryan quoted in Lawrence Levine, *The Unpredictable Past: Explorations in American Cultural History* (New York: Oxford University Press, 1993), 197.

11. Richard Hofstadter, *The Age of Reform: From Bryan to F.D.R.* (New York: Vintage Books, 1955), 289; Joseph Gusfield, *Symbolic Crusade: Status Politics and the American Temperance Movement* (Urbana: University of Illinois Press, 1963). In *Profits, Power, and Prohibition: Alcohol Reform and the Industrializing of America, 1880–1930* (Albany: State University of New York Press, 1989), John J. Rumbarger claims that conservative businessmen instigated the prohibition movement with their own economic interests in mind.

12. Jack S. Blocker, Jr., *Retreat from Reform: The Prohibition Movement in the United States, 1890–1913* (Westport, Conn.: Greenwood Press, 1976); see also Pegram, *Battling Demon Rum*, and his article "Hoodwinked: The Anti-Saloon League and the Ku Klux Klan in 1920s Prohibition Enforcement," *Journal of the Gilded Age and Progressive Era* 7, no. 1 (2008): 89–119.

13. Notable exceptions include David E. Kyvig, *Repealing National Prohibition* (Chicago: University of Chicago Press, 1979); Kenneth D. Rose, *American Women and the Repeal of Prohibition* (New York: New York University Press, 1996). For a case study of German American response to the movement, see Peter N. Stearns, "Social Movements and the Symbolism of Public Demonstrations: The 1874 Women's Crusade and German Resistance in Richmond, Indiana," *Journal of Social History* 32, no. 3 (1999): 557–88.

14. The book that arguably launched the debate about immigrant adaptation among ethnic historians was Oscar Handlin, *The Uprooted: The Epic Story of the Great Migrations That Made the American People* (New York: Little, Brown, 1951), which made a case that American society exerted an irresistibly powerful assimilative force on newcomers. This view was challenged in the 1970s and 1980s by scholars who emphasized immigrant agency and cultural continuity. Of note was John Bodnar's *The Transplanted: A History of Immigrants in Urban America* (Bloomington: Indiana University Press, 1985), which argued for the complexity and variety of immigrant experience. "Varying degrees of commitment to an assortment of cultures and ideologies were evident," he wrote. "Not everyone faced identical experiences" (xvi). Most immigration historians currently take a position that favors complexity and in-group variation; see, for example, George J. Sanchez, *Becoming Mexican American: Ethnicity, Culture, and Identity in Chicano Los Angeles, 1900–1945* (New York: Oxford University Press, 1993). A list of monographs on this subject is far too vast to include here, but for a useful discussion of trends in the historiography, see Alan M. Kraut, "A Century of Scholarship in American Immigration and Ethnic History," in *A Century of American Historiography*, ed. James M. Banner, Jr. (New York: Bedford/St. Martin's, 2010), 124–40.

15. Recent historians of the American Jewish experience have made a great effort to challenge previous scholarly assertions that Americanization was a linear process and relatively unproblematic. Becoming American, they assert, was a constant negotiation and sometimes required painful compromises. See, for instance, Eric L. Goldstein, *The Price of Whiteness: Jews, Race, and American Identity* (Princeton, N.J.: Princeton University Press, 2006).

16. The exception to this rule is kosher wine that has been made "mevushal" through boiling or, more recently, flash pasteurization. Cooked wine is unfit for "idolatrous" use, according to Jewish law, and can be handled by gentiles.

17. David Kraemer, *Jewish Eating and Identity through the Ages* (New York: Routledge, 2007), 129–31.

18. Salo W. Baron and Arcadius Kahan, *Economic History of the Jews* (New York: Schocken Books, 1975), 20.

19. Baron and Kahan, *Economic History of the Jews*, 132–33; Jane S. Gerber, *Jewish Society in Fez, 1450–1700* (Leiden: E. J. Brill, 1980), 180–82; *Medieval Islamic Civilization: An Encyclopedia*, ed. Josef W. Meri (New York: Routledge, 2006), vol. 1, p. 26, s.v. "alcohol."

20. Baron and Kahan, *Economic History of the Jews*, 136; Werner J. Cahnman, *German Jewry: Its History and Sociology* (New Brunswick, N.J.: Transaction, 1989), 44–45; Stefi Jersch-Wenzel, "Jewish Economic Activity in Early Modern Times," in *In and Out of the Ghetto: Jewish-Gentile Relations in Late Medieval and Early Modern Germany*, ed. R. Po-Chia Hsia and Hartmut Lehmann (New York: Cambridge University Press, 1995), 98–99; Jacob Katz, *Tradition and Crisis: Jewish Society at the End of the Middle Ages* (New York: New York University Press, 1993), 18–19; Yisrael Yaakov Yuval, "Nice Aroma, Complicated Bouquet: Review of 'Principles and Pressures: Jewish Trade in Gentile Wine in the Middle Ages' by Haym Soloveitchik," *Haʾaretz*, September 29, 2004. Communications to Dr. Hartmut Lehmann from Dr. Friedrich Battenberg and Dr. Sabine Ullmann, generously made available to the author by Dr. Lehmann, have served as an additional source.

21. Fernand Braudel's monumental scholarship on developments in European capitalism in the early modern period is especially instructive. On credit and the development of monetary economies, see his book *The Structures of Everyday Life*, vol. 1 of *Civilization and Capitalism, 15th–18th Century* (New York: Harper & Row, 1981), 436–78; on the development of trans-regional trade networks, see pp. 138–230. On Jewish involvement in global trade networks, see, for instance, Jonathan I. Israel, *European Jewry in the Age of Mercantilism, 1550–1750* (Oxford: Clarendon Press, 1985); Werner E. Mosse, *Jews in the German Economy: The German-Jewish Elite, 1820–1935* (Oxford: Clarendon Press, 1987); Sarah Abrevaya Stein, *Plumes: Ostrich Feathers, Jews, and a Lost World of Global Commerce* (New Haven, Conn.: Yale University Press, 2008).

22. Tun Yuan Hu, *The Liquor Tax in the United States, 1791–1947* (New York: Columbia University Press, 1950), appendix 1.

23. Passing reference can be found in, Lucy Dawidowicz, "The Business of American Jews (Notes on a Work in Progress)," in *What Is the Use of Jewish History?* (New York: Schocken Books, 1992), 251; Jacob Rader Marcus, *United States Jewry, 1776–1985* (Detroit: Wayne State University Press, 1993), vol. 3, pp. 228–29, 276–77; Deborah Weiner, *Coalfield Jews: An Appalachian History* (Urbana: University of Illinois Press, 2005), 34–37, 48–50; Lee Shai Weissbach, *Jewish Life in Small-Town America: A History* (New Haven, Conn.: Yale University Press, 2005), 105–23. This list does not include the scholarly and popular works that examine Jewish alcohol commerce during the era of national Prohibition, which will be examined more fully in chapters 5 and 6.

24. A representative sample of these works must include the following: Irving Howe, *World of Our Fathers: The Journey of the East European Jews to America and the Life They Found and Made* (New York: Harcourt Brace Jovanovich, 1976); Daniel Soyer, "*Landsmanshaftn* and the Jewish Labor Movement: Cooperation, Conflict, and the Building of Community," *Journal of American Ethnic History* 7, no. 2 (1988): 22–45; Susan Glenn, *Daughters of the Shtetl: Life and Labor in the Immigrant Generation* (Ithaca, N.Y.: Cornell University Press, 1990); Nan Enstad, *Ladies of Labor, Girls of Adventure* (New York:

Columbia University Press, 1999); Tony Michels, *A Fire in Their Hearts: Yiddish Socialists in New York* (Cambridge, Mass.: Harvard University Press, 2005); Eli Lederhendler, *Jewish Immigrants and American Capitalism, 1880–1920* (New York: Cambridge University Press, 2009).

25. Andrew R. Heinze, *Adapting to Abundance: Jewish Immigrants, Mass Consumption, and the Search for American Identity* (New York: Columbia University Press, 1990); Jenna Weissman Joselit, *The Wonders of America: Reinventing Jewish Culture, 1880–1950* (New York: Picador, 2002). For a contemporary analysis that extends beyond Jewish consumer practices in the United States, see Marilyn Halter, *Shopping for Identity: The Marketing of Ethnicity* (New York: Schocken Books, 2002). On European Jewish culture and modern consumption practices, see Gideon Reuveni and Nils Roemer, eds., *Longing, Belonging, and the Making of Jewish Consumer Culture* (Leiden: Brill, 2010).

26. Jonathan Karp, "It's the Economy, Shmendrick!: An 'Economic Turn' in Jewish Studies?," *AJS Perspectives*, Fall 2009, 8–11; Stein, *Plumes*, 6–9. Exceptions include (but are not limited to) Neal Gabler, *An Empire of Their Own: How the Jews Invented Hollywood* (New York: Crown Books, 1988); and Leon Harris, *Merchant Princes: An Intimate History of the Jewish Families Who Built Great Department Stores* (New York: Harper & Row 1979).

27. Dawidowicz, "Business of American Jews," 252.

28. Ibid. Sociologists refer to "middleman minority" populations, or ethnic groups who occupy intermediary roles in trade and commerce and whose socioeconomic concentration often provokes the suspicion of native-born locals. At the turn of the twentieth century, Max Weber designated such economic actors as "pariahs," and Georg Simmel referred to them as "strangers." For more recent examinations, see Edna Bonacich, "A Theory of Middleman Minorities," *American Sociological Review* 38, no. 5 (1973): 583–94; Ivan Light and Steven J. Gold, *Ethnic Economies* (San Diego: Academic Press, 2000); Walter Zenner, *Minorities in the Middle: A Cross-Cultural Analysis* (Albany: State University of New York Press, 1991). Simon Kuznets offers both cultural and quantitative analysis of Jewish economic activity in "Economic Structure and the Life of the Jews," in *The Jews: Their History, Culture, and Religion*, ed. Lewis Finkelstein, 3rd ed. (New York: Harper, 1960), vol. 2, pp. 1597–1666. An interesting and unconventional discussion of Jews and other middleman minorities is offered in Yuri Slezkine, "Mercury's Sandals: The Jews and Other Nomads," in *The Jewish Century* (Princeton, N.J.: Princeton University Press, 2004), 4–39. My own analysis of Jewish participation in the American alcohol trade suggests that broad categorizations fail to consider contextual details. Hostility toward Jewish alcohol entrepreneurs developed over time, in parallel with developments within anti-alcohol ideologies. While the sociological literature on middleman minorities can explain some aspects of this phenomenon, it elides too much to be useful as an organizing principle.

29. Dawidowicz, "Business of American Jews," 240. For an example of work that has been done on the sociology of Jewish ethnic entrepreneurial practices, see Ewa Morawska, *Insecure Prosperity: Small-Town Jews in Industrial America, 1890–1940* (Princeton, N.J.: Princeton University Press, 1996).

30. For scholarship that examines the relationship between anti-Semitism and specific commodities, see Jay A. Gertzman, *Bookleggers and Smuthounds: The Trade in Erotica, 1920–1940* (Philadelphia: University of Pennsylvania Press, 1999).

31. John Higham, "Anti-Semitism in the Gilded Age: A Reinterpretation," *Mississippi Valley Historical Review* 43, no. 4 (March 1957): 563–64.

32. Goldstein, *Price of Whiteness*, 102–8.

33. *Eleventh Census of the United States* (1890), vol. 2: *Population*, 304, 484–85. These numbers include both male and female saloonkeepers, but they do not include bartenders, who are counted as a separate category.

NOTES TO CHAPTER 1

1. Jack S. Blocker, Jr., "Introduction," in *Alcohol, Reform, and Society: The Liquor Issue in Social Context*, ed. Jack S. Blocker, Jr. (Westport, Conn.: Greenwood Press, 1979), 7.

2. A very selective list of general books on the topic: Blocker, *Retreat from Reform*; Clark, *Deliver Us from Evil*; Dannenbaum, *Drink and Disorder*; Epstein, *Politics of Domesticity*; Gusfield, *Symbolic Crusade*; Pegram, *Battling Demon Rum*; Madelon Powers, *Faces along the Bar: Lore and Order in the Workingman's Saloon, 1870–1920* (Chicago: University of Chicago Press, 1998); W. J. Rorabaugh, *The Alcoholic Republic: An American Tradition* (New York: Oxford University Press, 1979); Rumbarger, *Profits, Power, and Prohibition*; Timberlake, *Prohibition and the Progressive Movement*; Ian R. Tyrrell, *Sobering Up: From Temperance to Prohibition in Antebellum America, 1800–1860* (Westport, Conn.: Greenwood Press, 1979). The most recent addition to the shelves, and a worthy one, is Daniel Okrent, *Last Call: The Rise and Fall of Prohibition* (New York: Scribner, 2010).

3. See, for example, Stanley Baron, *Brewed in America: A History of Beer and Ale in the United States* (Boston: Little, Brown, 1962); Gerald Carlson, *The Social History of Bourbon: An Unhurried Account of Our Star-Spangled American Drink* (Louisville: University Press of Kentucky, 1963); Perry R. Duis, *The Saloon: Public Drinking in Chicago and Boston, 1880–1920* (Urbana: University of Illinois Press, 1983); Sarah Hand Meacham, *Every Home a Distillery: Alcohol, Gender, and Technology in the Colonial Chesapeake* (Baltimore: Johns Hopkins University Press, 2009); Amy Helaine Mittleman, "The Politics of Alcohol Production: The Liquor Industry and the Federal Government, 1862–1900" (Ph.D. diss., Columbia University, 1986); Maureen Ogle, *Ambitious Brew: The Story of American Beer* (Orlando: Harcourt, 2006); and Thomas Pinney's two-volume survey, *A History of Wine in America*, published by the University of California Press in 1989 and 2005.

4. On this wave of Jewish immigration to the United States, see Avraham Barkai, *Branching Out: German-Jewish Immigration to the United States, 1820–1914* (New York: Holmes and Meier, 1994); Hasia Diner, *A Time for Gathering: The Second Migration, 1820–1880* (Baltimore: Johns Hopkins University Press, 1992).

5. Frank H. Bunce, "Dreams from a Pack: Isaac Wolfe Bernheim and Bernheim Forest," *Filson Club History Quarterly* 47, no. 4 (1973): 323–26; Weissbach, *Jewish Life in Small-Town America*, 353; *A History of the Jews of Louisville, Ky.* (New Orleans: Jewish Historical Society, 1900), 33–34.

6. Isaac Wolfe Bernheim, *The Story of the Bernheim Family* (Louisville: John P. Morton and Company, 1910), 43–44; Bunce, "Dreams from a Pack," 323; Lee Shai Weissbach, "Stability and Mobility in the Small Jewish Community: Examples from Kentucky History," *American Jewish History* 79, no. 3 (1990): 355. Quote from Isaac Wolfe Bernheim, *The Closing Chapters of a Busy Life* (Denver: Welch-Haffner Printing Company, 1929), 114–17. Interview with Robert Paul in Oral Histories: Ethnic Communities part 4, Jewish Community Center Collection, University Archives and Records Center, University of Louisville.

7. *Bonfort's Wine and Liquor Circular* (New York), August 12, 1901, 11–12.

8. Mark Edward Lender and James Kirby Martin, *Drinking in America: A History* (New York: Free Press, 1982), 31–33; Peter Park, "The Supply Side of Drinking: Alcohol Production and Consumption in the United States before Prohibition," *Contemporary Drug Problems* 12, no. 4 (Winter 1985): 483–85; Rorabaugh, *Alcoholic Republic*, 54, 69, 80.

9. This fascination with Scots-Irish immigration's influence on American political history and racial identity is still present and powerful in American culture. For its most recent popular iteration, see James Webb, *Born Fighting: How the Scots-Irish Shaped America* (New York: Broadway Books, 2004).

10. Baron and Kahan, *Economic History of the Jews*, 139.

11. William L. Downard, *Dictionary of the History of the American Brewing and Distilling Industries* (Westport, Conn.: Greenwood Press, 1980), 24, 28, 157.

12. Interview with Herbert B. Ehrmann in American Jewish Committee Oral History Collection, Dorot Jewish Division, New York Public Library; *A History of the Jews of Louisville, Ky.*, 115.

13. The total population of Louisville in 1900 was 204,371, of whom approximately 7,000 were Jewish. The total number of whiskey producers, rectifiers, and wholesalers in 1900 was 99, of whom 25 were Jewish. These numbers refer only to proprietors of businesses that distilled, rectified, or wholesaled hard liquors, and do not include employees of such establishments, nor do they include proprietors or employees of breweries, wineries, saloons, or liquor stores. Percentages determined by consulting the following sources: Carol Ely, *Jewish Louisville: Portrait of a Community* (Louisville: Jewish Community Federation of Louisville's Foundation for Planned Giving, 2003), 49–63; John E. Kleber, ed., *The Encyclopedia of Louisville* (Lexington: University Press of Kentucky, 2001); *A History of the Jews of Louisville, Ky.*; Jacob Rader Marcus, *To Count a People: American Jewish Population Data, 1585–1984* (Lanham, Md.: University Press of America, 1990), 77; *Caron's Louisville City Directory for 1899* (Louisville: C. K. Caron, 1899), available at the University Archives and Records Center, University of Louisville; *Twelfth Census of the United States* (1900), vol. 1: *Population*, 180; U.S. Census Manuscript Schedules for 1900, Kentucky, Jefferson County, Louisville City, Ward 3, ED (Enumeration District) 32, no. 4; Ward 5, ED 55, no. 8; Ward 6, ED 62, nos. 3, 4; Ward 7, ED 67, nos. 9, 15; ED 68, no. 11; Ward 8, ED 75, no. 8. Archival holdings consulted include Louisville YMHA Records, Jewish Community Center Collection, and Jewish Community Oral Histories, all in University Archives and Records Center, University of Louisville; Kentucky vols. 24–29, R. G. Dun & Co. credit report volumes, Baker Library Historical Collections, Harvard Business School (hereafter cited as R. G. Dun & Co.). Many thanks also to Herman Meyer & Son Funeral Directors, and Marcia Hertzman at the Temple in Louisville. As with any work of American Jewish social history, because of the voluntary nature of American religious affiliation, some American Jews were never recorded as such. It is possible, therefore, that the numbers of alcohol entrepreneurs who were Jewish by birth are even higher than has been stated here.

14. Duis, *The Saloon*, 21–45.

15. In 1870, 6,780 of the 11,246 brewers working in the United States were German born. In 1880, 9,925 of the country's 16,278 brewers and maltsters were of German birth. *Ninth Census of the United States* (1870), vol. 1: *Population*, 680; *Tenth Census of the United States* (1880), vol. 1: *Population*, 748. Although Germany was not established as a unified nation until 1871, the U.S. census of 1870 lists fourteen central European principalities, collectively, as "Germany." Clearly, even though the country did not formally exist yet, it was generally accepted that these states were connected to one another by a common history, language, culture, and politics.

16. In Cincinnati in 1880, for instance, 527 of the 727 men working in the city's breweries were German natives; 365 of Brooklyn's 501 brewers were German born; and in Milwaukee, 370 of the total 508 local brewers and maltsters had emigrated from German-speaking central Europe. Newark's brewer community was particularly German in character, as only 42 of the city's 246 brewers were *not* German. *Tenth Census of the United States* (1880), vol. 1: *Population*, 865, 871, 886, 889.

17. *The History of Brewing and the Growth of the United States Brewers' Association* (New York: United States Brewers' Association, 1937), 6; Baron, *Brewed in America*, 175–78, 216–17; Ogle, *Ambitious Brew*, 13–14, 33–34; Rorabaugh, *Alcoholic Republic*, 109; Hermann Schluter, *The Brewing Industry and the Brewery Workers' Movement in America* (New York: Burt Franklin, 1910), 68–69. For more on the late nineteenth-century brewing industry, see Martin Stack, "Local and Regional Breweries in America's Brewing Industry, 1865 to 1920," *Business History Review* 74, no. 3 (Autumn 2000): 435–63.

18. Cahnman, *German Jewry*, 31, 39, 74.

19. Mosse, *Jews in the German Economy*, 105.

20. U.S. Census Manuscript Schedules for 1870, California, Anaheim Santa Ana Township, Los Angeles County, no. 24.

21. *Atlanta City Directory*, 1885 (Atlanta: Norwood, Connelly & Co., 1885); *Atlanta City Directory, 1890* (Atlanta: R. L. Polk and Co., 1890); *Atlanta City Directory, 1900* (Atlanta: Maloney Directory Co., 1900); *Jewish Sentiment and Echo* (Atlanta), August 12, 1898, 10; Todd Ashley Herring, "Saloons and Drinking in Mississippi from the Colonial Era to Prohibition" (M.A. thesis, Mississippi State University, 1991), v, 58–61, 76. On the anti-alcohol movement and religion in the late nineteenth-century South, see Joe L. Coker, *Liquor in the Land of the Lost Cause: Southern White Evangelicals and the Prohibition Movement* (Lexington: University Press of Kentucky, 2007). On German-Jewish sociality in nineteenth-century Atlanta, see Steven Hertzberg, *Strangers within the Gate City: The Jews of Atlanta, 1845–1915* (Philadelphia: Jewish Publication Society of America, 1978), 50–54.

22. Rolf Hoffman, "The Originators of Rheingold Beer: From Ludwigsburg to Brooklyn—a Dynasty of German-Jewish Brewers," http://www.beerhistory.com/library/holdings/hofmann-rheingold.shtml; Will Anderson, *The Breweries of Brooklyn: An Informal History of a Great Industry in a Great City* (Croton Falls, N.Y.: Self-published, 1976), 100–111.

23. *Ninth Census of the United States* (1870), vol. 3: *Wealth and Industry*, 396; *Tenth Census of the United States* (1880), vol. 2: *Manufacturing*, 52–53; *Eleventh Census of the United States* (1890), vol. 6: *Report on Manufacturing Industries in the United States*, 234–37.

24. Katz, *Tradition and Crisis*, 19; Yuval, "Nice Aroma, Complicated Bouquet." The scholar David Kraemer has found rabbinic approval of wines produced and handled by non-Jewish monotheists—by Muslims in particular—during the medieval period. Such leniencies were not universally granted, however, and concerns about the ability of alcohol to dissolve cultural boundaries remained a matter of rabbinic debate. Kraemer, *Jewish Eating and Identity through the Ages*, 129–32.

25. Jonathan Sarna, "Passover Raisin Wine, the American Temperance Movement, and Mordecai Noah," *Hebrew Union College Annual* 59 (1988): 271–76. A recipe notebook from late nineteenth-century Baltimore, compiled by an immigrant from eastern Europe, includes a recipe for raisin wine: "2 lbs raisins, 3 qts cold water, handful stick cinnamon, five tablespoon [*sic*] sugar, let this boil until raisins have swelled and water has been

reduced ½ . . . cold press and strain this bag." Recipe Notebook by "Grandma Seligman" (1992.259), date unknown, Collections of the Jewish Museum of Maryland, Baltimore.

26. Recipe Notebook by "Grandma Seligman"; Esther Levy, *Mrs. Esther Levy's Jewish Cookery Book* (Bedford, Mass.: Applewood Books, 1988), 5–8, 138–39. Levy's cookbook, originally published in Philadelphia in 1871, offered several recipes for homemade wine, though none for kosher wine specifically. She did insist, however, that the Jewish house-wife serve only kosher meat in her home. Passover wine, she wrote, was "usually made in this country with raisins."

27. Yitzchak Rivkind, "Wine from the Land of Israel for Sale in New York in 1848," in *Mekorot Chitzonim: Jubilee Anthology of the Mizrachi Organization of America* (New York: Mizrachi Organization of America, 1936), 4–8. Many thanks to Shalom Goldman for alerting me to this item, and to Joab Eichenberg Eilon for translation assistance.

28. *Jewish Messenger* (New York), February 18, 1859, 54. *The Gleaner* (San Francisco), July 5, 1861; Thomas Pinney, *From the Beginnings to Prohibition*, vol. 1 of *A History of Wine in America* (Berkeley: University of California Press, 1989), 254; *Daily News* (Charleston), March 29, 1866, 8.

29. See advertisement for I. Rosenstraus & Bros. in *American Israelite*, March 15, 1867, 3.

30. Emmanuel M. Myers, *The Jews, Their Customs and Ceremonies, with a Full Account of All Their Religious Observances from the Cradle to the Grave* (New York: R. Worthington, 1879), 27. Myers wrote that much kosher wine available in the United States was manufac-tured in "Germany and Australia," but this is undoubtedly a typographical error.

31. Pinney, *From the Beginnings to Prohibition*, 286–89.

32. Charles Stern, a Jew who emigrated from Mainz, worked for German American vintners in Los Angeles and went on to operate his own winery with a series of gentile partners. During the 1880s, Herman and Max Goldschmidt, brothers from Rheinhes-sen, worked with a gentile winemaking family they had known back in Germany. They eventually formed an independent wholesale wine and liquor business, and invested in a six thousand–acre vineyard owned by an Italian immigrant in San Bernardino County. Norton B. Stern and William M. Kramer, "The Wine Tycoon of Anaheim," *Western States Jewish Historical Quarterly* 9 (1977): 277. Interviews with Adlai Goldschmidt and Charles Stern, both in box 2802, Economic Life—Liquor Industry, AJA.

33. Stern and Kramer, "Wine Tycoon of Anaheim," 277; Justin G. Turner, "The First Decade of Los Angeles Jewry: A Pioneer History (1850–1860)," *American Jewish Historical Quarterly* 54, no. 2 (December 1964): 128. Further biographical materials made available to the author by the Orange County Jewish Historical Society, Irvine, California.

34. "Anaheim Wine," February 12, 1864, 8, and "Kosher Wines," April 20, 1864, 6, both from *The Hebrew* (San Francisco).

35. Pinney, *From the Beginnings to Prohibition*, 290–91; Stern and Kramer, "Wine Tycoon of Anaheim," 269; quote from *American Israelite* in Rudolf Glanz, *The Jews of California from the Discovery of Gold until 1880* (New York: Waldon Press, 1960), 108–10.

36. Lee Shai Weissbach points to this tendency in trades other than the wine industry, such as cattle, tourism, oil, and whiskey. Weissbach, *Jewish Life in Small-Town America*, 111–12.

37. Pinney, *From the Beginnings to Prohibition*, 292; Stern and Kramer, "Wine Tycoon of Anaheim," 277.

38. "Wanted," *Twice-a-Month* (Louisville), February 1, 1901; *Jewish Criterion* (Pitts-burgh), October 24, 1902, 7. Many thanks to Martha Berg of Rodef Shalom in Pittsburgh for making me aware of Pittsburgh's resources.

39. Light and Gold, *Ethnic Economies*; Min Zhou, "The Role of the Enclave Economy in Immigrant Adaptation and Community Building: The Case of New York's Chinatown," in *Immigrant and Minority Entrepreneurship: The Continuous Rebirth of American Communities*, ed. John Sibley Butler and George Kozmetsky (Westport, Conn.: Praeger, 2004); on Italian immigrants and the padrone system, see Andrew Rolle, *The Italian Americans: Troubled Roots* (New York: Free Press, 1980), 61–63; Donald R. Taft and Richard Robbins, *International Migrations: The Immigrant in the Modern World* (New York: Ronald Press, 1955), 486–87; on more recent Korean immigrants and *kye* money clubs, see Moon H. Jo, *Korean Immigrants and the Challenge of Adjustment* (Westport, Conn.: Greenwood Press, 1999), 65–66.

40. See the discussion of immigrant in-group hiring practices in Michael Reibel, "Immigrants at Work," in *Contemporary Ethnic Geographies in America*, ed. Ines M. Miyares and Christopher A. Airress (Lanham, Md.: Rowman & Littlefield, 2007), 355–74.

41. Interview with Robert Paul in Oral Histories: Ethnic Communities part 4, Jewish Community Center Records, University Archives and Records Center, University of Louisville. Dreyfuss eventually left the alcohol business and became owner of the Pittsburgh Pirates. "Barney Dreyfuss," in Sam Bernstein, *Deadball Stars of the National League*, ed. Tom Simon (Washington, D.C.: Brassey's, 2004), 147–48.

42. Freiberg & Workum, Hoffheimer & Company, Elias Block & Company, S. Levi & Bros., and Henry Block & Company, *Bonfort's Wine and Liquor Circular* (New York), February 3, 1875, 296.

43. The total population of Cincinnati in 1900 was 325,902, of whom approximately 16,000 were Jewish. The total number of whiskey producers, rectifiers, and wholesalers in 1900 was 152, of whom 36 were Jewish. These numbers refer only to proprietors of businesses that distilled, rectified, or wholesaled hard liquors, and do not include employees of such establishments, nor do they include proprietors or employees of breweries, wineries, saloons, or liquor stores. Percentages determined by consulting the following sources: *1880 Williams' Cincinnati Directory* (Cincinnati: Williams & Co., 1880); *1900 Williams' Cincinnati Directory* (Cincinnati: Williams & Co., 1900); U.S. Census Manuscript Schedules for 1900, Ohio, Hamilton County, Cincinnati City, Ward 26F, ED 227, no. 1; Ward 31B, ED 270, nos. 3–5; Ward 31C, ED 271, no. 9; Ward 31D, ED 242, no. 14; ED 272, no. 20.. Other sources consulted include Barnett Robert Brickner, "Jewish Community of Cincinnati: Historical and Descriptive" (Ph.D. diss., University of Cincinnati, 1933); Stephen G. Mostov, "A 'Jerusalem' on the Ohio: The Social and Economic History of Cincinnati's Jewish Community, 1840–1875" (Ph.D. diss., Brandeis University, 1981); Jonathan Sarna and Nancy H. Klein, *The Jews of Cincinnati* (Cincinnati: Center for the Study of the American Jewish Experience, 1989); and the generous assistance of Kevin Proffitt and his staff at the American Jewish Archives.

44. Nephews Henry Bernheim, Jacob Oppenheimer, and Reuben Levi, and Leopold's son-in-law Simon Hirsch all operated their own wholesaling businesses, as did another unrelated Levi employee, Louis Klein. Brickner, "Jewish Community of Cincinnati," 256; S. Levi & Bros, Ohio, vol. 82, p. 6–7, Hirsch & Loewenstein Wines Liq & Cigars, Ohio, vol. 88, p. 205, Klein & Bernheim, Ohio, vol. 85, p. 119, R. G. Dun & Co.

45. Herman Freiberg, Sigmund Freiberg, J. & A. Freiberg, and Solomon and Simon Klein. Brickner, "Jewish Community of Cincinnati," 254–56; Isaac Landman, ed., *Universal Jewish Encyclopedia* (New York: Universal Jewish Encyclopedia, 1941), vol. 4, pp. 434–35; Charles Frederic Goss, *Cincinnati: The Queen City* (Chicago: S. J. Clarke Publishing Company, 1912), vol. 3, pp. 862–67; Max Burgheim, *Cincinnati in Wort Und Bild* (Cincinnati:

M. & R. Burgheim, 1888), 465–67 (English translation by Stephen Farrelly); *Bonfort's Wine and Liquor Circular* (New York), February 3, 1875, 296; *1900 Williams' Cincinnati Directory*.

46. Charles Dellheim discusses the "demonstration effect," which can help explain "the existence of clusters of Jews within the same economic sector," in "The Business of Jews," in *Constructing Corporate America: History, Politics, Culture*, ed. Kenneth Lipartito and David B. Sicilia (London: Oxford University Press, 2004), 231. On the Westheimer family, see *St. Joseph (Mo.) Telegraph*, April 4, 1996, 1–3; Milton Westheimer, "Gold in Them Thar Hills" (unpublished autobiography), Robert C. and Jean Westheimer Rothenberg Family Papers, MS 684, box 15, AJA. Many thanks to Nancy Toff for making her genealogical research on the Bluthenthals available.

47. Barry Supple, "A Business Elite: German-Jewish Financiers in Nineteenth-Century New York," in *The American Jewish Experience*, ed. Jonathan Sarna (New York: Holmes and Meier, 1997), 107.

48. Burgheim, *Cincinnati in Wort Und Bild*, 465–67; Bunce, "Dreams from a Pack," 327; Hoffman, "Originators of Rheingold Beer"; "Steiner," published by S. S. Steiner in 1982, and made available to author in 2002 by Walter H. Liebman of Rheingold Breweries.

49. Barkai, *Branching Out*, 87.

50. *Bazaar Budget* (Louisville), December 4, 1895.

51. Ely, *Jewish Louisville*, 21–22; Herman Landau, *Adath Louisville: The Story of a Jewish Community* (Louisville: Herman Landau and Associates, 1981), 5–6; Ira Rosenwaike, "The First Jewish Settlers in Louisville," *Filson Club History Quarterly* 53, no. 1 (January 1979): 37–38.

52. Mark Bauman, "Factionalism and Ethnic Politics in Atlanta: The German Jews from the Civil War through the Progressive Era," *Georgia Historical Quarterly* 82, no. 3 (Fall 1998): 537; Hertzberg, *Strangers within the Gate City*, 18–24.

53. Landman, *Universal Jewish Encyclopedia*, vol. 4, pp. 434–35.

54. *A History of the Jews of Louisville, Ky.*; Ely, *Jewish Louisville*, 58–59.

55. *1880–81 Gould's Peoria City Directory* (Peoria, Ill.: D. B. Gould, 1880); *1900 Franks' Peoria City Directory* (Peoria, Ill.: J. W. Franks and Sons, 1900); Downard, *Dictionary of the History of the American Brewing and Distilling Industries*, 219; James M. Rice, *Peoria City and County: A Record of Settlement, Organization, Progress, and Achievement* (Chicago: S. J. Clarke Publishing Company, 1912), 167–68, s.v. "Samuel Woolner, Jr."

56. Isaac W. Bernheim, Louis Barkhouse, Samuel Ullman, M. Schwartz, Charles Goldsmith, and Nathan F. Block. Letter from Nathan F. Block to Simon A. Dreifus, November 21, 1892, made available to the author by Marcia Hertzman at the Temple of Louisville.

57. Levi Cohen, Morris Teitlebaum, Alex Dittler, Max Franklin, Aaron Haas, and Isaac Guthman. *Atlanta Constitution*, January 4, 1892, 6. Levi Cohen, then president of this organization, had also served as Atlanta's first mohel (ritual circumciser). Hertzberg, *Strangers within the Gate City*, 22. Thanks to Ann Abrams for sharing her genealogical research on Isaac Guthman and Aaron Haas. On Isaac Guthman as purveyor of "excellent cider," see *Atlanta Constitution*, February 8, 1876, 3.

58. *Thirty-Third Annual Report of the Union of American Hebrew Congregations* (Cincinnati: UAHC, 1907), 5708.

59. Moshe Davis, *The Emergence of Conservative Judaism: The Historical School in 19th Century America* (Philadelphia: Jewish Publication Society of America, 1963); Abraham Karp, *Jewish Continuity in America: Creative Survival in a Free Society* (Tuscaloosa: University of Alabama Press, 1998), 196–203, 205–14; Jonathan Sarna, *American Judaism* (New Haven, Conn.: Yale University Press, 2004), 124–34.

60. Diner, *A Time for Gathering*, 114–19.

61. Naomi W. Cohen, *Encounter with Emancipation: The German Jews in the United States, 1830–1914* (Philadelphia: Jewish Publication Society of America, 1984), 52–55.

62. Quote from Alfred Selligman in *Louisville Courier-Journal*, January 1, 1896.

63. Diner, *A Time for Gathering*, 142–60.

64. Brickner, "Jewish Community of Cincinnati," 255; Burgheim, *Cincinnati in Wort Und Bild*, 647; Sarna and Klein, *Jews of Cincinnati*, 141–43.

65. Carolyn Gray LeMaster, *A Corner of the Tapestry: A History of the Jewish Experience in Arkansas, 1820s–1990s* (Fayetteville: University of Arkansas Press, 1994), 125–26, 167; Jack E. Davis, *Race against Time: Culture and Separation in Natchez since 1930* (Baton Rouge: Louisiana State University Press, 2001), 110; Herring, "Saloons and Drinking in Mississippi from the Colonial Era to Prohibition," 64.

66. Stern and Kramer, "Wine Tycoon of Anaheim," 272.

67. James K. Mercer and C. N. Vallandigham, *Representative Men of Ohio, 1896–97* (Columbus, Ohio: Mercer and Vallandigham, 1896), 87; Goss, *Cincinnati*, vol. 4, p. 199.

68. "Committees Have Been Appointed." *Atlanta Constitution*, March 12, 1900, 5.

69. In 1900, the total population of Atlanta was 89,872, of whom approximately 2,000, or 2.2 percent, were Jews. That year, 29 of 411 participants in the local alcohol industry (7.0 percent) were Jewish. This number includes both proprietors and employees of all categories of alcohol production, distribution, and retail. Percentages and ethnic identities determined by consulting the following sources: *Atlanta City Directory, 1900*; U.S. Census Manuscript Schedules for 1900, Georgia, Fulton County, Atlanta City, Ward 1, ED 42, no. 17; Ward 2, ED 50, nos. 15, 20; ED 51, nos. 19, 24–25; ED 54, nos. 6, 8, 18; Interment Records of Oakland Cemetery and Westview Cemetery, and Hebrew Benevolent Congregation Membership Questionnaires, MSS 59, 20.7–10, all at the Ida Pearle and Joseph Cuba Community Archives of the William Breman Jewish Heritage Museum, Atlanta. Other sources consulted include Bauman, "Factionalism and Ethnic Politics in Atlanta"; Hertzberg, *Strangers within the Gate City*; Janice O. Rothschild, *As But a Day: The First Hundred Years, 1867–1967* (Atlanta: The Temple, 1967); Solomon Sutker, "The Jews of Atlanta: Their Structure and Leadership Patterns" (Ph.D. diss., University of North Carolina, 1950).

70. Cohen, *Encounter with Emancipation*, 130–31.

71. *Bonfort's Wine and Spirit Circular* (New York), June 25, 1880, 53.

72. Goss, *Cincinnati*, vol. 3, pp. 817–18, 862–65; vol. 4, pp. 224, 320–21, 436–39, 493, 716–17.

73. *Bonfort's Wine and Spirit Circular* (New York), May 25, 1880, 24, February 25, 1890, 230, December 25, 1889, 110. The word *Metziah* is also found on March 10, 1890, 259, and is used in a similarly friendly and joshing manner. On the ethnic heritage of *Bonfort's* founders, see the issue from February 1934, 12.

74. R. G. Dun & Co. was founded by Lewis Tappan in 1841 as the Mercantile Agency, and renamed in 1859. Much has been written about the company, and especially about the evangelical Protestant morality that guided its founder. See James D. Norris, *R. G. Dun & Co., 1841–1900: The Development of Credit-Reporting in the Nineteenth Century* (Westport, Conn.: Greenwood Press, 1978); Rowena Olegario, "Credit and Business Culture: The American Experience in the Nineteenth Century" (Ph.D. diss., Harvard University, 1998); Bertram Wyatt-Brown, "God and Dun & Bradstreet, 1841–1851," *Business History Review* 40, no. 4 (Winter 1966): 432–50. The name of the agency changed again, to Dun & Bradstreet, in 1933.

75. Hoffheimer Brothers, Ohio, vol. 78, pp. 382–83, R. G. Dun & Co.

76. Frank, Silverman & Co., Ohio, vol. 85, p. 244, R. G. Dun & Co.

77. Julius Isaacs, New Jersey, vol. 23, p. 66, R. G. Dun & Co.

78. See, for instance, Barkai, *Branching Out*, 87–88; Bodnar, *The Transplanted*, 135–36; Stephen G. Mostov, "Dun and Bradstreet Reports as a Source of Jewish Economic History, 1840–1875," *American Jewish History* 72, no. 3 (1983): 339; Howard M. Sachar, *A History of the Jews in America* (New York: Alfred A. Knopf, 1992), 50, 58. David A. Gerber, in his essay on R. G. Dun & Co.'s investigations of the Jews of Buffalo, asserts that anti-Semitic stereotypes permeated credit assessments of American Jewish businesses. Though his analysis of the local scene is nuanced and informative, his primary sources are limited to Buffalo only. "Cutting Out Shylock: Elite Anti-Semitism and the Quest for Moral Order in the Mid-Nineteenth-Century Market Place," *Journal of American History* 69, no. 3 (December 1982): 615–37. Among those who have written against this general historical analysis are Dawidowicz, "Business of American Jews," 243–47; Rowena Olegario, "'That Mysterious People': Jewish Merchants, Transparency, and Community in Mid-Nineteenth Century America," *Business History Review* 73, no. 2 (Summer 1999): 161–89.

79. L. Cohen, Georgia, vol. 13, p. 29, and Loeb & Bloom, Kentucky, vol. 32, p. 107, R. G. Dun & Co.

80. Higham, "Anti-Semitism in the Gilded Age."

81. For an excellent analysis of the cultural clashes between American and Jewish business practices, see Olegario, "That Mysterious People."

82. Dawidowicz, "Business of American Jews," 245.

83. Isaac Jacobs, Ohio, vol. 79, p. 131, H. Jacobs, Ohio, vol. 79, p. 131, C. H. Samuels, Ohio, vol. 82, p. 14, R. G. Dun & Co.

84. Selig & Bros., Georgia, vol. 14, p. 154, R. G. Dun & Co.

85. Wyatt-Brown, "God and Dun & Bradstreet," 440.

86. Fleischmann's summer resort did not remain the exclusive province of wealthy Jews for long. Within decades, his town and the surrounding area became a summer vacation destination for less moneyed and less acculturated eastern European Jewish immigrants as well; the region was so thoroughly associated with American Jews that it was referred to as the "Jewish Alps" and the "borscht belt." Phil Brown, *Catskill Culture: A Mountain Rat's Memories of the Great Jewish Resort Area* (Philadelphia: Temple University Press, 1998), 25. On Joseph Seligman at Saratoga Springs, see "A Sensation at Saratoga," *New York Times*, June 19, 1877.

NOTES TO CHAPTER 2

An earlier version of chapter 2 has been previously published as "'No Whisky Amazons in the Tents of Israel': American Jews and the Gilded Age Temperance Movement," *American Jewish History* 94, no. 3 (September 2008): 143–73.

1. Sarah F. Ward, *The White Ribbon Story: 125 Years of Service to Humanity* (Evanston, Ill.: Signal Press, 1999), 10.

2. *American Jewess*, November 1895, 101. See also *New York Times*, October 24, 1895, 15.

3. *American Jewess*, November 1895, 101.

4. Gaines M. Foster, *Moral Reconstruction: Christian Lobbyists and the Federal Legislation of Morality, 1865–1920* (Chapel Hill: University of North Carolina Press, 2002), 40–46;

Jonathan Sarna, "Christian America or Secular America? The Church-State Dilemma of American Jews," in *Jews in Unsecular America*, ed. Richard John Neuhaus (Grand Rapids, Mich.: Eerdmans, 1987), 8–19.

5. Rorabaugh, *Alcoholic Republic*, 20–21.

6. Edward Behr, *Prohibition: Thirteen Years That Changed America* (New York: Arcade Publishing, 1996), 13–17; Pegram, *Battling Demon Rum*, x; Rorabaugh, *Alcoholic Republic*, 25–57. Rorabaugh's work remains the standard for scholarly analysis of early American discussions of alcohol consumption, though his quantifications of alcohol consumption have been disputed. See Jack S. Blocker, "Consumption and Availability of Alcoholic Beverages in the United States, 1863–1920," *Contemporary Drug Problems* 21 (Winter 1994): 631–66.

7. Dannenbaum, *Drink and Disorder*; Paul E. Johnson, *A Shopkeeper's Millennium: Society and Revivals in Rochester, New York, 1815–1837* (New York: Hill and Wang, 1978); Rorabaugh, *Alcoholic Republic*; Tyrrell, *Sobering Up*. For a helpful synthesis of this literature, see Pegram, *Battling Demon Rum*, 3–42.

8. The most totalized and successful legislation in this vein was the Maine Law, a statewide total prohibition law passed in 1851 and copied by a dozen other northeastern and midwestern states—though rarely without ugly and factionalizing political battles. By the 1870s, only Maine, Vermont, and New Hampshire still had their prohibition laws on the books. Tyrrell, *Sobering Up*, 252–89. On the shift from moral suasion to no-license legislation in Cincinnati, see Dannenbaum, *Drink and Disorder*, 106–55. Sometimes temperance coercion took extralegal forms; Paul E. Johnson's study of Rochester, New York, shows that socioeconomic coercion was also a powerful tool, especially when imposed on workingmen by their employers. See Johnson, *Shopkeeper's Millennium*, 116–28.

9. Tyrrell, *Sobering Up*, 54–86.

10. Gerrit Smith quoted in ibid., 145.

11. Sarna, "Passover Raisin Wine, the American Temperance Movement, and Mordecai Noah," 272–76.

12. Jonathan D. Sarna, *Jacksonian Jew: The Two Worlds of Mordecai Noah* (New York: Holmes and Meier, 1981), 104, 159–60.

13. Morton Borden, *Jews, Turks, and Infidels* (Chapel Hill: University of North Carolina Press, 1984), 42–52; Cohen, *Encounter with Emancipation*, 72–90; Jonathan Sarna and David G. Dalin, *Religion and State in the American Jewish Experience* (Notre Dame, Ind.: University of Notre Dame Press, 1997), 4–6.

14. James G. Heller, *Isaac M. Wise: His Life, Work, and Thought* (New York: Union of American Hebrew Congregations, 1965), 267–68.

15. Isaac Mayer Wise, *An Essay on the Temperance Question* (Cincinnati: Bloch Publishing Company, 1880), 7.

16. Foster, *Moral Reconstruction*, 27–30, 94–117; Batya Miller, "Enforcement of the Sunday Closing Laws on the Lower East Side, 1882–1903," *American Jewish History* 91, no. 2 (2003): 269–85; Pegram, *Battling Demon Rum*, 45–46.

17. Egal Feldman, *Dual Destinies: The Jewish Encounter with Protestant America* (Urbana: University of Illinois Press, 1990), 115–16.

18. *American Israelite*, March 6, 1868, 4; Marcus Jastrow, *A Lecture on Temperance, Delivered March 28, 1874, at Broad Street Synagogue of Philadelphia* (New York: Hebrew Orphan Asylum Printing Establishment, 1874), 6; Gustav Gottheil, "Judaism and Temperance," in

Central Conference of American Rabbis, *Sermons by American Rabbis* (Chicago: Central Conference Publication Committee, 1896), 178.

19. In 1865 and 1900, the total number of alcohol dealers per 1,000 in the United States was between 2.4 and 2.6. During the 1870s, that number was consistently 3.0 and over, and peaked in 1873 at 4.2. Blocker, "Consumption and Availability of Alcoholic Beverages in the United States," 642–43.

20. Pittsburgh Platform quoted in Cohen, *Encounter with Emancipation*, 198. See also Arthur Hertzberg, *The Jews in America: Four Centuries of an Uneasy Encounter: A History* (New York: Columbia University Press, 1997), 135–37.

21. American Jewish commitments to social justice activism became more pronounced during the first two decades of the twentieth century. An earlier exception, Rabbi Emil Hirsch of Chicago, was responsible for this above-quoted plank in the Pittsburgh Platform. See Cohen, *Encounter with Emancipation*, 194–202; Feldman, *Dual Destinies*, 132–38.

22. Ernest H. Cherrington, *The Evolution of Prohibition in the United States of America* (Montclair, N.J.: Patterson Smith, 1969), 184–236.

23. Ibid., 167.

24. Ibid. On state prohibition laws, see pp. 176–82; for a chronology of temperance achievements from 1869 to 1893, see pp. 184–248.

25. Wise, *An Essay on the Temperance Question*, 7.

26. Moshe Davis has written that "Jastrow considered Wise flippant," which suggests that their differences were personal as well as theological. Jastrow was one of the leaders of the "Historical School" of American Judaism, which was a precursor of the Conservative movement. Davis, *Emergence of Conservative Judaism*, 138–46, 342–44; Sarna, *American Judaism*, 184.

27. *Jewish Exponent* (Philadelphia), April 12, 1889, 5. This issue also includes a short summary of a sermon by the Italian-born Rabbi Sabato Morais of Mikveh Israel Synagogue in Philadelphia. Morais was an ally of Jastrow's in efforts to maintain a traditionalist practice in American Judaism, and though he did not share Jastrow's anti-prohibition fervor, he agreed with Jastrow's position on the matter. See also Naomi W. Cohen, *What the Rabbis Said: The Public Discourse of Nineteenth-Century American Rabbis* (New York: New York University Press, 2008), 41.

28. Foster, *Moral Reconstruction*, 80–81; Rumbarger, *Profits, Power, and Prohibition*, 57–59, 66–68.

29. Cohen, *Encounter with Emancipation*, 195.

30. Ibid., 130; Diner, *A Time for Gathering*, 144–47.

31. Jastrow, *A Lecture on Temperance*, 1.

32. Catherine Gilbert Murdock, *Domesticating Drink: Women, Men, and Alcohol in America, 1870–1940* (Baltimore: Johns Hopkins University Press, 1998), 16–18.

33. Jack S. Blocker, *"Give to the Winds Thy Fears": The Women's Temperance Crusade, 1873–1874* (Westport, Conn.: Greenwood Press, 1985); Epstein, *Politics of Domesticity*, 93; Murdock, *Domesticating Drink*, 18–25; Pegram, *Battling Demon Rum*, 58–65.

34. Faith Rogow, *Gone to Another Meeting: The National Council of Jewish Women, 1893–1993* (Tuscaloosa: University of Alabama Press, 1993); William Toll, "A Quiet Revolution: Jewish Women's Clubs and the Widening Female Sphere, 1870–1920," *American Jewish Archives* 41, no. 1 (Spring/Summer 1989): 7–26; *American Jewess*, February 1898, 251–52.

35. Jastrow, *A Lecture on Temperance*, 4, 6.

36. *American Israelite*, March 13, 1874, 4.

37. *New York Times*, February 14, 1874, 5.

38. *Chicago Daily Tribune*, April 1, 1874, 4. Freudenthal, who arrived in the United States in 1865 from Germany, held a doctorate in addition to rabbinical ordination. In 1886, after serving congregations in Pennsylvania for nineteen years, he became the superintendent of the Hebrew Orphans Asylum in Baltimore. See Nurith Zmora, *Orphanages Reconsidered: Child Care Institutions in Progressive Era Baltimore* (Philadelphia: Temple University Press, 1994), 25–26.

39. *Jewish South* (Atlanta), April 19, 1878, 4.

40. Much appreciation to my colleague Dr. Jacqueline Rouse, who inspired me to think more deeply about both Jewish women's attitudes toward temperance and the meaning of their relative silence in the face of their community's general anti-prohibitionist ardor.

41. Jastrow, *A Lecture on Temperance*, 6.

42. Kant quoted in Glazer, "Why Jews Stay Sober," 184. Many thanks to Dr. Sander Gilman, who generously made his unpublished work on this topic, "Race (again) and Medicine (again): The Jews and Alcoholism," available to me.

43. *Life*, January 7, 1886, 30; *Christian Advocate* (New York), October 24, 1889, 685; Richard Wheatley, "The Jews of New York," *Century Magazine*, January 1892, 328; Richard Wheatley, "The Jews of New York II," *Century Magazine*, February 1892, 512–32.

44. *American Israelite*, June 17, 1881, 396, May 19, 1882, 372. Wise's claim was mostly true, though not devoid of exception: he neglected to include the Nazarites, an ascetic sect that included Samson and Samuel, within his analysis of ancient Israel's attitudes toward wine.

45. *American Israelite*, May 24, 1872, 8.

46. *American Israelite*, April 20, 1888, 4.

47. Gottheil, "Judaism and Temperance." See also Cohen, *What the Rabbis Said*, 29–30.

48. Joseph Krauskopf, *Does Prohibition Prohibit?* (Cincinnati: Bloch Publishing, 1889), 19, 21.

49. Jastrow, *A Lecture on Temperance*, 10–11.

50. J. J. Peres, "Temperance among Israelites," *The Occident* (Philadelphia), June 2, 1859, 56–57.

51. P. Wiernik, "Jewish Temperance Men," *Jewish Gazette* (New York), November 25, 1898.

52. Esther J. Ruskay, *Hearth and Home Essays* (Philadelphia: Jewish Publication Society of America, 1902), 94.

53. Ibid.

54. Ibid, 95.

55. Goldstein, *Price of Whiteness*, 22–23. This idealization of gender roles and the circumscription of the public and private spheres was by no means unique to the middle-class American Jewish experience. American Jews adopted Victorian-era ideas about the proper place of women, which they reconfigured for their own religious and cultural purposes. On the creation of the female sphere in the nineteenth-century United States, and shifting gender ideologies during the expansion of the market economy, see Carroll Smith-Rosenberg, *Disorderly Conduct: Visions of Gender in Victorian America* (New York: Oxford University Press, 1985).

56. Wheatley, "The Jews of New York," 327, 332; Wheatley, "The Jews of New York II," 513, 515.

57. Gusfield, *Symbolic Crusade*, 55–57; Lender and Martin, *Drinking in America*, 58–63; Pegram, *Battling Demon Rum*, 41–42. W. J. Rorabaugh has criticized Gusfield's analysis of the relationship between temperance and nativism, claiming that Gusfield gives nativism too much causal power in the development of the temperance movement, when in fact the anti-liquor movement predated mass immigration by decades. This useful critique does not obviate the fact that anti-immigrant sentiment became a factor in the temperance movement. See Rorabaugh, *Alcoholic Republic*, 188. Ian Tyrrell points out that though "temperance served as a vehicle for the expression of nativist tensions," there is copious evidence to suggest that many nativists "were either indifferent or hostile to temperance." See Tyrrell, *Sobering Up*, 264–65.

58. Hasia Diner writes that Irish immigrants embraced the stereotype as an assertion of ethnic identity, and as a way to cope with dire poverty, squalid living conditions, and the hostility they encountered from native-born Americans. Hasia Diner, *Hungering for America: Italian, Irish, and Jewish Foodways in the Age of Migration* (Cambridge, Mass.: Harvard University Press, 2001), 133–41. See also James R. Barrett, "Why Paddy Drank: The Social Importance of Whiskey in Pre-famine Ireland," *Journal of Popular Culture* 11, no. 1 (1977): 155–66. On anti-Catholicism and its conflation with anti-liquor sentiment, see Dannenbaum, *Drink and Disorder*, 114–17; John Higham, *Send These to Me: Jews and Other Immigrants in Urban America* (New York: Atheneum, 1975), 68–69.

59. Paul Boyer, *Urban Masses and Moral Order in America, 1820–1920* (Cambridge, Mass.: Harvard University Press, 1978), 77; Timberlake, *Prohibition and the Progressive Movement*, 152–53; Peter Conolly-Smith, *Translating America: An Immigrant Press Visualizes American Popular Culture, 1895–1918* (Washington, D.C.: Smithsonian Books, 2004), 31; Raymond Michael Ralph, "From Village to Industrial City: The Urbanization of Newark, New Jersey, 1830–1860" (Ph.D. diss., New York University, 1978), 152, 95; Pegram, *Battling Demon Rum*, 77–78. Some who sympathized with the temperance movement were quite openly nativist, as suggested by a sample of doggerel from Worcester, Massachusetts: "The Irish and the Dutch; they don't amount to much / For the Micks have their whiskey and the Germans guzzle the beer / And all we Americans wish they had never come here." Roy Rosenzweig, *Eight Hours for What We Will: Workers and Leisure in an Industrial City, 1870–1920* (Cambridge: Cambridge University Press, 1983), 50.

60. Blocker, *Give to the Winds Thy Fears*, 62–64; Kathleen Neils Conzen, *Immigrant Milwaukee, 1836–1860* (Cambridge, Mass.: Harvard University Press, 1976), 210; Dannenbaum, *Drink and Disorder*, 224–25; Pegram, *Battling Demon Rum*, 77–78; Carl Wittke, *The German-Language Press in America* (Lexington: University of Kentucky Press, 1957), 131, 62–63.

61. Cohen, *Encounter with Emancipation*, 58–61; Diner, *A Time for Gathering*, 162–65.

62. Interview with Iphigne Molony Bettman recorded on May 13, 1964, available at AJA. Though *American Jewess* praised leaders of the women's suffrage movement in the 1890s, and the National Council of Jewish Women supported women's right to vote, Jewish women's organizations did not openly and actively take up the suffrage cause until the 1910s. Rogow, *Gone to Another Meeting*, 78–85.

63. For more on the "Germanness" of central European Jews in the United States, see Barkai, *Branching Out*, 184–88; Rudolf Glanz, *Jews in Relation to the Cultural Milieu of the Germans in America up to the Eighteen Eighties* (New York: YIVO, 1947); Michael A. Meyer,

"German-Jewish Identity in Nineteenth-Century America," in *Toward Modernity: The European Jewish Model*, ed. Jacob Katz (New Brunswick, N.J.: Transaction, 1987); Stanley Nadel, "Jewish Race and German Soul in Nineteenth-Century America," *American Jewish History* 77, no. 1 (1987): 6–26.

64. Wolf's political efforts on behalf of German American anti-prohibition organizations, which continued until World War I, will be discussed in greater depth in chapter 5.

65. Esther L. Panitz, *Simon Wolf: Private Conscience and Public Image* (Rutherford, N.J.: Fairleigh Dickinson University Press, 1987), 56–57, 70.

66. Annie Wittenmyer, *History of the Woman's Temperance Crusade* (Boston: James H. Earle, ca. 1882), 314.

67. Ibid., 156, 279–80.

68. Carry Nation, *The Use and Need of the Life of Carry A. Nation* (Topeka, Kans.: F. M. Steves and Sons, 1905), 50.

NOTES TO CHAPTER 3

1. "No Jew Trade Wanted," *Jewish Sentiment and Echo* (Atlanta), September 8, 1899, 4.

2. *Jewish Sentiment and Echo* (Atlanta), November 18, 1898, 1.

3. Baron and Kahan, *Economic History of the Jews*, 134–35; Simon Dubnow, *History of the Jews in Russia and Poland from the Earliest Times until the Present Day*, trans. I. Friedlaender (Philadelphia: Jewish Publication Society of America, 1918), vol. 1, p. 67; Gershon David Hundert, "Comparative Perspectives on Economy and Society: The Jews of the Polish Commonwealth—a Comment," in Hsia and Lehmann, *In and Out of the Ghetto*, 103; John Doyle Klier, *Russia Gathers Her Jews: The Origins of the "Jewish Question" in Russia, 1772–1825* (DeKalb: Northern Illinois University Press, 1986), 15. For more on the *arenda* leasing system of assets, monopolies, and government functions, see Baron and Kahan, *Economic History of the Jews*, 125–28.

4. Baron and Kahan, *Economic History of the Jews*, 134–37; Benjamin Nathans, *Beyond the Pale: The Jewish Encounter with Late Imperial Russia* (Berkeley: University of California Press, 2002), 40–44; Michael Stanislawski, *Tsar Nicholas I and the Jews: The Transformation of Jewish Society in Russia, 1825–1855* (Philadelphia: Jewish Publication Society of America, 1983), 173–74.

5. Baron and Kahan, *Economic History of the Jews*, 136; Hans Rogger, *Jewish Policies and Right-Wing Politics in Imperial Russia* (Berkeley: University of California Press, 1986), 127.

6. Klier, *Russia Gathers Her Jews*, 57; Jack Kugelmass, "Native Aliens: The Jews of Poland as a Middleman Minority" (Ph.D. diss., Graduate Faculty of Political and Social Science of the New School for Social Research, 1980), 112; Rogger, *Jewish Policies and Right-Wing Politics in Imperial Russia*, 148.

7. Translation from Michael Wex, *Born to Kvetch: Yiddish Language and Culture in All Its Moods* (New York: St. Martin's Press, 2005), 67; Glenn Dynner, "Tavernkeepers and Crypto-tavernkeepers: Reconsidering the Demise of the Polish Village Jew" (unpublished paper made available by author, 2009), 30–39.

8. Quote from Klier, *Russia Gathers Her Jews*, 87.

9. Dynner, "Tavernkeepers and Crypto-tavernkeepers," 8–11, 16; Klier, *Russia Gathers Her Jews*, 140–42.

10. Stanislawski, *Tsar Nicholas I and the Jews*, 171–74.

11. Kugelmass, "Native Aliens," 79–120. For synopses of a number of Polish novels that include Jewish tavern-keeper characters, see Magdalena Opalski, *The Jewish Tavern-Keeper and His Tavern in Nineteenth-Century Polish Literature* (Jerusalem: Zalman Shazar Center, 1986).

12. Michael Stanislawski, "Russian Jewry, the Russian State, and the Dynamics of Jewish Emancipation," in *Paths of Emancipation: Jews, States, and Citizenship*, ed. Pierre Birnbaum and Ira Katznelson (Princeton, N.J.: Princeton University Press, 1995), 277–78.

13. Alexander Orbach, "The Development of the Russian Jewish Community, 1881–1903," in *Pogroms: Anti-Jewish Violence in Modern Russian History*, ed. John Doyle Klier and Shlomo Lambroza (New York: Cambridge University Press, 1992), 141–42; Rogger, *Jewish Policies and Right-Wing Politics in Imperial Russia*, 135–39.

14. Adam Schupack, "Vodka in the Pale: The Jews, Russian Drinking, and the State Liquor Monopoly" (unpublished seminar paper, Brown University, 1999), 11; Maurice Fishberg, *The Jews: A Study of Race and Environment* (New Brunswick, N.J.: Transaction, 2008), 397; Patricia Herlihy, *The Alcohol Empire: Vodka and Politics in Late Imperial Russia* (New York: Oxford University Press, 2002), 6–7.

15. Isaac M. Rubinow, *The Economic Conditions of the Jews in Russia* (Washington, D.C.: U.S. Government Printing Office, 1907; repr., New York: Arno Press, 1975), 556–57.

16. Dynner, "Tavernkeepers and Crypto-tavernkeepers," 19–22.

17. Quotation from Dubnow, *History of the Jews in Russia and Poland*, vol. 2, pp. 23–24; poem from Baron and Kahan, *Economic History of the Jews*, 138.

18. Estimates of unemployed Jewish tavernkeepers from Rubinow, *Economic Conditions of the Jews in Russia*, 557; Dubnow, *History of the Jews in Russia and Poland*, vol. 2, pp. 23–24.

19. Lederhendler, *Jewish Immigrants and American Capitalism*, 35–37.

20. An overview of the factors that went into immigrants' occupational choices during the late nineteenth and early twentieth centuries is offered in chapter 2 of Bodnar, *The Transplanted*.

21. Joel Perlmann, "Selective Migration as a Basis for Upward Mobility? The Occupations of the Jewish Immigrants to the United States, ca. 1900" (unpublished working paper, 1996), 7–8.

22. For examples of vague language in pre-migrational occupation descriptions, see, for example, Alexander E. Cance, *Recent Immigrants in Agriculture*, part 24 of *Immigrants in Industries*, ed. William P. Dillingham (Washington, D.C.: U.S. Government Printing Office, 1911), vol. 2, part 3, "Recent Immigrants in Agriculture: Hebrews," pp. 86–87, 120–22.

23. Lederhendler, *Jewish Immigrants and American Capitalism*, 41–47.

24. This particular immigrant soon found employment with a produce wholesaler in Atlanta, though there is no record of how long he stayed at that job or what he did next. Letter from David Bressler to Benjamin Wildauer, November 29, 1907, letter from Wildauer to Bressler, December 7, 1907, both in IRO Records, box 34, folder 21, American Jewish Historical Society, New York.

25. *Tenth Census of the United States* (1880), vol. 2: *Manufacturing*, 52–53; *Twelfth Census of the United States* (1900), vol. 7: *Manufactures*, 278; Rumbarger, *Profits, Power, and Prohibition*, 17–20; Downard, *Dictionary of the History of the American Brewing and Distilling Industries*, 28; Hu, *The Liquor Tax in the United States*, 46–47.

26. According to Shelly Tenebaum, by 1918 the most generous Jewish loan associations capped borrowers at $500 a year, and most applicants were loaned less than $100. In many states, that would not even cover the costs of the manufacturing licenses. Shelly Tenenbaum, *A Credit to Their Community: Jewish Loan Societies in the United States, 1880–1945* (Detroit: Wayne State University Press, 1993), 56–58; *Bonfort's Wine and Spirit Circular* (New York), March 25, 1890, 291.

27. *Boston Daily Globe*, August 15, 1897, 6; *Chicago Daily Tribune*, February 17, 1889, 16; *Los Angeles Times*, July 28, 1895, 11; *New York Times*, February 16, 1889, 1, and February 24, 1889, 16.

28. *New York Times*, March 6, 1910, 6; Cance, *Recent Immigrants in Agriculture*, 16, 73, 86–87, 102, 20–23, 30, 39–40.

29. Pinney, *From the Beginnings to Prohibition*, 214–15.

30. Cance, *Recent Immigrants in Agriculture*, 116.

31. William Chazanof, *Welch's Grape Juice: From Corporation to Co-operative* (Syracuse, N.Y.: Syracuse University Press, 1977); Robert C. Fuller, *Religion and Wine: A Cultural History of Wine Drinking in the United States* (Knoxville: University of Tennessee Press, 1996), 87–89.

32. *New York Times*, March 31, 1996, 6; Harvey Finkel, "Kosher Wines," *Massachusetts' Beverage Business*, March 2005, http://www.beveragebusiness.com/archives/article.php?cid=1&eid=23&aid=166; and various materials made available by Norman Schapiro, in possession of author.

33. Sarna, *American Judaism*, 169–70.

34. Alan M. Kraut, "The Butcher, the Baker, the Pushcart Peddler: Jewish Foodways and Entrepreneurial Opportunity in the East European Immigrant Community, 1880–1940," *Journal of American Culture* 6, no. 4 (Winter 1983): 71–83.

35. Moses Rischin, author of a seminal social history of the Jewish Lower East Side, cites an 1899 study that counted thirteen "wine shops" and fifteen "grape wine shops" in the quarter. See *The Promised City: New York's Jews, 1870–1914* (New York: Harper & Row, 1970), 56. For wine and liquor advertisements, see, for instance, from *Di Idishe Gazetn* (New York): I. Bloch & Co., January 6, 1899, 15; I. Goldberg, January 13, 1899, 10; D. Shapiro, January 20, 1899, 6; Strunsky Wine and Liquor, January 5, 1900, 14; and London & Bro. (*sic*), February 2, 1900, 10.

36. On Jewish immigrant adaptation of American consumer practices, see Heinze, *Adapting to Abundance*, 42–48; Harold P. Gastwirt, *Fraud, Corruption, and Holiness: The Controversy over the Supervision of Jewish Dietary Practice in New York City, 1881–1940* (Port Washington, N.Y.: Kennikat Press, 1974), 5–6.

37. Letter from Dov Behr Manischewitz, April 1887, SC-7705, AJA. The Manischewitz Company was not involved in the commercial wine trade until after Repeal, when they licensed their brand name to Monarch Wine in Brooklyn. For more on Dov Behr Manischewitz and his family's matzo industry, see Jonathan Sarna, "Manischewitz Matzah and the Rabbis of the Holy Land: A Study in the Interrelationship of Business, Charity, and Faith" (unpublished paper, 1999), available in Manischewitz Company nearprint file, AJA.

38. Arthur A. Goren, *New York Jews and the Quest for Community: The Kehillah Experiment, 1908–1922* (New York: Columbia University Press, 1970), 77.

39. Advertisement for Rev. H. Rubin, *Di Idishe Gazetn*, February 9, 1900, 10.

40. *Pacific Wine and Spirit Review* (San Francisco), December 31, 1910, 45, November 30, 1911, 49.

41. Ran Aaronsohn, "The Beginnings of Modern Jewish Agriculture in Palestine: 'Indigenous' versus 'Imported,'" *Agricultural History* 69, no. 3 (1995): 438–53; Baron and Kahan, *Economic History of the Jews*, 139–40; Derek J. Penslar, *Zionism and Technocracy: The Engineering of Jewish Settlement in Palestine, 1870–1918* (Bloomington: Indiana University Press, 1991), 18–27.

42. *New York Times*. November 23, 1901, 1, December 14, 1903, 2; *The Federal Reporter: Cases Argued and Determined in the Circuit Courts of Appeals and Circuit and District Courts of the United States* (St. Paul: West Publishing, 1907), vol. 154, pp. 157–59; Simon Schama, *Two Rothschilds and the Land of Israel* (New York: Alfred A. Knopf, 1978), 120–26, 54–55; Jeffrey Shandler, "*Di toyre fun skhoyre*; or, I Shop, Therefore I Am: The Consumer Cultures of American Jews," in Reuveni and Roemer, *Longing, Belonging, and the Making of Jewish Consumer Culture*, 183–200. On Sarasohn's general efforts to introduce modern forms of advertising and merchandizing into New York's Yiddish publications, see Heinze, *Adapting to Abundance*, 150–51, 155–56.

43. *Federal Reporter*, vol. 154, pp. 157–58; *Pacific Wine and Spirit Review* (San Francisco), December 31, 1914, 42.

44. Kraut, "The Butcher, the Baker, the Pushcart Peddler," 80. For an account of a scandal in New York's kosher meat industry by a contemporary observer, see Jonathan Sarna, ed., *People Walk on Their Heads: Moses Weinberger's Jews and Judaism in New York* (New York: Holmes and Meier, 1982), 46–50.

45. Blocker, "Consumption and Availability of Alcoholic Beverages in the United States," 646–47.

46. Jon Kingsdale, "The 'Poor Man's Club': Social Functions of the Urban Working-Class Saloon," *American Quarterly* 25, no. 4 (October 1973): 472–89; Powers, *Faces along the Bar*, 48–71.

47. Clark, *Deliver Us from Evil*, 55–57; Duis, *The Saloon*, 25–29; Kingsdale, "Poor Man's Club," 474; Pegram, *Battling Demon Rum*, 94–97.

48. Okrent, *Last Call*, 26–30.

49. *The Liquor Problem: A Summary of Investigations Conducted by the Committee of Fifty, 1893–1903* (Boston: Houghton Mifflin, 1905; repr., New York: Arno Press, 1970), 23.

50. Ibid., 210–40.

51. Ibid., 125–26; Duis, *The Saloon*, 143–51.

52. *Liquor Problem*, 125–26. For a critical assessment of the Committee of Fifty, see Rumbarger, *Profits, Power, and Prohibition*, 89–101.

53. "Of a Friday in the Jewish Quarter of New York," *Harper's Weekly*, April 19, 1890; *Yidishes Tageblat* quoted in Charles S. Bernheimer, ed., *The Russian Jew in the United States* (Philadelphia: John C. Winston Co., 1905; repr., New York: Augustus M. Kelley Publishers, 1971), 222–23.

54. "Hebrew Advancement in American Business," *Phrenological Journal of Science and Health*, September 1885, 140.

55. Rubinow was using statistics from Russia's 1897 census and the U.S. census of 1900. See Rubinow, *Economic Conditions of the Jews in Russia*, 557.

56. Rischin, *Promised City*, 272.

57. *Social Statistics of a City Parish* (New York: Church Temperance Society, 1894), 45–49, 24.

58. Howe, *World of Our Fathers*, 209; John Kobler, *Ardent Spirits: The Rise and Fall of Prohibition* (London: Michael Joseph, 1974), 179.

59. *Liquor Problem*, 125–26.

60. John Koren, *Economic Aspects of the Liquor Problem: An Investigation Made for the Committee of Fifty* (Boston: Houghton Mifflin, 1899), 224–25; Rischin, *Promised City*, 88, 141; Eric L. Goldstein, "'Sociability and Bright Talk': East Side Cafes and the Jewish Immigrant Public Sphere" (paper presented at the Association of Jewish Studies, Washington, D.C., 2002); Luc Sante, *Low Life: Lures and Snares of Old New York* (New York: Vintage Books, 1991), 329–30; "New York's Jewish Saloons," *New York Sun*, September 29, 1895, 24.

61. This Yiddish drinking song, and others, quoted in Ruth Rubin, *Voices of a People: The Story of Yiddish Folksong*, 2nd ed. (Urbana: University of Illinois Press, 2000), 169–79. The Yiddishist and folklorist Ruth Rubin has pointed out that the *Maskilim*—comparatively secular and integrationist European Jews—might have written some of these drinking songs in order to discredit the exuberantly pious Hasidic movement. The Hasidim's reputation for being overly eager to "gladden the soul" struck the *Maskilim* as degenerate, inappropriate, and offensive. Simon Dubnow articulated the *Maskil*'s impatience for this "ugly passion for alcohol": "Originally tolerated as a means of producing cheerfulness and religious ecstasy, drinking gradually became the standing feature of every gathering. . . . The habit resulted in drowsiness of thought, idleness and economic ruin, insensibility to the outside world and to the social movements of the age, as well as in stolid opposition to cultural progress in general." On the other end of this spectrum are Mark Zborowski and Elizabeth Herzog, whose 1952 ethnography of shtetl life celebrates the Hasid's culture of drinking. "They drink but do not get drunk to a point where they would lose their *yiddishkayt*, their 'human' aspect," the social scientists insisted. "When a *hasid* drinks . . . he merely grows happier and more joyful. . . . They are drunk partly from alcohol and partly from their love and devotion" to their rabbi. Written in the immediate aftermath of the Holocaust, Zborowski and Herzog's *Life Is with People* idealizes eastern European Jewish village culture to such an extent that they ignore the possibility that some Hasidim might actually have had an unhealthy relationship with liquor. Dubnow, *History of the Jews in Russia and Poland*, 124–25; Mark Zborowski and Elizabeth Herzog, *Life Is with People: The Culture of the Shtetl* (New York: Schocken Books, 1973), 175–76.

62. Stories #5 (University Café), #6 (Segal's), #25 (17 Rivington), # 37 and #42 (Jake Wolf's), #49 (Russian Casino), #50 (J. Cohen's), from Vigilantes Committee Reports, 1912–14, Judah Magnes Papers, AJA; Albert Fried, *The Rise and Fall of the Jewish Gangster in America* (New York: Holt, Rinehart and Winston, 1980), 5; Jean Ulitz Mensch, "Social Pathology in Urban America: Desertion, Prostitution, Gambling, Drugs, and Crime among Eastern European Jews in New York City between 1881 and World War I" (Ph.D. diss., Columbia University, 1983), 150, 208, 72–73; Rischin, *Promised City*, 90; Timothy J. Gilfoyle, *City of Eros: New York City, Prostitution, and the Commercialization of Sex, 1790–1920* (New York: Norton, 1992), 244.

63. Michels, *Fire in Their Hearts*, 43.

64. Gerald Sorin, *A Time for Building: The Third Migration, 1880–1920* (Baltimore: Johns Hopkins University Press, 1992), 136–37; Nathan Goldberg, "Occupational Patterns of American Jews," *Jewish Review* 3, no. 1 (1945): 3–24; Morawska, *Insecure Prosperity*, 31–32. See also Aaron Michael Glazer, "Entrepreneurship among Eastern European Jewish Immigrants in Baltimore, 1881–1914" (M.A. thesis, Johns Hopkins University, 2002); Weissbach, *Jewish Life in Small-Town America*, 102–6.

65. Baron and Kahan, *Economic History of the Jews*, xi; Deborah R. Weiner, "The Jews of Keystone: Life in a Multicultural Boomtown," *Southern Jewish History* 2 (October 1999): 4, 7. See also Simon Kuznets, "Economic Structure and the Life of the Jews," in Finkelstein, *The Jews*.

66. Weiner, "Jews of Keystone," 6.

67. In 1900, Newark's population was 246,070—less than a tenth of New York City's population, and not even 20 percent of Philadelphia's. Likewise, Newark's Jewish population, at 15,000, was 3 percent the size of New York's, and a fifth of Philadelphia's. *Twelfth Census of the United States* (1900), vol. 1: *Population*, 268; Marcus, *To Count a People*.

68. Marcus, *To Count a People*, 130; William B. Helmreich, *The Enduring Community: The Jews of Newark and MetroWest* (New Brunswick, N.J.: Transaction, 1999), 14–20; Gary M. Klein, *A Study of the Economic Activity of the Jewish Community of Newark, New Jersey, 1861–1875* (Cincinnati: Hebrew Union College–Jewish Institute of Religion, 1972), 12–14. To determine who among Newark's alcohol purveyors were Jews, the following sources were used: U.S. Census Manuscript Schedules for 1870, New Jersey, Essex County, Newark City, Ward 2, no. 148; U.S. Census Manuscript Schedules for 1880, ED 32, no. 10; U.S. Census Manuscript Schedules for 1900, New Jersey, Essex County, Newark City, Ward 3, ED 27, nos. 4, 7, 8, 32; Ward 4, ED 35, no. 4; Ward 8, ED 79, no. 9; Ward 14, ED 139, no. 11; Ward 15, no. 9; U.S. Census Manuscript Schedules for 1910, New Jersey, Essex County, Newark City, Ward 2, ED 13, no. 18; Ward 3, ED 18, no. 19; ED 19, no. 45; Ward 13, ED 109, no. 28; U.S. Census Manuscript Schedules for 1920, Ward 3, ED 122, no. 16; ED 125, no. 37; the *Israel Kranken Untersteutzung Verein* Collection (4701–4705), Jewish Historical Society of MetroWest, Parsippany, New Jersey (hereafter cited as JHSMW; "*Oheb Shalom* Fair Journal of 1911" and "Jewish Community Blue Book of Newark of 1926," both in collection 6701, folder 21, JHSMW; oral history transcripts made available to JHSMW by William B. Helmreich; Helmreich, *Enduring Community*; online databases of Jewish cemeteries (http://www.jewishgen.org/databases/cemetery/); and the help of several Newark historians and archivists, including Dr. David Cowen, Nat Bodian, Joseph Settani, and Linda Forgosh. This data, and all of the Newark data that follows, should be regarded as fairly impressionistic. None of the sources available represented the majority of Newark's Jewish community at any given time. To find Jewish Newarkers who were not active in the city's Jewish community, information available in censuses—wife and children's names, place of birth, and, when available, native language—helped to determine ethnicity. But this sort of historical investigatory work is necessarily interpretive, and therefore statistically imprecise.

69. Ralph, "From Village to Industrial City," 13, 40–45; Samuel H. Popper, "Newark, New Jersey, 1870–1910: Chapters in the Evolution of an American Metropolis" (Ph.D. diss., New York University, 1951), 23.

70. Popper, "Newark, New Jersey, 1870–1910," 32, 63.

71. Marcus, *To Count a People*, 130.

72. Marilyn R. Kussick, "School Reform as a Tool of Urban Reform: The Emergence of the Twentieth-Century Public School in Newark, New Jersey, 1890–1920" (Ph.D. diss., Rutgers University, 1974), 29.

73. Helmreich, *Enduring Community*, images insert.

74. Ibid., 55, Willard D. Price, *The Ironbound District: A Study of a District in Newark, N.J.* (Newark: Neighborhood House, 1912), 9.

75. Price, *Ironbound District*, 4–5.

76. Ibid., 8.

77. Charles Stephenson, "The Process of Community: Class, Culture, and Ethnicity in Nineteenth-Century Newark," in *New Jersey's Ethnic Heritage: Papers Presented at the Eighth Annual New Jersey History Symposium*, ed. Paul Stellhorn (Trenton: New Jersey Historical Commission, 1978), 95–96.

78. *Twelfth Census of the United States* (1900), vol. 1: *Population*, 268, 612, 666.

79. This was not for lack of trying. In the first decade of the twentieth century, the all-white governments of several southern states attempted to recruit foreign-born settlement. They hoped that immigrant workers would provide energetic labor for the region's growing manufacturing sector, as well as take over farming and sharecropping from black laborers. These were controversial measures, and many southerners suggested that native-born white northerners be invited south instead. "One northern immigrant," declaimed Henry W. Grady, editor in chief of the *Atlanta Constitution*, "is worth fifty foreigners." In the end, these attempts proved mostly unsuccessful, and the recruiting programs were all suspended by 1910. See Rowland T. Berthoff, "Southern Attitudes toward Immigration, 1865–1914," *Journal of Southern History* 17, no. 3 (1951): 342; Dewey Grantham, *Southern Progressivism: The Reconciliation of Progress and Tradition* (Knoxville: University of Tennessee Press, 1982), 299–300; Steve Oney, *And the Dead Shall Rise: The Murder of Mary Phagan and the Lynching of Leo Frank* (New York: Pantheon Books, 2003), 14; C. Vann Woodward, *Origins of the New South, 1877–1913* (Baton Rouge: Louisiana State University Press, 2006), 297–301.

80. *Twelfth Census of the United States* (1900), vol. 1: *Population*, 268, 666. Newark's African American population would increase dramatically over the next several decades, as southern blacks migrated north to find wage labor in northern and midwestern industrial cities. In 1930, Newark's black population numbered 38,800, and many of these new Newarkers moved into the Third Ward, which Jewish Newarkers were in the process of abandoning for the suburbs. See Clement Price, "The Afro-American Community of Newark, 1917–1947: A Social History" (Ph.D. diss., Rutgers University, 1975), 1, 71–72.

81. Gregory Mixon, *The Atlanta Riot: Race, Class, and Violence in a New South City* (Gainesville: University Press of Florida, 2005), 42–43.

82. *Atlanta Constitution*, January 22, 1906; Mark Bauerlein, *Negrophobia: A Race Riot in Atlanta, 1906* (San Francisco: Encounter Books, 2001); 45–46; Hertzberg, *Strangers within the Gate City*, 110–15.

83. *Atlanta City Directory, 1905* (Atlanta: Foote and Davies Co. and Joseph W. Hill, 1905). To determine who among the Decatur Street neighborhood's alcohol purveyors were Jews, the following sources were used: U.S. Census Manuscript Schedules for 1900, Georgia, Fulton County, Atlanta City, Ward 4, ED 61; Hertzberg, *Strangers within the Gate City*; Rothschild, *As But a Day*, 11–19; and Interment Records of Oakland Cemetery and Westview Cemetery; Ahavath Achim Congregation, MSS 21, 20.1–4; and Hebrew Benevolent Congregation Membership Questionnaires, MSS 59, 20.7–10, all at the Ida Pearle and Joseph Cuba Community Archives of the William Breman Jewish Heritage Museum, Atlanta

84. All data on business locations comes from *Atlanta City Directory, 1900* and *Atlanta City Directory, 1905*. Immigration data comes from U.S. Census Manuscript Schedules for 1900, Georgia, Fulton County, Atlanta City, Ward 4, ED 61, and from Hertzberg, *Strangers within the Gate City*. Hyman Mendel later went back into the dry goods business and became the city's largest dry goods wholesaler. See Mark Bauman, "Jewish Community of Atlanta," in *New Georgia Encyclopedia*, http://www.georgiaencyclopedia.org/nge/Article.jsp?id=h-2731&hl=y.

85. *Atlanta Constitution*, January 11, 1896, 9, and November 8, 1905, 4.

86. Atlanta Chamber of Commerce, *Annual Reports of Officers* (Atlanta: Chamber of Commerce, 1906), 32.

NOTES TO CHAPTER 4

1. "Of a Friday in the Jewish Quarter of New York," *Harper's Weekly*, April 19 1890, 306.

2. Burton J. Hendrick, "The Jewish Invasion of America," *McClure's*, March 1913, 154; George Kibbe Turner, "Beer and the City Liquor Problem," *McClure's*, September 1909, 537; John Foster Fraser, *The Conquering Jew* (New York: Funk and Wagnalls, 1915), 108–9; *Atlanta Constitution*, July 15, 1907, 7.

3. Henry A. Scomp, *King Alcohol in the Realm of King Cotton; or, A History of the Liquor Traffic and of the Temperance Movement in Georgia from 1733 to 1887* (Chicago: Blakely, 1888), 765.

4. *The Committee of Twenty-Five, Appointed at the Mass Meeting of Citizens Who Are Not Interested in the Manufacture or Sale of Liquors* (Atlanta: n.p., 1885), 6–8.

5. *Atlanta Constitution*, July 31 1886, 8, August 15, 1886, 7. Hawthorne's comment elicited an angry response from Jacob Jacobson, then rabbi of the Temple, who scolded the minister for "ridicul[ing] and belittl[ing] the Jew." Jacobson also conjured the same image of the Jewish relationship with alcohol as did his rabbinic contemporaries: "With certainly justifiable pride," he wrote, "we claim for the Jew the habit of temperance, for which Dr. H claims to labor." *Atlanta Constitution*, August 17, 1886, 5. On Rabbi Jacobson, see Rothschild, *As But a Day*, 19.

6. According to local newspaper reports, Adolph Brandt, Elias Haiman, Joseph Menko, Julius Dreyfus, and Isaac Haas all participated in rallies organized by the "Antis." The merchant Jacob Haas wrote an open letter to Henry W. Grady criticizing Grady's prohibitionist stance, and signed it "Your anti-prohibition friend." Several of these men had relatives in the city's alcohol trade, but none were themselves so engaged. *Atlanta Constitution*, November 22, 1885, 9, November 24, 1885, 7, November 22, 1887, 5. For membership and leadership rosters of the Conservative Citizens Association, see *Atlanta Constitution*, July 31, 1886, 8, August 19, 1886, 5.

7. Hertzberg, *Strangers within the Gate City*, 160.

8. *Atlanta Journal*, November 1, 1886, 4. The biblical quote cited by the "plain business man" comes from Habakkuk 2:15: "Woe unto him that giveth his neighbor drink, that putteth thy bottle to *him*, and maketh *him* drunken also, that he may look on their nakedness!" *The Holy Scriptures: A Jewish Bible according to the Masoretic Text* (Tel Aviv: Sinai Publishing, 1996), 1096. The *New Oxford* revision of the Old and New Testaments, however, uses "wrath" instead of "bottle," suggesting that drunkenness is intended as a metaphor for loss of reason. See *The New Oxford Annotated Bible* (New York: Oxford University Press, 1973), 1138. For a modern exegetical analysis of the text, see C. F. Whitley, "A Note on Habakkuk 2:15," *Jewish Quarterly Review* 66, no. 3 (January 1976): 143–47.

9. On Grant's Order #11, see Diner, *A Time for Gathering*, 158–60; Leonard Dinnerstein, *Anti-Semitism in America* (New York: Oxford University Press, 1994), 32–33. Dinnerstein's book is the best known and most commonly referenced scholarly monograph on American anti-Semitism. Other important works that engage the topic in its broadest terms are David A. Gerber, ed., *Anti-Semitism in American History* (Urbana: University of Illinois Press, 1986); John Higham, "Social Discrimination against Jews in America, 1830–1930," *Publications of the American Jewish Historical Society* 47, no. 1 (1957): 1–33; Louise A. Mayo, *The Ambivalent Image: Nineteenth-Century America's Perception of the Jew* (Rutherford, N.J.: Fairleigh Dickinson University Press, 1988); Carey McWilliams, *A Mask for Privilege: Anti-Semitism in America* (Boston: Little, Brown, 1949); Robert Rockaway and Arnon Gutfield, "Demonic Images of the Jew in the Nineteenth Century United States," *American Jewish History* 89, no. 4 (2002): 355–81. For a sociological interpretation of economic anti-Semitism spanning back to the ancient period, see Werner J. Cahnman, "Socio-economic Causes of Antisemitism," *Social Problems* 5, no. 1 (1957): 21–29.

10. Higham, *Send These to Me*, 121–22.

11. When spelled with an uppercase *P*, Populism here refers only to the Populist Party, more correctly known as the People's Party, which was founded in 1892. A lowercase *p* refers to populism as a political and ideological system that was taken up by a wide range of political actors, including the Grangers, Farmers' Alliances, and other radical agrarians; advocates of the free coinage of silver; and those workingmen's advocates, such as the Knights of Labor, who aligned themselves with causes such as public ownership of utilities, a graduated income tax, and opposition to the gold standard. Two well-regarded works of scholarship on the history of populism/Populism in the United States are Lawrence Goodwyn, *Democratic Promise: The Populist Moment in America* (New York: Oxford University Press, 1976); and Michael Kazin, *The Populist Persuasion* (New York: Basic Books, 1995). For a useful and thought-provoking inquiry into populists' attraction to the movement and its ideologies in Texas, see James Turner, "Understanding the Populists," *Journal of American History* 67, no. 2 (1980): 354–73.

12. Richard D. Heffner, ed., *A Documentary History of the United States*, 7th ed. (New York: New American Library, 2002), 235–39.

13. Rockaway and Gutfield, "Demonic Images," 378–81; Sorin, *A Time for Building*, 52–55. Historians also take care to point out that American anti-Semitism was not the province of Populists alone. The economic elite, who also feared that the era's changes would destabilize their status, expressed hostility toward Jews as well. The private writings of the Boston Brahmin and turn of the century intellectual Henry Adams, the great grandson of John Adams, were filled with diatribes against Jewish economic behavior. But his brother Brooks was even more open in his hatred. The 1893 financial crisis, he wrote, was the fault of "the rotten, unsexed, swindling, lying Jews represented by J. P. Morgan and the gang." See T. J. Jackson Lears, *No Place of Grace: Antimodernism and the Transformation of American Culture* (Chicago: University of Chicago Press, 1981), 133.

14. See, for example, Frederic Cople Jaher, *Doubters and Dissenters: Cataclysmic Thought in America, 1885–1918* (London: Free Press of Glencoe, 1964), 135; Norman Pollack, "The Myth of Populist Anti-Semitism," *American Historical Review* 68, no. 1 (1962): 76.

15. Dinnerstein, *Anti-Semitism in America*, 48–50; William F. Holmes, "Whitecapping: Agrarian Violence in Mississippi," *Journal of Southern History* 35, no. 2 (1969): 165–85.

16. See Higham, *Send These to Me*, 124–32; Kazin, *Populist Persuasion*, 296n38; Mayo, *Ambivalent Image*, 128–32.

17. Hofstadter, *Age of Reform*, 80.

18. Richard Hofstadter famously defined the populists by their tendency to see themselves as not merely oppressed, but as oppressed "consciously, continuously, and with wanton malice by 'the interests.'" Ibid., 70. He claimed that the populists were unconsciously driven by "status anxiety"—by fear, inspired by downward economic mobility, that they were losing control of American culture and of their own future—toward paranoid and irrational visions of political and economic power struggles. This interpretation of the populist mentalité has been criticized since Hofstadter first offered it in 1955; his critics accuse him of having been blinkered by his own McCarthy-era anxieties.

19. Gusfield, *Symbolic Crusade*, 94–98; Pegram, *Battling Demon Rum*, 107.

20. Rumbarger, *Profits, Power, and Prohibition*, 104; Sam W. Small, *Pleas for Prohibition* (Atlanta: Self-published, 1890), 59.

21. Small, *Pleas for Prohibition*, 54.

22. K. Austin Kerr, *Organized for Prohibition: A New History of the Anti-Saloon League* (New Haven, Conn.: Yale University Press, 1985), 15.

23. The sociologist Joseph R. Gusfield has written that both populism and prohibitionism attracted those who suffered from "a sense of economic and political powerlessness," and who either feared or had experienced a decline in economic and cultural status. Unconsciously motivated by "status anxiety" (a concept Gusfield borrows from Hofstadter; see above), they viewed their adversaries from an irrational, paranoid perspective, interpreting their opponents' successes as evidence that "the people" were victimized by a corrupt political and economic system. This assessment would certainly describe neither every prohibitionist nor every populist. It does, however, point to the uncontroversial fact that both groups feared that the nation was being steered off track by powerful, malevolent forces. See Gusfield, *Symbolic Crusade*, 97–102.

24. Kazin, *Populist Persuasion*, 92. For a similar analysis of southern prohibitionists' hatred of "liquor power," see William A. Link, *The Paradox of Southern Progressivism, 1880–1930* (Chapel Hill: University of North Carolina Press, 1992), 39–49.

25. The issue of prohibitionism's rural or urban character has inspired much scholarly debate. Assertions of its essential rural identity can be found in Gusfield, *Symbolic Crusade*; and Hofstadter, *Age of Reform*. Opposing claims that prohibitionism was the product of middle-class concerns, and that the movement's leaders were on the whole "more urban in origin and residence than the general population," are asserted, quantitatively and convincingly, in Blocker, *Retreat from Reform*, 8–14.

26. On populism's religious commitments, see Bruce Palmer, *"Man over Money": The Southern Populist Critique of American Capitalism* (Chapel Hill: University of North Carolina Press, 1980), 24–25, 126–37. On those of turn of the century prohibitionists, see Blocker, *Retreat from Reform*, 82–88; Kazin, *Populist Persuasion*, 82–96; Timberlake, *Prohibition and the Progressive Movement*, 4–17.

27. Blocker, *Retreat from Reform*, 77–78; Paul E. Isaac, *Prohibition and Politics: Turbulent Decades in Tennessee, 1885–1920* (Knoxville: University of Tennessee Press, 1965), 65–69, 77.

28. The Knights of Labor barred liquor dealers and saloonkeepers from membership in its organization, but the members themselves were of mixed opinion about temperance, and often held their meeting in saloons and other establishments where alcohol was sold.

See Kazin, *Populist Persuasion*, 35. For a contemporary account of the Knights' debate over saloons and temperance, see "The Magnetism of Beer Drawing to Itself Knights of Labor Committees," *New York Times*, July 4, 1886, 5.

29. On the interactions between prohibitionists and the populist movement at the national level, see Blocker, *Retreat from Reform*, 39–61; Clark, *Deliver Us from Evil*, 87; Rumbarger, *Profits, Power, and Prohibition*, 85–88.

30. "Wasson Experiment Station Bulletin," date unknown, in possession of author. For more on Wasson and the Ohio Agricultural Experiment Station, see Christopher Cumo, *A History of the Ohio Agricultural Experiment Station, 1882–1997* (Akron, Ohio: Midwest Press, 1997), 51. On James G. Blaine, see Cyrus Adler, *Jews in the Diplomatic Correspondence of the United States* (New York: Publications of the American Jewish Historical Society, 1906), 86–104.

31. The combine was originally called the "Distillers' and Cattle Feeders' Trust," so named because they also dealt in cooked grain mash, a waste product of alcohol distilling commonly used as livestock feed. The trust was organized in 1887 and included sixty-five distilleries at its peak; they briefly dominated the American whiskey industry, producing two-thirds of the nation's whiskey during the years it was in operation. The Illinois Supreme Court declared the trust an illegal combination in restraint of trade in 1895. Nevertheless, the industry continued to undergo reorganization and consolidation. In 1902, the Distillers Securities Corporation, an outgrowth of the dissolved trust, became the nation's leading producer and distributor of liquor through vertical integration, purchasing and consolidating several large distilleries and alcohol-marketing firms. See Alfred D. Chandler, "The Beginnings of 'Big Business' in American Industry," *Business History Review* 33, no. 1 (1959): 10–11; Downard, *Dictionary of the History of the American Brewing and Distilling Industries*, 128–29, 213–14; Ernest E. East, "The Distillers' and Cattle Feeders' Trust, 1887–1895," *Journal of the Illinois State Historical Society* 45, no. 2 (Summer 1952): 17–20.

32. Many thanks to Dr. Rebecca Edwards for suggesting this possible connection between Wasson and Coxey.

33. *Chicago Daily Tribune*, March 14, 1885, 8.

34. *Chicago Daily Tribune*, June 21 1884, 11. On the newspaper's approach to the prohibition debate, see Duis, *The Saloon*, 63; Kobler, *Ardent Spirits*, 97–113.

35. *Atlanta Constitution*, March 1, 1908, A5; Charles Dickens, Jr., "The Jew in Russia," *All the Year Round: A Weekly Journal*, June 3, 1882, 378–80. See also *The World's Work*, June 1915, 205–6. On Russia's prohibition movement, see *American Issue*, April 28, 1917, 136.

36. According to Perry Duis, once Slavic immigrants themselves began opening saloons that catered to their own communities, the assumption of a natural association between Jews and alcohol purveyance diminished. Duis, *The Saloon*, 150–51.

37. Kingsdale, "Poor Man's Club," 476, 480, 485, 487–88.

38. These statements come from late 1880s issues of the journal *Public Opinion*, and are quoted in Higham, *Strangers in the Land*, 55.

39. Quote from the Constitution of the Immigration Restriction League, quoted in Jerome Karabel, *The Chosen: The Hidden History of Admission and Exclusion at Harvard, Yale, and Princeton* (Boston: Houghton Mifflin, 2005), 48.

40. Michael McGerr, *A Fierce Discontent: The Rise and Fall of the Progressive Movement in America* (New York: Oxford University Press, 2003), 77–117.

41. John Marshall Barker, *The Saloon Problem and Social Reform* (Boston: Everett Press, 1905), 49–50.

42. Blocker, *Retreat from Reform*, 39.

43. Howe, *World of Our Fathers*, 185.

44. *New York Times*, July 20, 1894, 9. For more regarding the diversity of American Catholic opinion on the liquor question, see *The Chautauquan*, October 1894, 95, November 1894, 233; *The Review of Reviews*, September 1894, 257.

45. *Eleventh Census of the United States* (1890), vol. 2: *Population*, 304, 484; quotation from Barker, *Saloon Problem and Social Reform*, 28–29.

46. Duis, *The Saloon*, 163; *Thirteenth Census of the United States* (1910), vol. 4: *Population*, 430–33.

47. *The Political Prohibitionist for 1888* (New York: Funk and Wagnalls, 1888), 137.

48. Wittenmyer, *History of the Woman's Temperance Crusade*, 27, 206.

49. According to Jenna Weissman Joselit's study of Jewish immigrants and crime in New York City, a 1912 study showed that Jews constituted 17 percent of all women charged with procurement. At that time, about 25 percent of the city's population was Jewish. "Though probably underrepresented as far as their proportion of the population is concerned," Joselit asserts, "Jewish prostitution was fairly widespread." Jenna Weissman Joselit, *Our Gang: Jewish Crime and the New York Jewish Community, 1900–1940* (Bloomington: Indiana University Press, 1983), 45–53.

50. Frank Moss, *The American Metropolis from Knickerbocker Days to the Present Time: New York City Life in All Its Various Phases* (New York: Peter Fenelon Collier, 1897), vol. 3, pp. 166–67. In New York, anti-saloon sentiment grew after the 1896 passage of the Raines Law, an anti-vice statute that was intended to curtail the saloon trade but in fact had the opposite effect. The legislation dramatically increased the fees for saloon licenses, but it allowed hotels with ten or more beds to serve alcohol to their customers. "In a matter of weeks" after the passage of the law, the historian Timothy Gilfoyle has written, "over one thousand saloons became 'hotels' by adding beds." This not only allowed saloonkeepers to subvert the law, but also created spaces that the saloonkeepers could rent out to prostitutes and their clients. Alcohol retail was barely curtailed, and the sex trade grew. See Gilfoyle, *City of Eros*, 243–47.

51. Theodore Bingham, "Foreign Criminals in New York," *North American Review* 188, no. 634 (September 1908): 383–84. An in-depth analysis of the Bingham article and Jewish reaction to it can be found in chapters 3 and 4 of Joselit, *Our Gang*.

52. *Chicago Daily Tribune*, June 21 1884, 11.

53. *Atlanta Constitution*, August 6, 1900, 5; see also July 13, 1902, A29; Chad Heap, *Slumming: Sexual and Racial Encounters in American Nightlife, 1885-1940* (Chicago: University of Chicago Press, 2009), 2.

54. Clifford Kuhn, Harlon Joye, and E. Bernard West, *Living Atlanta: An Oral History of the City, 1914-1948* (Athens: University of Georgia Press, 1990), 172.

55. Timberlake, *Prohibition and the Progressive Movement*, 119–20.

56. Quotation from John E. White, "Prohibition: The New Task and Opportunity of the South," *South Atlantic Quarterly*, January–October 1908, 136. See also Thomas R. Pegram, "Temperance Politics and Regional Political Culture: The Anti-Saloon League in Maryland and the South, 1907–1915," *Journal of Southern History* 63, no. 1 (February 1997): 75–77.

57. David F. Godshalk, *Veiled Visions: The 1906 Atlanta Race Riot and the Reshaping of American Race Relations* (Chapel Hill: University of North Carolina Press, 2005), 47–51; Denise A. Herd, "Prohibition, Racism, and Class Politics in the Post-Reconstruction South," *Journal of Drug Issues* 13, no. 1 (1983): 84; Joel Williamson, *The Crucible of Race: Black-White Relations in the American South since Emancipation* (New York: Oxford University Press, 1984), 209–33.

58. Gail Bederman, *Manliness and Civilization: A Cultural History of Gender and Race in the United States, 1880–1917* (Chicago: University of Chicago Press, 1995), 65.

59. David E. Ruth, "The Georgia Prohibition Act of 1907: Its Proponents and Their Arguments" (B.A. thesis, Emory University, 1984), 63.

60. *Atlanta Journal*, September 22, 1906, 1; *Atlanta Evening News*, September 22, 1906, 1; *Atlanta Constitution*, September 22, 1906, 1; Godshalk, *Veiled Visions*, 52. On the founding of the Georgia branch office of the ASL, see the *Atlantic Constitution*, March 6, 1904, 4, April 18, 1904, 3.

61. The Atlanta Race Riot of 1906 has received a great deal of scholarly attention in recent years. See Godshalk, *Veiled Visions*; Bauerlein, *Negrophobia*; Mixon, *Atlanta Riot*. See also the website that Clifford Kuhn has organized to educate both scholars and the general public about the Atlanta Riot: http://www.1906atlantaraceriot.org/.

62. Frank Foxcroft, "Prohibition in the South," *Atlantic Monthly*, May 1908, 628; Ruth, "Georgia Prohibition Act of 1907," 79–97.

63. Studies of early twentieth-century voting patterns show a causal relationship between the removal of blacks from southern voter rolls and prohibitionist successes in ballot referenda. See Michael Lewis, "Access to Saloons, Wet Voter Turnout, and Statewide Prohibition Referenda, 1907–1919," *Social Science History* 32, no. 3 (2008): 379–80.

64. Ibid., 381.

65. See George Kibbe Turner in *McClure's*, quoted above, as well as "The City of Chicago: A Study of the Great Immoralities," *McClure's*, April 1907, 575–92, and "The Daughters of the Poor," *McClure's*, November 1909, 45–61.

66. Goldstein, *Price of Whiteness*, 75–85; Jeffrey Melnick, *Black-Jewish Relations on Trial: Leo Frank and Jim Conley in the New South* (Jackson: University Press of Mississippi, 2000), 33. Other essays on Jewish commercial activity in the South, and specifically to African American patrons, include Arnold Shankman, "Friend or Foe? Southern Blacks View the Jew, 1880–1935," in *Turn to the South: Essays on Southern Jewry*, ed. Nathan M. Kaganoff and Melvin I. Urofsky (Waltham, Mass.: American Jewish Historical Society, 1979), 105–23; Clive Webb, "Jewish Merchants and Black Customers in the Age of Jim Crow," *Southern Jewish History* 2 (October 1999): 55–80.

67. Eric L. Goldstein, "Race and the Construction of Jewish Identity in America, 1875–1945" (Ph.D. diss., University of Michigan, 2000), 130–31.

68. *Atlanta Constitution*, September 28, 1906, 7.

69. *Atlanta Journal*, September 26, 1906, 2.

70. Yampolsky quoted in Hertzberg, *Strangers within the Gate City*, 191. Black and white journalists occasionally made this comparison between European anti-Semitic violence and American antiblack violence. For an example from the mainstream press, see quote from the *Augusta Tribune* in the *Atlanta Constitution*, September 26, 1906, 6.

71. *Atlanta Constitution*, October 6, 1906, 3.

72. *Atlanta Journal*, September 26, 1906, 5; *Atlanta Constitution*, September 30, 1906, 2.

73. Thomas Gibson, "The Anti-Negro Riots in Atlanta," *Harper's Weekly*, October 13, 1906, 1457–59; also cited in Hertzberg, *Strangers within the Gate City*, 161.

74. Ray Stannard Baker, *Following the Color Line: American Negro Citizenship in the Progressive Era* (New York: Doubleday, Page & Co., 1908).

75. Will Irwin, "Who Killed Margaret Lear?," *Collier's*, May 16 1908, 10; *U.S. v Lee Levy and Adolph Asher* (1908), U.S. District Court, Eastern Division of the Eastern Judicial District of Missouri. Trial records generously made available to author by Daniel Okrent. See also Okrent, *Last Call*, 44–46.

76. Isaac, *Prohibition and Politics*, 147–49.

77. Will Irwin, "More about 'Nigger Gin,'" *Collier's*, August 15, 1908, 27–30.

78. Will Irwin, "Tainted News Methods of the Liquor Interests," *Collier's*, March 13, 1909, 30. See also *The American Prohibition Yearbook for 1910* (Chicago: National Prohibition Press, 1910), 523.

79. *Atlanta Constitution*, July 15, 1907, 7.

80. J. N. T. Cawhern, "Souvenir of Georgia's Victory," Anti-Semitism File, American Jewish Historical Society, New York; also cited in Hertzberg, *Strangers within the Gate City*, 162.

81. Simon Wolf, letter to editor of the *Washington Herald*, May 18, 1908, Simon Wolf Papers (P-25), box 1, American Jewish Historical Society, New York.

82. S. Mays Ball, "Prohibition in Georgia: Its Failure to Prevent Drinking in Atlanta and Other Cities," *Putnam's Monthly*, March 1909, 694–701.

83. *Der Southern Veg-Vayzer* (Atlanta), March 10, 1908, 6b (English translation by Marni Davis and Mollie Lewis).

84. *Atlanta City Directory, 1910* (Atlanta: Atlanta City Directory Co., 1910); *Atlanta Constitution*, August 20, 1907, 2, December 27, 1907, 1.

85. Mr. Alexander served in the Georgia General Assembly from 1909 to 1910. See *Atlanta Constitution*, November 10, 1907, A3; Hertzberg, *Strangers within the Gate City*, 158,

86. Changes in the businesses along Decatur Street were determined by consulting Atlanta city directories published between 1905 and 1910.

87. *Atlanta Constitution*, March 1, 1908, C1, March 24, 1908, 9.

88. Communication between Dr. B. Wildauer (Atlanta) and David Bressler (New York), November 26 and 29, 1907, Papers of the Industrial Removal Office (I-91), folder 21, box 34, American Jewish Historical Society, New York.

89. *Atlanta City Directory*, 1910.

90. While his case was on appeal, both Cohen and his new son-in-law, Sam Loeb, were arrested and charged with violating the prohibition law. See *Atlanta Constitution*, August 19, 1908, 7, February 21, 1909, 1, May 22, 1909, 6, June 2, 1909, 7, October 18, 1909, 2; *State v. Morris Cohen*, Clemency Applications, loc. 1-4-42, 2849-12, box 24, Georgia State Archives, Morrow.

91. *Atlanta Constitution*, February 18, 1888; *Madisonian* (Madison, Ga.), February 21, 1908, 2; Testimony of Loeb, April 28, 1909, and letter from Joseph Pottle, Milledgeville, May 4, 1909, both in *State v. D.C. Loeb*, Clemency Applications, loc. 1-4-42, 2854-11, box 75, Georgia State Archives, Morrow. See also H. Paul Thompson, "Race, Temperance, and Prohibition in the Postbellum South: Black Atlanta, 1865–1900" (Ph.D. diss., Emory University, 2005).

92. On the trial and lynching of Leo Frank, see Leonard Dinnerstein, *The Leo Frank Case* (New York: Columbia University Press, 1968); Nancy MacLean, "The Leo Frank Case

Reconsidered: Gender and Sexual Politics in the Making of Reactionary Populism," *Journal of American History* 78, no. 3 (December 1991): 917–48; Melnick, *Black-Jewish Relations on Trial*; Oney, *And the Dead Shall Rise*.

93. Bernheim, *The Story of the Bernheim Family*, 62–63.

94. Ibid.

95. Ibid., 64.

NOTES TO CHAPTER 5

1. Okrent, *Last Call*, 54–58.

2. On the Georgia law, see *New York Times*, November 17, 1915.

3. Letter to Sam Cronheim, April 17, 1916, folder 2 (Correspondence), container 1, Joseph Benjamin Jacobs Papers (MS 165), Ida Pearle and Joseph Cuba Community Archives of the William Breman Jewish Heritage Museum, Atlanta (hereafter cited as Joseph Benjamin Jacobs Papers).

4. Letters from Edward Jacobs to Joe Jacobs: April 13, 21, and 26, 1916, folder 2 (Correspondence), container 1, Joseph Benjamin Jacobs Papers. Lichtenstein was a leader of Atlanta's Russian Jewish community and in 1916 was the president of the Atlanta branch of the Jewish Educational Alliance. See Hertzberg, *Strangers within the Gate City*, 128–29.

5. Letters from Edward Jacobs to Joe Jacobs: June 7 and 8, 1916, folder 2 (Correspondence), container 1, Joseph Benjamin Jacobs Papers.

6. Kerr, *Organized for Prohibition*, 200–206; Okrent, *Last Call*, 98–103; Pegram, *Battling Demon Rum*, 140–48.

7. "What Nationality Are Saloon-Keepers?," *The Independent* (New York), December 1915, 387; *American Issue* (New York), October 13, 1917, 301; Ogle, *Ambitious Brew*, 172–73; Okrent, *Last Call*, 101.

8. *The Year Book of the United States Brewers' Association* (New York: USBA, 1909), 22; *American Brewer*, July 1909, 356.

9. Charles Thomas Johnson, *Culture at Twilight: The National German-American Alliance, 1901–1918* (New York: Peter Lang, 1999), 84–85; Kerr, *Organized for Prohibition*, 177–84; Ogle, *Ambitious Brew*, 167.

10. 1st Session, 66th Congress, *Brewing and Liquor Interests and German and Bolshevik Propaganda: Report of the Committee on the Judiciary, United States Senate, Submitted pursuant to S. Res. 307 and 436* (Washington, D.C.: U.S. Government Printing Office, 1919); Einstein, *Prohibition Agent No. 1*, 191; Johnson, *Culture at Twilight*, 142, 150–58; Kristie Taylor, "Consequences of Countermovement Collapse: German-American Anti-Prohibition Activism against U.S. Alcohol Prohibition, 1904–1919" (paper presented at the annual meeting of the American Sociological Association, 2003).

11. Simon Wolf, *The Presidents I Have Known from 1860 to 1918* (Washington, D.C.: Press of B. S. Adams, 1918).

12. 66th Congress, *Brewing and Liquor Interests*, 901; Nuala McGann Drescher, "The Opposition to Prohibition, 1900–1919. A Social and Institutional Study" (Ph.D. diss., University of Delaware, 1964), 326; Johnson, *Culture at Twilight*, 84–87; "Plea for Liberty by Simon Wolf before the Senate Judiciary Committee" (1914), Simon Wolf Papers, box 2, "Congress" folder, *P-25, American Jewish Historical Society, New York.

13. 66th Congress, *Brewing and Liquor Interests*, 901.

14. Kerr, *Organized for Prohibition*, 161–65; Timberlake, *Prohibition and the Progressive Movement*, 158; *Pacific Wine, Brewing, and Spirit Review* (San Francisco and Los Angeles), December 31, 1915, 30; *Collier's*, August 15, 1908, 29.

15. Okrent, *Last Call*, 118–19.

16. Ibid.

17. Bud Johns, *The Ombibulous Mr. Mencken: A Drinking Biography* (New York: Synergistic Press, 1968), 8–10; Garrett Peck, *Prohibition in Washington, D.C.: How Dry We Weren't* (Charleston: History Press, 2011), 37–47.

18. Michael Alexander, *Jazz Age Jews* (Princeton, N.J.: Princeton University Press, 2001), 66; Asbury, *Great Illusion*, 289; E. P. Sanford, "The Illegal Liquor Traffic," *Annals of the American Academy of Political and Social Science* 163 (1932): 42; *Newark Evening News*, August 14, 1920, 5.

19. Constantine Panunzio, "The Foreign Born and Prohibition," *Annals of the American Academy of Political and Social Science* 163 (1932): 147–48. According to a 1932 study, 60 percent of prohibition violations occurred in cities, 35 percent occurred in rural areas, and the remainder happened in transport between the two. See Sanford, "Illegal Liquor Traffic," 42.

20. Joselit, *Our Gang*, 94.

21. Ibid.; Panunzio, "Foreign Born and Prohibition," 148.

22. Historians have noted that bootlegging resembles the motion picture industry in this way. Both fields were shunned by "respectable" businessmen and taken up by ambitious young immigrants. See Gabler, *Empire of Their Own*; Michael E. Parrish, *Anxious Decades: America in Prosperity and Depression, 1920–1941* (New York: Norton, 1992), 72.

23. Sean Dennis Cashman, *Prohibition: The Lie of the Land* (New York: Free Press, 1981), 122–25; Fried, *The Rise and Fall of the Jewish Gangster in America*, 111; Joselit, *Our Gang*, 95. See also Kyvig, *Repealing National Prohibition*, 26–27; David E. Ruth, *Inventing the Public Enemy: The Gangster in American Culture, 1918–1934* (Chicago: University of Chicago Press, 1996).

24. Mark H. Haller, "Bootleggers and American Gambling, 1920–1950," in *Gambling in America* (Washington, D.C.: Commission on the Review of the National Policy toward Gambling, 1976), 110–14.

25. Fried, *The Rise and Fall of the Jewish Gangster in America*, 12–18; Haller, "Bootleggers and American Gambling," 110–14; Helmreich, *Enduring Community*, 27–28; Joselit, *Our Gang*, 95–97; John Starr, *The Purveyor: The Shocking Story of Today's Illicit Liquor Empire* (New York: Holt, Rinehart and Winston, 1961), 16–18; Mark A. Stuart, *Gangster #2: Longy Zwillman, the Man Who Invented Organized Crime* (Secaucus, N.J.: Lyle Stuart, 1985), 20–21; Brad R. Tuttle, *How Newark Became Newark: The Rise, Fall, and Rebirth of an American City* (New Brunswick, N.J.: Rutgers University Press, 2009), 97–112.

26. Nicholas Faith, *The Bronfmans: The Rise and Fall of the House of Seagram* (New York: St. Martin's Press, 2006), 23–54, 64–70; Michael R. Marrus, *Samuel Bronfman: The Life and Times of Seagram's Mr. Sam* (Hanover, N.H.: Brandeis University Press, 1991), 19–34; Okrent, *Last Call*, 146–49.

27. Stephen Birmingham, *The Rest of Us: The Rise of America's Eastern European Jews* (Syracuse, N.Y.: Syracuse University Press, 1984), 163.

28. Cashman, *Prohibition*, 115; Fried, *The Rise and Fall of the Jewish Gangster in America*, 120–22.

29. Rich Cohen, *Tough Jews* (New York: Simon & Schuster, 1998), 61.

30. Ibid., 20–21; Rachel Rubin discusses this phenomenon in her essay "Gangster Generation: Crime, Jews, and the Problem of Assimilation," in *"Jewishness" and the World of "Difference" in the United States*, ed. Marc Lee Raphael (Williamsburg, Va.: College of William and Mary Press, 2001), 65–77.

31. Fried, *The Rise and Fall of the Jewish Gangster in America*, 94, 109. Even the American Jewish Historical Society's website boasts that Jewish gangsters disrupted American Nazi Party rallies in the 1930s, and that Meyer Lansky contributed $50,000 to the Haganah in Jewish Palestine during the 1940s. See "But They Were Good to Their People," http://www.ajhs.org/publications/chapters/chapter.cfm?documentID=260; Warren Grover, *Nazis in Newark* (Newark: Transaction, 2003), 39–71. See also Birmingham, *Rest of Us*; Robert A. Rockaway, *But—He Was Good to His Mother: The Lives and Crimes of Jewish Gangsters* (Jerusalem: Gefen Publishing House, 1993); Stuart, *Gangster #2*. This recent fascination with Jewish gangsters has also been inspired by the popularity of Francis Ford Coppola's *Godfather* movies and Sergio Leone's *Once upon a Time in America*. Celebrations of Jewish criminals serve as proof that Jews, too, belong in the American cultural pantheon of beloved outlaws and tough guys. The HBO series *The Sopranos*, in fact, includes a scene in which the Jewish psychoanalyst treating the Italian American therapist of the mobster Tony Soprano boasts of a relative's relationship with the Murder Inc. member Louis "Lepke" Buchalter. "Those were some tough Jews," the doctor proudly exclaims, to the bafflement and dismay of his patient.

32. Rockaway, *But—He Was Good to His Mother*, 254.

33. Asbury, *Great Illusion*, 227–30; Jess Carr, *The Second Oldest Profession: An Informal History of Moonshining in America* (Englewood Cliffs, N.J.: Prentice-Hall, 1972) 95–96.

34. Martha Bensley Bruere, *Does Prohibition Work? A Study of the Operation of the Eighteenth Amendment Made by the National Federation of Settlements, Assisted by Social Workers in Different Parts of the United States* (New York: Harper & Brothers, 1927), 102.

35. Clifford Kuhn, "'The Full History of the Strike as I Saw It': Atlanta's Fulton Bag and Cotton Mills Workers and Their Representations through the 1914–15 Strike" (Ph.D. diss., University of North Carolina, 1993), 88; Leonard Rogoff, *Homelands: Southern Jewish Identity in Durham and Chapel Hill, North Carolina* (Tuscaloosa: University of Alabama Press, 2001), 147–48; Letter from Dale Rosengarten, March 27 and April 25, 1995, in "Fieldwork Files," Jewish Heritage Collection, Addlestone Library, College of Charleston, South Carolina.

36. Questionnaire responses from Harry Merfeld, George Solomon, and Isaac Marcuson in Morris S. Lazaron Papers (MS 71), box 38, 1926 Prohibition Survey folder, AJA.

37. *The Anti-Saloon League Year Book* (Columbus: Anti-Saloon League, 1917), 8–9; Joseph K. Willing, "The Profession of Bootlegging," *Annals of the American Academy of Political and Social Science* 125 (May 1926): 40–48.

38. Letters from Simon Wolf to Rabbi George Zepin, March 6 and 17, 1919, in Collections of the Union of American Hebrew Congregations (MS 72), box 44, AJA.

39. Letter from Daniel Roper to J. Walter Freiberg, July 5, 1919, in Collections of the Union of American Hebrew Congregations (MS 72), box 43, AJA.

40. Letters from Rabbi Leo M. Franklin, Daniel Roper, and Rabbi J. D. Schwartz, all from July 1919, in Collections of the Union of American Hebrew Congregations (MS 72), box 43, AJA; Joselit, *Our Gang*, 89; Daniel Roper, C., *Fifty Years of Public Life* (Durham, N.C.: Duke University Press, 1941), 190–95; Letter from R. Lewin-Epstein to Louis Wolsey, August 17, 1920, box 12, folder 5, Collection of the Central Conference of American Rabbis (MS 34), AJA.

41. Jonathan Sarna makes the important point that Jewish communal leaders worked to reduce Jewish criminality not only because of "a fear that criminals would jeopardize the status of American Jews generally," but also because they felt that criminal behavior went against Jewish morality, and because "they felt deeply ashamed" of Jews who broke the law. Jonathan Sarna, "The Jewish Way of Crime," *Commentary*, August 1984, 53–55.

42. Laurence F. Schmeckbier, *The Bureau of Prohibition: Its History, Activities, and Organization* (Washington, D.C.: Brookings Institution, 1929), 98; Hannah Sprecher, "Let *Them* Drink and Forget *Our* Poverty: Orthodox Rabbis React to Prohibition," *American Jewish Archives* 43, no. 2 (1991): 140.

43. Sprecher, "Let *Them* Drink and Forget *Our* Poverty," 165–68; Kimmy Caplan, "In God We Trust: Salaries and Income of American Orthodox Rabbis, 1881–1924," *American Jewish History* 86, no. 1 (1998): 77–106.

44. Schmeckbier, *Bureau of Prohibition*, 98; Survey of Prohibition Unit (1924), Correspondence of the Office of the Secretary of the Treasury, entry 191, box 115, Prohibition Survey folder, National Archives and Records Administration, College Park, Maryland; *American Hebrew* (New York), March 20, 1925, 571; Okrent, *Last Call*, 181–85.

45. Einstein, *Prohibition Agent No. 1*, 136–40; Letter from Jerome Mark to Morris Lazaron, February 16, 1926, in Morris S. Lazaron Papers (MS 71), box 38, 1926 Prohibition Survey folder, AJA.

46. Joselit, *Our Gang*, 97–99; Sprecher, "Let *Them* Drink and Forget *Our* Poverty," 143–47; Interview of Norman Schapiro by author, September 23, 2003; *New York Times*, March 31, 1996, 6; *American Issue* (New York), November 14, 1925, 7.

47. *New York Times*, March 30, 1920, 17; Rudolph I. Coffee, "Stamping Out Wine Congregations," *Jewish Chronicle* (Newark), February 9, 1923, 10 (originally published in *Survey*, December 15, 1922, 366–67); Sprecher, "Let *Them* Drink and Forget *Our* Poverty," 152–53.

48. *Baltimore Jewish Times*, March 16, 1923, 4.

49. *Newark Star-Eagle*, October 3, 1921, 3, October 4, 1921, 15; Imogen B. Oakley, "The American People vs. the Alien Bootlegger," *The Outlook* (New York), May 5, 1926, 18.

50. Burton J. Hendrick, "The Jews in America, Part III: The 'Menace' of the Polish Jew," *World's Work*, February 1923, 370–71.

51. Dinnerstein, *Anti-Semitism in America*, 81–82; Henry L. Feingold, *A Time for Searching: Entering the Mainstream, 1920–1945* (Baltimore: Johns Hopkins University Press, 1992), 8–10. See also Neil Baldwin, *Henry Ford and the Jews: The Mass Production of Hate* (New York: Public Affairs, 2001); Leo P. Ribuffo, "Henry Ford and *The International Jew*," *American Jewish History* 69, no. 4 (June 1980): 437–77

52. "How Jews Gained American Liquor Control," *Dearborn (Mich.) Independent*, December 17, 1921; "Gigantic Jewish Liquor Trust and Its Career," *Dearborn (Mich.) Independent*, December 24, 1921; "The Jewish Element in Bootlegging Evil," *Dearborn (Mich.) Independent*, December 31, 1921. All three articles reprinted in Ford, *Aspects of Jewish Power in the United States*.

53. Ford, "The Jewish Element in Bootlegging Evil," 34.

54. *Colonel Mayfield's Weekly* (Dallas), February 4, 1922.

55. For more on Ford's view of Jews and popular music, see "Jewish Jazz Becomes Our National Music," *Dearborn (Mich.) Independent*, August 6 1921; and "How the Jewish Song Trust Makes You Sing," *Dearborn (Mich.) Independent*, August 13, 1921. Both reprinted in

Henry Ford, *Jewish Influences in American Life*, vol. 3 of *The International Jew: The World's Foremost Problem* (Dearborn, Mich.: Dearborn Publishing Co., 1921), 64–87.

56. Dinnerstein, *Anti-Semitism in America*, 78–104; Feingold, *A Time for Searching*, 15–20; Karabel, *The Chosen*.

57. For scholarship on the importance of urban politics to the 1920s Klan, and a refutation of earlier historical claims that the Klan was a rural and small-town phenomenon, see Kenneth T. Jackson, *The Ku Klux Klan in the City, 1915–1930* (New York: Oxford University Press, 1967). Studies of regional Klan activity include Charles C. Alexander, *The Ku Klux Klan in the Southwest* (Lexington: University of Kentucky Press, 1965); David Horowitz, *Inside the Klavern: The Secret History of a Ku Klux Klan of the 1920s* (Carbondale: Southern Illinois University, 1999); William D. Jenkins, *Steel Valley Klan: The Ku Klux Klan in Ohio's Mahoning Valley* (Kent, Ohio: Kent State University Press, 1990); Nancy MacLean, *Behind the Mask of Chivalry: The Making of the Second Ku Klux Klan* (New York: Oxford University Press, 1994); Leonard J. Moore, *Citizen Klansmen: The Ku Klux Klan in Indiana, 1921–1928* (Chapel Hill: University of North Carolina Press, 1991). These historians come to a range of conclusions about the Klan's nature; some see it as a mainstream interest group of its time, a fraternal association with retrograde political goals, while others—MacLean especially—regard the Klan as a proto-fascist organization with an appetite for vigilante violence.

58. Pegram, "Hoodwinked," 91.

59. William E. Leuchtenburg, *The Perils of Prosperity, 1914–1932* (Chicago: University of Chicago Press, 1958), 211; MacLean, *Behind the Mask of Chivalry*, 139; *Saturday Press* (Minneapolis), November 19, 1927.

60. *Colonel Mayfield's Weekly* (Dallas), January 14, 1922. The actual ethnicity of the song's lyricist is unknown.

61. *New York Age*, May 18, 1889, quoted in Philip S. Foner, "Black-Jewish Relations in the Opening Years of the Twentieth Century," *Phylon* 36, no. 4 (Winter 1975): 360n8.

62. Hasia Diner, *In the Almost Promised Land: American Jews and Blacks, 1915–1935* (Baltimore: Johns Hopkins University Press, 1995), 72–74; Cheryl Lynn Greenberg, *Troubling the Waters: Black-Jewish Relations in the American Century* (Princeton, N.J.: Princeton University Press, 2006), 61–69.

63. Michael A. Lerner, *Dry Manhattan: Prohibition in New York City* (Cambridge, Mass.: Harvard University Press, 2007), 35, 199–226.

64. *New York Age*: September 30, 1922, 1; February 17, 1923, 1; June 30, 1923, 1; July 14, 1923, 1; November 3, 1932, 1. See also Steven Bloom, "Interactions between Blacks and Jews in New York City, 1900–1930, as Reflected in the Black Press" (Ph.D. diss., New York University, 1973); David Johns Hellwig, "The Afro-American and the Immigrant, 1880–1930: A Study of Black Social Thought" (Ph.D. diss., Syracuse University, 1973).

65. Cheryl Lynn Greenberg, *Or Does it Explode? Black Harlem in the Great Depression* (New York: Oxford University Press, 1991), 38–39.

66. Shane White, Stephen Garton, Stephen Robertson, and Graham White, "The Envelope, Please," *The Cultural Turn in U.S. History: Past, Present, and Future*, ed. James W. Cook, Lawrence B. Glickman, and Michael O'Malley (Chicago: University of Chicago Press, 2008), 147; Joselit, *Our Gang*, 93–95; Lewis Erenberg, "Impresarios of Broadway Nightlife," in *Inventing Times Square: Commerce and Culture at the Crossroads of the World*, ed. William R. Taylor (Baltimore: Johns Hopkins University Press, 1991), 165; Einstein, *Prohibition Agent No. 1*, 139–40.

67. Letter from Elias Cohen to Louis Marshall, January 26, 1923, Judah Magnes Papers, Central Archives for the History of the Jewish People, Jerusalem.

NOTES TO CHAPTER 6

1. 2nd Session, 67th Congress, *Hearings before the Committee on Immigration and Naturalization* (Washington, D.C.: U.S. Government Printing Office, 1922), 338–39; Sprecher, "Let *Them* Drink and Forget *Our* Poverty," 169.

2. "The Peril of Racial Prejudice: A Statement to the Public," *American Jewish Year Book* (hereafter cited as *AJYB*) (Philadelphia: Jewish Publication Society of America, 1922), vol. 23, p. 332.

3. Ford, "The Jewish Element in Bootlegging Evil," 34.

4. Louis Marshall (hereafter LM) to Sieg Natenberg, November 9, 1925, box 1597, Louis Marshall Collection, AJA.

5. Ibid.

6. LM to William Travers Jerome, January 7, 1904, box 1573, Louis Marshall Collection, AJA; LM to Herbert S. Carpenter, February 6, 1926, box 1598, Louis Marshall Collection, AJA; Jonathan Sarna, "Two Jewish Lawyers Named Louis," *American Jewish History* 94, nos. 1–2 (2008): 9–10.

7. LM to Emanuel Celler, May 24, 1924, box 1595, Louis Marshall Collection, AJA. See also Louis Marshall, "Preservation of Law and Its Significance to American Democracy," in *Law versus Lawlessness: Citizenship Conference Addresses*, ed. Fred Smith (New York: Fleming H. Revell, 1924), 149–62.

8. Felix Frankfurter, "A National Policy for Enforcement of Prohibition," *Annals of the American Academy of Political and Social Science* 109 (September 1923): 193; Melvin Urofsky, ed., *Elder Statesman (1921–1941)*, vol. 5 of *Letters of Louis D. Brandeis* (Albany: State University of New York Press, 1978), 91, 103.

9. Solomon Foster, "Sacramental Wine Abuses," *Jewish Chronicle* (Newark), December 30, 1921, 4.

10. Questionnaire response from Israel Heinberg in Morris Lazaron Papers (MS 71), box 38, 1926 Prohibition Survey folder, AJA.

11. Elias Cohen to LM, January 26, 1923, Papers of the Kehillah of New York City, Central Archives for the History of the Jewish People, Jerusalem.

12. *HUC Songs and Yells*, Boards of the Student Body and Literary Society, Hebrew Union College, AJA. The likely date of this document's publication was between 1915 and 1917.

13. Ibid.

14. The original author of the song is unknown. The song has been updated over the years, and now has dozens of verses, almost all of which are parodic. For example: "We never eat cookies, because they have yeast / And one little bite turns a man to a beast / Can you imagine such a sorry disgrace / As a man in the gutter with crumbs on his face?" It was briefly repopularized during the folk revival of the 1950s and 1960s, and performed by Theodore Bikel and the Chad Mitchell Trio under the title "Away with Rum (The Song of the Temperance Union)."

15. Ibid. This song, "Kotalti, Kotaltoh," was sung to the tune of "Upidee-Upida," which was written in 1859 and adopted by the Army of the Confederacy during the Civil War.

The meaning of the words *kotalti* and *kotaltoh* are unclear, and could have meant to stand as Hebraic-sounding and rhythmic nonsense syllables.

16. *Yearbook of the Central Conference of American Rabbis* (hereafter cited as *YBCCAR*) (Cincinnati: Central Conference of American Rabbis, 1914), vol. 24, pp. 117–18.

17. Naomi W. Cohen, "Commissioner Williams and the Jews," *American Jewish Archives* 61, no. 2 (2009), 110, 119–20; Rischin, *Promised City*, 232–33, 273.

18. *New York Times*, January 29, 1917, 17; "Prohibition Concerns the Jew," date unknown, http://dl.lib.brown.edu/catalog/catalog.php?verb=render&id=1111169646036250&view=showmods.

19. On Stephen Wise, see Mark A. Raider, "The Aristocrat and the Democrat: Louis Marshall, Stephen S. Wise, and the Challenge of American Jewish Leadership," *American Jewish History* 94, nos. 1–2 (2008): 91–113; Sarna, *American Judaism*, 195–96.

20. Stephen S. Wise, "World War I: What Are We Fighting For?," available from the Library of Congress at http://www.loc.gov/teachers/classroommaterials/lessons/great-war/gallery.html.

21. Stephen S. Wise, "A Jewish View of Prohibition," *Scientific Temperance Journal* 30, no. 3 (August 1921): 148–51.

22. Beryl Williams, *Lillian Wald: Angel of Henry Street* (New York: Julian Messner, 1948), 187; R. L. Duffus, *Lillian Wald: Neighbor and Crusader* (New York: Macmillan, 1939), 271.

23. Marjorie N. Feld, *Lillian Wald: A Biography* (Chapel Hill: University of North Carolina Press, 2008), 139.

24. Arthur Weyne, "The First Jewish Governor: Moses Alexander of Idaho," *Western States Jewish Historical Quarterly* 9, no. 1 (1976): 22, 35, 38.

25. In 1920, approximately 2,500 Jews lived in Salt Lake City, which had a total population of just over 116,000. Boise's Jewish population was around 300, not even 2 percent of the city's total 21,000. Marcus, *To Count a People*.

26. S. George Ellsworth, "Simon Bamberger, Governor of Utah," *Western States Jewish Historical Quarterly* 5, no. 4 (1973): 231–42.

27. *The Anti-Saloon League Year Book* (1917), 232–35; Mark Edward Lender, *Dictionary of American Temperance Biography: From Temperance Reform to Alcohol Research, the 1600s to the 1980s* (Westport, Conn.: Greenwood Press, 1984), 24–26.

28. Jonathan Sarna argues against interpretation of Jewish vigilance against Jewish crime as too focused on their insecurity and communal self-defensiveness. See Sarna, "Jewish Way of Crime," 53–55.

29. "An American Layman on Zionism," *American Israelite*, July 18, 1918, n.p., in "Zionism, Judaism" folder; "Wants American Jews to Speak for an Undiluted American Citizenship," *American Hebrew*, January 24, 1919, n.p., "Biographical—Judaism" folder: both in box 2, Bernheim Papers, University Archives and Records Center, University of Louisville (hereafter cited as Bernheim Papers).

30. Isaac Wolfe Bernheim, "The Reform Church of American Israelites" (address delivered in Buffalo, May 1921), in "Reprints of IWB Speeches" folder, box 2, Bernheim Papers.

31. Edgar Magnin, "To Be or Not to Be Is the Question," *Jewish Review and Observer* (Cleveland), in "Biographical—Judaism" folder, box 2, Bernheim Papers; Mosessohn quote from Klaus J. Herrmann, "Isaac Wolfe Bernheim: A Crusader for a Prophetically Universalist 'Israelitism,'" *American Council for Judaism*, Summer 1996, http://www.acjna.org/acjna/articles_detail.aspx?id=71.

32. Stephen Wise, "Shall We Be Jews—Or Members of the Reform Church of American Israelites?," *Free Synagogue Pulpit* 6, no. 10 (1920–21), in "Reprints of IWB Speeches" folder, box 2, Bernheim Papers; Magnin, "To Be or Not To Be Is the Question"; "Reform Church of American Israelites," *Baltimore Jewish Times*, October 14, 1921, in "Biographical—Judaism" folder, box 2, Bernheim Papers.

33. Stephen S. Wise, "Integrity of Law: Essential to the Morality of the Nation," in Smith, *Law versus Lawlessness*, 64–65.

34. 1920 Diary, 83, box 1, Samuel Price Papers (P-95), American Jewish Historical Society, New York; U.S. Census Manuscript Schedules for 1920, Massachusetts, Hampden County, Springfield City, Ward 6, ED 149, no. 2. Section 29 of the National Prohibition Act grants dispensation for home use of "nonintoxicating cider, etc."

35. 1920 Diary, 85, and 1921 Diary, 67–74, both in box 1, Samuel Price Papers (P-95), American Jewish Historical Society, New York.

36. LM to Elias Cohen, January 25, 1923, box 1590, Louis Marshall Collection, AJA.

37. Memo by Leo M. Franklin, March 19, 1920, CCAR Papers (MS 34), box 12, folder 6, AJA; *YBCCAR* (Cincinnati: Central Conference of American Rabbis, 1920), vol. 30, pp. 18, 74; Moses Hyamson, *The Jewish Concept of Wine and Its Use* (New York: n.p., 1920).

38. LM to Moses Z. Margolies, March 20, 1920, box 1597, Louis Marshall Collection, AJA; Joselit, *Our Gang*, 91; Sprecher, "Let *Them* Drink and Forget *Our* Poverty," 139.

39. Einstein, *Prohibition Agent No. 1*, 143–51.

40. I have relied greatly on Hannah Sprecher's article "Let *Them* Drink and Forget *Our* Poverty" for her account of the Menorah Wine Company scandal.

41. Ibid., 153.

42. *YBCCAR* (Cincinnati: Central Conference of American Rabbis, 1922), vol. 32, p. 107; *AJYB* (Philadelphia: Jewish Publication Society of America, 1923), vol. 24, pp. 377–79.

43. "Jews Proffer Aid to End Wine Abuses," *New York Times*, December 23, 1921, 1; Notes from CCAR executive board meeting, January 31, 1922, CCAR Papers (MS 34), folder 3, box 13, AJA; *YBCCAR* (1922), vol. 32, pp. 107–8.

44. Leonard Landes, *Di Drey Leydenshaften* (New York: Self-published, n.d.), 90, 91, 95 (English translation by Marni Davis and Mollie Lewis). On Dr. Landes, see Michael M. Davis, *Immigrant Health and the Community* (New York: Harper & Brothers, 1921).

45. Isidore Koplowitz, *Midrash Yayin Veshechor: Talmudic and Midrashic Exegetics on Wine and Strong Drink* (Detroit: n.p., 1923), 6, 13.

46. Einstein, *Prohibition Agent No. 1*, 2; "Books: Izzy the Agent," *Time*, October 24, 1932, 48.

47. *Time*, November 23, 1925, 9–10; *Atlanta Constitution*, July 24, 1923, 1.

48. Asbury, *Great Illusion*, 211–13; Einstein, *Prohibition Agent No. 1*, 30.

49. Einstein, *Prohibition Agent No. 1*, 57, 24.

50. Okrent, *Last Call*, 262–63.

51. Elias Cohen to Louis Marshall, January 26, 1923, Papers of the Kehillah of New York City, Central Archives for the History of the Jewish People, Jerusalem.

52. Joselit, *Our Gang*, 88, 92. Recordings of numerous comedy routines that include jokes about Prohibition, as well as several versions of "Vi Bist Du Geveyzn Far Prohibishn?" (Where were you before Prohibition?), are available at the Ellis Island Immigration Museum, New York.

53. "Plan to Bar Wine and Use Fruit Juice in All Churches," *New York Times*, December 24, 1921, 1; "Sacramental Wine Is Not in Danger," *The Catholic News* (New York), January 7, 1922, 7; Sprecher, "Let *Them* Drink and Forget *Our* Poverty."

54. "Sacramental Wine Is Not in Danger," 7; *YBCCAR* (1922), vol. 32, pp. 107–8.

55. *New York Times*, October 15, 1922, 1.

56. *New York Times*, July 17, 1922, January 18, 1925.

57. *New York Times*, August 27, 1926, March 23, 1926; "Import of Palestine Wine for Passover Denied by Prohibition Authorities," *Jewish Telegraphic Agency*, March 24, 1926.

58. *AJYB* (Philadelphia: Jewish Publication Society of America, 1927), vol. 28, p. 31; Joselit, *Our Gang*, 102–3; Sprecher, "Let *Them* Drink and Forget *Our* Poverty," 160–62; *New York Times*, August 29, 1926, 1.

59. Joselit, *Our Gang*, 103–5; *New York Times*, February 8, 1927; *Regulations 2: Relating to Permits as Provided in Title II, National Prohibition Act for the Manufacture of and Traffic in Intoxicating Liquors for Nonbeverage Purposes (Effective October 1, 1927)* (Washington, D.C.: U.S. Government Printing Office, 1927), 139.

60. Charles Reznikoff, ed., *Louis Marshall: Champion of Liberty* (Philadelphia: Jewish Publication Society of America, 1957), 935.

61. Joselit, *Our Gang*, 90–91; Sprecher, "Let *Them* Drink and Forget *Our* Poverty," 157.

62. *Baltimore Jewish Times*, March 16, 1923.

63. Michael A. Meyer, "American Reform Judaism and Zionism: Early Efforts at Ideological Rapprochement," *Judaism within Modernity* (Detroit: Wayne State University Press, 2001), 362–77.

64. Thomas A. Kolsky, *Jews against Zionism: The American Council for Judaism, 1942–1948* (Philadelphia: Temple University Press, 1992), 32.

65. "Prohibition Dept. Allows Import of Palestine Wine for Sacramental Uses," *Jewish Telegraphic Agency*, December 23, 1926; "Permission Granted to Import Palestine Wine," *Jewish Telegraphic Agency*, February 2, 1928; Fred Goldberg to H. G. Enelow, May 21 and 31, 1928, Papers of H. G. Enelow (MS 11), box 7, folder 10, AJA. Neither the Enelow Collection, the CCAR Papers, nor the records from the Department of the Treasury contain any further communications regarding this matter, and no "Fred Goldberg" with ties to either Zionist organizations or wine importation businesses is listed in the New York City business directories of the time.

66. H. G. Enelow to Fred Goldberg, June 7 and 22, 1928, Papers of H. G. Enelow (MS 11), box 7, folder 10, AJA; *YBCCAR* (Cincinnati: Central Conference of American Rabbis, 1928), vol. 38, pp. 39–40.

67. Hyman G. Enelow, "Prohibition, Judaism, and the Jew," n.d., H. G. Enelow Papers, box 30, folder 4, AJA.

68. Kyvig, *Repealing National Prohibition*, 71–97. Louis Marshall shared the AAPA's critique of Prohibition law. According to Charles Reznikoff, who compiled and edited Marshall's papers, Marshall corresponded with William Stayton, the founder of the AAPA, in 1924. Unfortunately, that correspondence seems to have been lost. See Reznikoff, *Louis Marshall*.

69. All the quotes from questionnaires that follow are in 1926 Prohibition Survey folder, box 38, Morris Lazaron Papers (MS 71), AJA.

70. Louis Wolsey to Morris Lazaron, February 12 and May 20, 1926, both in CCAR Papers (MS 34), box 14, folder 4, AJA.

71. Letter from Morris Lazaron to Colonel W. H. Stayton, n.d., Morris S. Lazaron Papers (MS 71), 1926 Prohibition Survey folder, box 38, AJA. For more on Stayton and the AAPA, see Kyvig, *Repealing National Prohibition*, 39–46. For a less sympathetic view, see Fletcher Dobyns, *The Amazing Story of Repeal: An Expose of the Power of Propaganda* (Chicago: Willett, Clark, 1940).

72. Lizabeth Cohen, *Making a New Deal: Industrial Workers in Chicago, 1919–1939* (New York: Cambridge University Press, 1990), 255; Lender and Martin, *Drinking in America*, 166–67; Rose, *American Women and the Repeal of Prohibition*. Cohen claims that Prohibition was *the* deciding factor in Chicago politics during the interwar period, since it unified the city's ethnic workers around the Democratic machine.

73. Kyvig, *Repealing National Prohibition*, 111–14.

74. Lender and Martin, *Drinking in America*, 162; Parrish, *Anxious Decades*, 208–15. Cannon quote is from Cashman, *Prohibition*, 197.

75. Lerner, *Dry Manhattan*, 252–54.

76. Cashman, *Prohibition*, 221–27; Pegram, *Battling Demon Rum*, 169–73.

77. "Prohibition in Chicago: Speech of Hon. Adolph J. Sabath of Illinois," *Congressional Record*, 70th Congress, 2nd Session, February 28 (Washington, D.C.: U.S. Government Printing Office, 1929), 1. See also box 3 of Adolph Joachim Sabath Papers (MS 43), AJA.

78. Hu, *The Liquor Tax in the United States*, 63; Joseph F. Kett, "Temperance and Intemperance as Historical Problems," *Journal of American History* 67, no. 4 (1981): 881; Kyvig, *Repealing National Prohibition*, 177; Pegram, *Battling Demon Rum*, 169; Morris Victor Rosenbloom, *The Liquor Industry: A Survey of Its History, Manufacture, Problems of Control, and Importance* (Braddock, Penn.: Ruffsdale Distilling Company, 1937), 70–71.

79. Thomas M. Coffey, *The Long Thirst: Prohibition in America, 1920–1933* (New York: Norton, 1975), 316; Kyvig, *Repealing National Prohibition*, 177–78.

80. Kobler, *Ardent Spirits*, 352.

81. Ferdinand Isserman, "After Prohibition, What?," Ferdinand Isserman Papers (MS 6), box 22, folder 3, AJA.

82. Press Release No. 26 (June 5, 1936), Department of the Treasury, Federal Alcohol Administration Division, Washington, D.C. (available at the Science, Industry, and Business Library branch of the New York Public Library); Ann McGahan, "The Emergence of the National Brewing Oligopoly: Competition in the American Market, 1933–58," *Business History Review* 65, no. 2 (Summer 1991): 229–84.

83. Ogle, *Ambitious Brew*, 240–41.

84. "Palestine Wine Export Increases," *Jewish Telegraphic Agency*, April 12, 1934; Thomas Pinney, *From Prohibition to the Present*, vol. 2 of *A History of Wine in America* (Berkeley: University of California Press, 2005), 173–75; Morris Freedman, "Wine Like Mother Used to Make: The Neighbors Make a Discovery," *Commentary*, May 1954, 481–89; Okrent, *Last Call*, 359–61, 364–66.

85. Birmingham, *Rest of Us*, 244–48; Mark H. Haller, "Bootleggers as Businessmen: From City Slums to City Builders," in *Law, Alcohol, and Order: Perspectives on National Prohibition*, ed. David E. Kyvig (Westport, Conn.: Greenwood Press, 1985), 143–46; Rosenbloom, *Liquor Industry*, 63–64; Anthony Summers, *Official and Confidential: The Secret Life of J. Edgar Hoover* (New York: G. P. Putnam's Sons, 1993), 226, 47–48. *Louisville Courier-Journal*, February 19, 1937, 1; "Abe 'Longey' Zwillman," n.d., box 9244, William O'Dwyer Papers, Municipal Archives, New York.

86. Haller, "Bootleggers as Businessmen," 146.

87. Faith, *The Bronfmans*, 125–27; Oscar Getz, *Whiskey: An American Pictorial History* (New York: David McKay, 1978), 193.

88. "Whiskey," *Fortune*, November 1933, 28–45; "Jews in America," *Fortune*, February 1936, 134; Okrent, *Last Call*, 359.

89. Pegram, *Battling Demon Rum*, 187.

90. Goldberg, "Occupational Patterns of American Jews," 3–24; Barry R. Chiswick, "The Postwar Economy of American Jews," *Studies in Contemporary Jewry* 8 (1992): 85–101.

91. Okrent, *Last Call*, 358.

NOTES TO THE CONCLUSION

1. Philip Roth, *The Human Stain* (New York: Vintage Books, 2000), 22–23, 84.

2. According to his wife, Diana, Lionel Trilling's early appointment as instructor of English at Columbia University was terminated because he was "a Freudian, a Marxist, and a Jew." Trilling was eventually reinstated, and he became the first Jewish member of Columbia's English department. See Diana Trilling, "Lionel Trilling, A Jew at Columbia," *Commentary*, March 1979, 414–16, quoted in Edward Alexander, *The Jewish Idea and Its Enemies* (New Brunswick, N.J.: Transaction, 1988), 31–34.

3. Herb Gardner, *Conversations with My Father* (New York: Pantheon Books, 1992). See also Frank Rich, "Review/Theater: Two Generations (and Cultures) at War," *New York Times*, March 30, 1992.

4. Ernest Gordon, *The Wrecking of the Eighteenth Amendment* (Francestown, N.H.: Alcohol Information Press, 1943), 16, 104, 156–58, 161–62.

5. Ibid., 161–63, 230–31.

6. John Benedict, "Who Controls the Whiskey Trust?," *American Mercury*, December 1959, 3–18. A further example of post-Repeal condemnation of Jewish alcohol entrepreneurs can be found in LeMaster, *A Corner of the Tapestry*, 325.

7. Murdock, *Domesticating Drink*, 159–74; Jay L. Rubin, "The Wet War: American Liquor Control, 1941–1945," in Blocker, *Alcohol, Reform, and Society*, 235–58.

8. http://www.shmaltz.com/HEBREW/index.html.

9. Malamud's *The Assistant* (1957) includes a Jewish alcohol entrepreneur as well: the liquor store owner Julius Karp's ill-gotten success is juxtaposed with the precarious economic situations of the other Jews in their multiethnic immigrant neighborhood.

10. Today, more recent immigrant groups have replaced Jews as visible and clustered liquor store owners in urban ghettos. Tensions between Korean liquor store owners and their black customers in poor city neighborhoods have erupted into violence over the past twenty years, in both New York City and Los Angeles. See Jennifer Lee, *Civility in the City: Blacks, Jews, and Koreans in Urban America* (Cambridge, Mass.: Harvard University Press, 2002), 25; Pyong Gap Min, "Korean Immigrants in the United States," in *Handbook of Research on Ethnic Minority Entrepreneurship*, ed. Leo Paul Dana (Northampton, Mass.: Edward Elgar, 2007), 212–27.

Index

A. & M. Moses General Store (Natchez), *35*
Abelsky, Abram, 127, *128*
acculturation of American Jews: entry into professional middle class, 196; flouting Prohibition, 164; Jewish alcohol entrepreneurs in, role of, 2–3, 5–6, 15, 31–33; pressure on Orthodox Jews to modernize, 79, 176–183, 184; promotion of social justice and aid to the poor, 49; Reform Judaism, 23; Young Men's Hebrew Association (YMHA), 32
Adams, Brooks, 229n13
Adams, Henry, 229n13
Adas Israel congregation (Louisville), 30, 31
African Americans: American Jews, commerce with, 120, 122–127, *128*, 162, 164; in Atlanta, 98; Atlanta race riot (1906), 120, 122–127, *128*; black men's access to alcohol, 121–123; disenfranchisement of, 121, 124; Harlem, 162–163; Jewish alcohol entrepreneurs, 202–203; middle-class Southern whites' fears of black men, 121; Volstead Act (National Prohibition Act, 1919), 162
alcohol abuse, 41–42
alcohol industry: American Jews in (*see* Jewish alcohol entrepreneurs); beer (*see* brewing industry); consolidation, 231n31; distilled liquor (*see* whiskey industry); eastern European Jewish immigrants, 72, 78–79, 90–95, 102; election-day campaigns, 142–143; farming as alternative to, 80; federal tax revenues, 7, 139, 191; as force for inclusion in American society, 10; as force for marginaliza-

tion in American society, 11; growth of, 204; Jewish alcohol entrepreneurs (*see* Jewish alcohol entrepreneurs); lobbying organizations, 35–36 (*see also* National Model License League; United States Brewers' Association); middlemen, 17, 208n28; municipal corruption, 116; per capita consumption (1890-1900), 86; post-Civil War era, 49, 110–111; post-Repeal revival, 193, 195–197; premigrational skills, 78–79; scholarly production on, 15; sectors, 16–17; Sunday commerce, 64; vertical integration, 17, 231n31; wholesalers, 17, 28–29; wine (*see* wine; wine industry); during World War I, 141–142
alcohol's menace, neutralization of, 201
Alexander, Henry, 132–133
Alexander, Moses, 171–172
Alexander II, Czar, 76
Alexander III, Czar, 76
All the Year Round (journal), 114–115
The American Hebrew (magazine), 156
American Israelite (newspaper), 24, 47, 56
American Issue (magazine), 12, 169
American Jewess (magazine), 41, 54, 60
American Jewish Committee (AJC), 165, 166, 173
American Jewish Historical Society, 237n31
American Jews: acculturation of (*see* acculturation of American Jews); African Americans, commerce with, 120, 122–127, *128*, 162, 164; in alcohol industry (*see* Jewish alcohol entrepreneurs); antebellum United States, status

246

Bill of Rights, 46
Bingham, Theodore, 119
Black Cock Vigor Gin, 129–130
"Black Is My Favorite Color" (Malamud), 202
Blaine, James G., 113
Block, Nathan, 30
Blocker, Jack S., Jr., 15
Bloom, Loeb, and Co., 16
Bloom, Moses, 16
Bluthenthal, Aaron, 34, 71, 126
Bluthenthal and Bickart, 34, 130, 132
Bluthenthal Brothers, 28–29
Bokritzky, Joel, 100
Bonfort's Wine and Liquor Circular (trade publication), 28, 36, 144
bootlegging: Bronfman family, 148–149; division of labor, 149; ethnicity of, 141, 148, 150–151; in Harlem, 163; interethnic bootlegging, 149; Jewish bootlegging (*see* Jewish bootlegging); pervasiveness of, 146; pluralism, 141; profits, 150; Schapiro's House of Kosher Wines, 156–157; in the South, 151–152
"Bottled-in-Bond" Act (1897), 17, 79
bourbon, 17
Brandeis, Louis, 166
Brandeis University, 194
brauerstern, 19–20
brewing industry, 18–23; anti-German sentiment, 142–143; in Atlanta, 22; *brauerstern,* 19–20; in Brooklyn, 22–23, 211n16; in central Europe, 19; in Cincinnati, 211n16; consolidation, 196; dollar value of production (1870-1890), 23; German Americans, 18–19, 211n16; hexagram, 19–20; Jewish alcohol entrepreneurs, 18–23, 193; logo designs, 19–20; National German-American Alliance (NGAA), 143; in Newark, New Jersey, 95; post-Repeal revival, 193, 196; power, 111; production (1936), 193; prohibition movement, 110; "rushing the growler," 18; "tied-house" system, 18, 86–87, 195
Bronfman, Abe, 148

Bronfman, Harry, 148
Bronfman, Samuel, 148, 193–194
Bronfman, Yechiel (Ekiel), 148
Bronfman family, 148–149, 194
Brooklyn, New York, 22–23, 211n16
Browne, Edward B. M., 56, 205n4
Browne Vintners, 194
Bruce, Lenny, 202
Bryan, William Jennings, 4
Buchalter, Louis "Lepke," 237n31
Bureau of Internal Revenue, 152, 153
Bureau of Prohibition, 155–156, 182–183, 185
Business Men's Club (Cincinnati), 35

Caddo Adviser (circular), 130, 142
Cahan, Abraham, 92
California, 20, 25–26, 84
Cannon, James, Jr., 190
Capone, Alphonse, 147
Carmel Wine Company, 85
Catholic Church, 117, 181–182, 200
Catskill Mountains, 40, 216n86
Cawhern, John, 131
Census Bureau, 9
Central Conference of American Rabbis (CCAR): Enelow, Hyman, 184–185, 186; Franklin, Leo, 159–160; grape juice as replacement for wine, 176, 178, 182; Prohibition, questionnaire about, 185–189; rabbis as distributors of wine during Prohibition, 153–154, 159–160; Reform Jews, 184; sacramental wine scandals, 177–178; Wise, Isaac Mayer, 168–169; Zionism, 173, 184, 185
central Europe: alcohol industry in, 6; brewing industry in, 19; Jewish alcohol entrepreneurs in, 6; Jewish immigrants from, 10, 95, 102
Century Magazine, 57, 61, 62
Cherrington, Ernest, 50
Chicago, "Jew saloons" in, 119
Chicago Daily Tribune (newspaper), 113–114, 119
Chicago Jewish Educational Alliance, 165
Christian Advocate (newspaper), 57

entrepreneurship. *See* Jewish alcohol entrepreneurs

Episcopal Church, 182

Episcopalians, 50

Europe: alcohol industry in medieval and early modern, 7; attitudes toward alcohol, 115–116; Galicia, alcohol industry in, 6. *See also* central Europe; eastern European Jewish immigrants; Pale of Settlement; Russia

Evening News (newspaper), 122

Evening Star (newspaper), 46

Feldman, Jake, 100–101

First Amendment, 152, 153

Fleischmann, Charles, 34, 40, 216n86

Food and Fuel Control Act (1917), 141

Ford, Henry: anti-Semitism, 158–160, 165, 188; on Jews, 2–3, 160; Prohibition, 159

Fortune (magazine), 195

Foster, Solomon, 167

Frank, Leo, 134–135, 152, 160

Frankfurter, Felix, 166

Franklin, Leo, 159–160, 165

Free Synagogue (New York City), 169

Freiberg, J. Walter, 30, 153

Freiberg, Julius, 28, 29, 30, 34

Freiberg & Workum, 28

Freiberg family, 31, 67, 194

Freudenthal, Samuel, 56, 219n38

Fried, Albert, 150

Gainesville, Texas, 127

Galicia, alcohol industry in, 6

Gardner, Herb, 199, 201–202

General Conference of Methodists, 50

George Ehret's brewery, 19

Georgia, prohibition movement in, 123–124, 126, 130–132, 139

Georgia House of Representatives, 124

German Americans, 61–65; American Jews, 64–65; anti-alcohol movement, 61; anti-German sentiment, 142–143; brewing industry, 18–19, 211n16; garment trade, 19; German Jews, 169; merchandising, 19; in Newark, New Jersey, 95; reputation/image of, 65; Sunday leisure habits, 63–64; temperance movement, 61–64; Wolf, Simon, 65; women's political activism, 64–65

Gibson, Thomas, 127

Gilfoyle, Timothy, 232n50

Gilmore, T. M., 144

Ginzberg, Louis, 178

Glazer, Nathan, 3

Godfather movies, 237n31

Goldberg, Fred, 184–185

Goldman, Emma, 92

Goldschmidt, Herman, 212n32

Goldschmidt, Max, 212n32

Goldstein, Max, 140

Goldstein, Solomon, 20–22

Gordon, Ernest, 200–201

Gordon, Waxey, 148

Goren, Arthur, 83

Gottheil, Gustav, 48, 58

Grabfelder, Samuel, 30

Grant, Ulysses S., 65, 107

Granville, Ohio, 66

Great Awakening, Second, 44–45

Great Depression, 191

Greenberg, Cheryl Lynn, 163

Greenberg, Maxie, 148

Greenhut, Joseph B., 113

Griffin's Corner, New York, 40, 216n86

Gusfield, Joseph R., 230n23

Habakkuk 2:15, 228n8

Haller, Mark, 148

Harding, Warren G., 145

Harlem, 162–163

Harper's Weekly (magazine), 104, 127

Harris, Bloom, 38, 113–114

Harvey, William "Coin," 109

Hasidim, 225n61

Hassell, Max, 148

Hawthorne, J. B., 106–107

Hayes, Lucy, 66

Hayes, Rutherford B., 65–66

Heap, Chad, 120

He'Brew ("The Chosen Beer"), 202

Hebrew Benevolent Association (Louisville), 31

176–178, 188; skepticism about, 190–191; tension between Orthodox and Reform Jews, 176–177; urban/rural split in sentiment, 192; Volstead Act (*see* Volstead Act); Wickersham Commission report, 189–190; xenophobic patriotism, 141

prohibition movement, 104–124, 130–135; alarm about economic stratification and commercial nature of society, 11; Alexander, Moses, 171–172; anti-German sentiment, 142; Anti-Saloon League (ASL), 105; anti-Semitism, 11, 105–106, 120; in Atlanta, 106–107, 132–134; Bamberger, Simon, 172; black men's access to alcohol, 121–123; brewing industry, 110; Catholic Church, 117; Christianization of American society and politics, 40; collapse of, 204; commercial nature of American economy, dissatisfaction with, 105; definition, 205n3; disenfranchisement of African Americans, 121, 124; economic base, 112; erosion of WASP power, dominance, 11; in Georgia, 123–124, 126, 130–132, 139; German Jews, 169; Hofstadter on, Richard, 11; immigrants, 116–119, 172; industrialization's effects on American life, 111; "Jew saloons," 114; Jewish alcohol entrepreneurs, 104; Jewish prohibitionists, 169, 171–173; nativism, 116, 118; opposition to, 5; populist movement, 110–112, 118; progressive movement, 172–173; Protestantism, 111; in Russia, 114; saloons, 87, 116; in the South, 120, 121, 124; statewide prohibitions, 50, 120, 124, 139, 217n8; status anxiety, 230n23; temperance movement, 47; tenets, 3–4; transformation of, 105; Wald, Lillian, 171, 172; Webb-Kenyon Act (1913), 139, 143, 158; wine industry, 110; Wise, Isaac Mayer, 50–51; Wise, Stephen S., 169–172

Prohibition Party, 117, 168

Protestantism: Christianization of American society and politics, 48; populist movement, 111; prohibition movement, 111; Sunday laws, 48

The Protocols of the Elders of Zion, 158

Pure Food and Drug Administration, 85

"Purple Gang," 149

Quakers, 50

R. G. Dun & Co., 36–40, 215n74

The Rabbinical Assembly, 154

rabbis: attitudes toward Prohibition, 184, 187, 188; Central Conference of American Rabbis (*see* Central Conference of American Rabbis); as distributors of wine during Prohibition, 153–156, 159–160, 182, 183; Hebrew Union College, 31; income, 83; as intermediaries between Jews and others, 175; Union of Orthodox Rabbis, 154, 176; wine industry, 83–84

Raines Law (New York State, 1896), 232n50

raisin wine, 46, 82, 83

rectifiers, 17, 28

Reform Church of American Israelites, 173–174

Reform Jews: acculturation, 23; Central Conference of American Rabbis (CCAR), 184; Jewish alcohol entrepreneurs, 31–32; Orthodox Jews, 176–177, 181; Pittsburgh Platform (1885), 49; Prohibition, 168; Wise, Isaac Mayer, 24; Zionism, 173. *See also* Central Conference of American Rabbis; Union of American Hebrew Congregations

Reformed Episcopal Church, 50

Reinfeld, Joseph, 148, 149–150, 194, 198

Republican Party, 110

Rheingold Beer, 23, 193

Rise and Fall of the Jewish Gangster in America (Fried), 150

Rodeph Shalom congregation (Philadelphia), 48, 53

Roosevelt, Franklin Delano, 189, 191–192

Roper, Daniel, 153–154

Rorabaugh, W. J., 43

Rose, Rufus M., 71–72, 98

Rosen, Nig, 149

Rosenberg, Mark, 114

Rosenfield Bros. & Co., 123

Sound Money (newspaper), 113
"sour wine," 80
the South: attitudes toward alcohol, 22; bootlegging in, 151–152; disenfranchisement of African Americans, 121, 124; immigrant population, 98; Jewish bootlegging, 151; Jewish communities, 72, 152; Jewish merchants, 125; Jews as sexual threats to white women, 134–135; middle-class whites' fears of black men, 121; populist movement, 109; prohibition movement, 120, 121, 124
Southern Interstate Fair, 34
stam yeinam, 6
Star Whiskey advertisement, *20*
Stayton, William H., 189
Steiner, Albert, 22, 34
Steiner, Samuel Simon, 29
Stern, Charles, 212n32
Sullivan, Ellen, 113–114
Sulzer, William, 168
Sunday laws, 48
Sunny Brook and Willow Creek Distillery, *123*

Tappan, Lewis, 39, 215n74
teetotalism, 63
temperance movement, 41–68; 1830s and 1840s, 43–44; alcohol as a burden on the community, 44; American Jews, 41–43, 45–47, 48, 68; American Party (Know-Nothings), 63; antebellum temperance activists, 43–44; anti-Catholic sentiment, 63; Christianization of American society and politics, 40, 42, 49–50; church networks, 50; coercion, 217n8; constitutional opposition to, 51–53; consumers as victims of a wicked industry, 50; dangers of excessive alcohol consumption, 48; definition, 205n3; eradication of alcohol commerce, 50; German Americans, 61–64; immigrants, 63; Irish immigrants, 63; Jastrow, Marcus, 51–52, 54–55; Jewish religious practices, 51; Jewish women, 60–61; Jews as a model of moderate drinking, 43, 56–61; moderation rather

than abstention, 43; nativism, 64, 220n57; Noah, Mordecai M., 45–46, 47; post-Civil War era, 47–50; prohibition, 47; property rights, 51–52; religious opposition to, 51; saloons, 87; Second Great Awakening, 44–45; Sunday commerce, 64; supersessionist claims that Christians had replaced Jews as God's chosen people, 66; Wise, Isaac Mayer, 47, 52–53; women's political activism, 53–56
Temple Emanu-El (New York), 48, 186
The Tenants (Malamud), 202
Tenebaum, Shelly, 223n26
"tied-house" system, 18, 86–87, 195
"tiger customers," 140
Tillman, Cassius, 34
Time (magazine), 179
tirosh, 45, 176
Twenty-First Amendment, 192, 195

Ullman, David, 30
Union Hotel (Saratoga), 40
Union of American Hebrew Congregations (UAHC): Bernheim, Isaac Wolfe, 30, 31; Freiberg, J. Walter, 30; Freiberg, Julius, 30; Wise, Isaac Mayer, 30; Wolf, Simon, 65, 153; Zionism, 173
Union of Orthodox Rabbis, 154, 176
Unitarians, 50
United Presbyterians, 50
United States Brewers' Association (USBA): founding, 35; German language usage, 18; National Association of Commerce and Labor (NACL), 143; National German-American Alliance (NGAA), 144; responsible alcohol consumption, promotion of, 142, 192
United States Constitution: First Amendment, 152, 153; Sixteenth Amendment, 139; Eighteenth Amendment (*see* Eighteenth Amendment); Twenty-First Amendment, 192, 195; amendment acknowledging Christ's moral authority, proposed, 48; anti-alcohol movement, 42, 51–53; Anti-Saloon League (ASL), 120; civil liberties guaranteed by, 42, 52; property rights, 52

About the Author

MARNI DAVIS is Assistant Professor of History at Georgia State University.